HOW ANCIENT EUROPEANS SAW THE WORLD

HOW ANCIENT EUROPEANS
SAW THE WORLD

Vision, Patterns, and the Shaping of the Mind in Prehistoric Times

PETER S. WELLS

Princeton University Press ◆ Princeton and Oxford

Copyright © 2012 by Princeton University Press
Published by Princeton University Press, 41 William Street, Princeton, New Jersey 08540
In the United Kingdom: Princeton University Press, 6 Oxford Street, Woodstock, Oxfordshire OX20 1TW

press.princeton.edu

Jacket Photograph: *Arm and neck rings*. Gold. Iron Age. Erstfeld UR Ribitäler. Inventory number: A-52044-A-52050. *Courtesy of the Swiss National Museum, Zurich.*

Library of Congress Cataloging-in-Publication Data
Wells, Peter S.
How ancient Europeans saw the world : vision, patterns, and the shaping of the mind in prehistoric times / Peter S. Wells.
    p.   cm.
Includes bibliographical references and index.
ISBN-13: 978-0-691-14338-5 (alk. paper)
ISBN-10: 0-691-14338-2 (alk. paper)
1. Prehistoric peoples—Europe, Western. 2. Material culture—Europe, Western.
3. Antiquities, Prehistoric—Europe, Western. 4. Symbolism. 5. Bronze age—Europe, Western. 6. Iron age—Europe, Western. I. Title.
GN803.W44 2012
936—dc23   2012001534

British Library Cataloging-in-Publication Data is available

This book has been composed in Minion

Printed on acid-free paper. ∞

Printed in the United States of America

10 9 8 7 6 5 4 3 2 1

CONTENTS

ILLUSTRATIONS

PREFACE

> If you want to know how someone once perceived and understood
> the world then you need to know what they saw and what they made
> (formed) from it. (Stafford 2007:17)

Why does an Early Bronze Age cup look different from one made in the Late Bronze Age? Why were Middle Bronze Age sword scabbards decorated only with simple vertical lines, while those of the Middle Iron Age were incised with sweeping S-curves and haunting animal heads? Why were Late Iron Age brooches plain and mass-produced, whereas those of earlier centuries had been handcrafted into enchanting forms ornamented with bizarre creatures?

To pose the question more broadly: why did the visual character of objects change so fundamentally during the final millennium of European prehistory, the last thousand years before the Roman conquests brought writing and literacy to the lands now occupied by France, Germany, the United Kingdom, and the rest of western and southern temperate Europe? And what can these changes tell us about how early Europeans perceived their world and their place in it?

When the peoples of temperate Europe first appear in written historical sources, such as Caesar's account of his war in Gaul and Tacitus's description of the peoples he called "Germans," they had already developed into complex societies. The archaeological evidence shows that efficient techniques of agricultural production, elaborate religious practices, long-distance trade, the mass production of goods, and fine art styles had all developed well before Caesar's armies entered Gaul.

The complex societies of temperate Europe emerged without creating a system of writing. We members of twenty-first-century societies are accustomed to studying the past through written history, but most of us are not as well versed in understanding how to reconstruct and understand the past on the basis of the material evidence of archaeology. For most of the million years that humans have inhabited Europe, however, the only evidence we have of the development of economic, social, and religious systems is material evidence. It consists of the objects people made and decorated, the structures that they built in the landscape, and the ways in which they arranged their settlements, graves, and ritual places.

Ever since archaeology became a systematic discipline during the nineteenth century, practitioners have tried to understand the prehistoric societies of Europe on the basis of what they know about later, historical peoples. But what if prehistoric societies were so different from the societies of historical times that those models simply do not fit?

In this book I take a different approach. I use the objects that people made and decorated, and the ways that they arranged things, to study the patterning in their material culture as a key to understanding how they saw objects in the natural and cultural environments in which they lived. Two fundamental changes took place in the structure of design and ornament during this two-thousand-year period from the start of the Bronze Age to the end of the Iron Age.

In the past, these changes have been explained by such causes as "the arrival of the Celts," the rise of new elites throwing off the shackles of old aristocracies, or the adoption of Roman urban lifestyles. But none of these explanations fits the archaeological data. In this book, I argue that the changes were much more comprehensive than past studies have suggested, and that they were part of fundamental shifts in perception and adaptation among the peoples of temperate Europe. I argue that understanding the nature of these changes helps us to understand the character of societies in Europe before writing became a common technology of communication.

As members of modern industrialized societies with literacy rates around 99%, we assume that writing is a "good thing" and that a society without writing must have been severely hampered. But near universal literacy is a modern phenomenon. As recently as the late seventeenth century, only some 20% of the population of Western Europe was literate, and degrees of literacy varied greatly. (In the European parts of the Roman Empire, only 5 to 10% of the population was literate.) By 500 BC, many communities in temperate Europe had been exposed to writing through contact with societies in the Mediterranean world, yet none of them created or adopted a system of writing for their own use, except for legends on coins and a few other inscriptions at the very end of the Iron Age. They managed their systems of communication in ways other than writing.

Physically, the peoples of Bronze and Iron Age Europe were like us, and in some respects their lives were similar to ours. They lived in houses built of wood with clay plaster, grew cereals and vegetable crops, raised cattle, pigs, sheep, and goats, made pottery for preparing and serving food, wore personal ornaments made of metal, glass, and other materials, and crafted their tools and weapons of bronze and iron. When a member of a community died, funerary rituals were performed, sometimes bodies were cremated, and the dead or their ashes were commonly buried in graves in the ground.

But in some fundamental ways their experiences were very different from ours. They had much less stuff than we do—fewer objects of all kinds. They saw many fewer images than we see every day. And their means of communicating were different from those of literate societies such as ours.

In this book, I take a long-term perspective, examining material over a period of two thousand years, in order to explore changes that, though gradual from the perspective of any individual's lifetime, were profound when viewed from the vantage point of the year AD 2012. Needless to say, I have had to be highly selective in the topics and the objects that I have chosen to examine.

It will be useful to explain some terms at the outset.

In this book, I shall not use the words "art" or "artifact" to designate the objects that are the focus of this investigation. "Art" in our modern world is so loaded with meanings that it cannot serve as a useful designation of objects from other cultural contexts. To me, using the term implies that we know the purpose of an object, and that we want to assign it to a category that belongs to our way of thinking about the world. Likewise, when we use the word "artist," it carries all kinds of implications about the motives and status of the individual producer of "art objects." Perhaps most importantly, we tend to think of an "art object" as something produced to serve one specific purpose, to express whatever it is that the artist wants to express. When we study objects made three thousand years ago, we need to approach them and think about them with as little of the mental baggage of our own world as possible.

"Temperate Europe" is the part of the continent in the temperate climate zones, between the shores of the Mediterranean Sea and the Arctic Circle.

I use the term "later prehistory" to designate the period of concern in this book, the Bronze and Iron Ages, from 2000 BC to the time of the Roman conquests during the first century BC and the first century AD.

"Bronze Age" and "Iron Age" are terms created in the first half of the nineteenth century to designate those times when bronze (a copper alloy, in temperate Europe usually about 90% copper and 10% tin) and subsequently iron came into common use. In temperate Europe the Bronze Age is dated from roughly 2200 to 800 BC, the Iron Age from 800 BC to the Roman conquests. There are no fixed dates for these periods, since investigators disagree on exactly when the metals first came into general use.

In temperate Europe, the "Roman Period" refers to the time between the Roman conquest and the end of Roman political control in the different regions. In Gaul (France, Belgium, parts of the Netherlands, Germany, and

Switzerland), the Roman Period began in 51 BC, after Caesar's conquest of that part of Europe. In Britain, it began during the Roman conquest of that island between AD 43 and 47. The "Roman Iron Age" refers to the time of the Roman Period, but in the lands beyond the Roman frontier (east of the lower Rhine, north of the *limes* boundary and of the Danube).

The Iron Age peoples (and sometimes even the Bronze Age populations) of temperate Europe are often referred to by names such as "Celts," "Gauls," "Germans," and "Scythians," but I avoid using those names in this book, because they are not helpful in our attempts to understand what was happening in late prehistoric Europe. These are all designations applied by outsiders, Greek and Roman writers, to the peoples of temperate Europe. For discussion of the issues involved, see my book *Beyond Celts, Germans and Scythians: Archaeology and Identity in Iron Age Europe* (London: Duckworth, 2001).

Two main methods of dealing with bodies of deceased persons are well documented in prehistoric Europe. "Inhumation" is the term used for burying the body. "Cremation" is burning the body. Other means of disposing of the dead were probably also used, but traces of those methods are scarce.

Throughout the text I use BC and AD instead of BCE and CE, because the former are more familiar to the majority of readers.

For the sake of convenience, I refer to locations by their modern place names, without the qualifications "now known as . . ." or "situated in . . . ," but the reader should remember that the modern place names rarely derive from the place names used in the period covered in this book.

Some of the issues that I consider in this book I touched on in *Image and Response in Early Europe* (London: Duckworth, 2008). But that book focused specifically on images, whereas my main concern here is on visual patterning more generally, and on shapes and motifs of decoration.

In order to provide as broad and comprehensive a picture of changes during the Bronze and Iron Ages as possible, without sacrificing detailed analysis of specific patterns and practices, I bring into the discussion sites from all parts of Europe but focus more detailed treatment on the central regions of the continent—the lands that are now France, Germany, Switzerland, Austria, and the Czech Republic. In significant ways, the styles of material culture (pottery, ornaments, tools, weapons), types of settlements, funerary practices, and other cultural behaviors were similar in the communities throughout this broad central part of the European land mass. Over time, with the gradual growth in trade and in movements of people, both as individuals and as communities, more cultural traits came to be shared in different regions of Europe than had been the case earlier.

In two chapters, 5 and 8, my discussion focuses on developments in what is now southern Germany and the surrounding areas. Communities in each region of Europe produced locally distinctive pottery. Unlike bronze, iron, and glass objects, pottery was little traded—it was heavy, fragile, and easily produced by most communities. In order to be able to examine changes in the forms and decoration of pottery through time without the complication of spatial variation, Chapter 5 focuses on pottery from sites in this region of the continent.

The same applies to Chapter 8 as regards the arrangement of objects in graves. Funerary practices tended to be shared by neighboring communities, but communities elsewhere often practiced different kinds of rituals. Again, in order to examine change through time, I focus the discussion on the central part of the continent.

For the detailed analysis of changes in both pottery and funerary practices, concentrating on this region in the center of the continent has the advantage of allowing connections to be drawn with neighboring regions in all parts of Europe.

This book touches on many themes that might have been elaborated upon further. But my aim was to keep the book as concise as possible, while presenting my argument in sufficient detail and bringing into the discussion enough archaeological evidence to back up my statements.

ACKNOWLEDGMENTS

Many colleagues and friends have contributed to this book, especially by sending me their publications, sharing their knowledge of European archaeology, hosting me in studying museum collections, and taking me to archaeological sites. Support for trips during which I was able to study objects in museums and to participate in relevant conferences was generously supplied by the Department of Anthropology, the Faculty Summer Research Fellowship Program, the McKnight Summer Fellowships, the Imagine Fund, the European Studies Consortium, and the Office of International Programs, all of the University of Minnesota. The excavations at Hascherkeller, Altdorf, and Kelheim referred to in the text were supported by the National Science Foundation (BNS78-07349, BNS82-09930, BNS900416402), the National Geographic Society, Earthwatch and the Center for Field Research, and Research Explorations of the University of Minnesota. The interlibrary loan service of Wilson Library at the University of Minnesota obtained for me a great many books and articles that were essential for this research.

Among individuals who have offered helpful materials, advice, and hospitality I want to thank especially David Anthony, William Beeman, Jörg Biel, Jan Bouzek, Joanna Brück, Rainer Christlein, Ton Derks, Stephen Dyson, Bernd Engelhardt, Lothar von Falkenhausen, Franz Fischer, Andrew Fitzpatrick, Christof Flügel, Hermann Gerdsen, Melanie Giles, Kristina Golubiewski, Giles Guthrie, Anthony Harding, Colin Haselgrove, Lotte Hedeager, Nancy Herther, J. D. Hill, Richard Hingley, Nicolle Hirschfeld, Fraser Hunter, Simon James, Henrik Jansen, Kristina Jennbert, Hans-Eckart Joachim, Andy Jones, Jody Joy, Wolfgang Kimmig, Werner Krämer, Kristian Kristiansen, Lars Larsson, Silas Mallery, Sonja Marzinzik, David Mattingly, Timothy McNiven, Vincent Megaw, Petra Neumann-Eisele, Conor Newman, Johannes Prammer, Ian Ralston, Michael Rind, Ben Roberts, Nico Roymans, Siegmar von Schnurbein, Peter Schröter, Niall Sharples, Susanne Sievers, Joanna Sofaer, Berta Stjernquist, Simon Stoddart, Bernard Wailes, Christopher Wells, Joan

Wells, Nicholas Wells, Günter Wieland, David Wigg-Wolf, Willem Willems, Stefan Winghart, Greg Woolf, and Werner Zanier.

At Princeton University Press, Rob Tempio, Julia Livingston, Karen Fortgang, Eva Jaunzems, Dimitri Karetnikov, and the two anonymous reviewers of the original manuscript have all provided excellent advice and information at all stages of preparation of this book.

I thank the Trustees of the British Museum, the Römisch-Germanische Kommission, and the Rheinisches Landesmuseum Trier for permission to use photographs and drawings.

Unless otherwise noted, all photographs are by the author.

CHAPTER 1

∞∞∞∞∞∞∞∞∞∞∞∞∞∞∞∞

OF MONSTERS AND FLOWERS

A NEW STYLE FOR IRON AGE EUROPE

A dramatic new style of imagery appeared in Europe twenty-five hundred years ago (Figure 1). Strange creatures, part human, part beast, were crafted onto gold and bronze jewelry and cast onto the handles and lids of bronze vessels. Metalsmiths created lush new forms of decoration—incised and relief ornament based on floral motifs such as leaves and petals, with spirals, S-curves, and whirligigs decorating objects ranging from pottery to sword scabbards.

This style was a radical departure from the forms of representation and decoration that preceded it. Throughout the Bronze Age and the Early Iron Age, representations of humans and animals had been rare, and those few that existed tended to be simple and naturalistic. There was no mistaking a waterbird or a stag for any other creature—their simple attributes made plain what animal was intended. Linear ornament was geometric, based on rectangles, rhomboids, triangles, and circles.

The reasons for the appearance of the new style, named La Tène after a site in western Switzerland, have been the source of endless controversy since the latter half of the nineteenth century. At that time archaeologists decided to divide the European Iron Age into an earlier stage called the "Hallstatt Period" (800–400 BC), after the great cemetery discovered at Hallstatt in Upper Austria, and a later stage designated the "La Tène Period" (from 400 BC to the Roman conquests), after the lakeshore site near Neuchâtel in Switzerland, where large numbers of metal objects, especially iron swords and their scabbards, had been found (see map, Figure 2). Debate has been dominated by two main questions. What was the source of the new style? And how was the new style related to social and political changes evident in the richly outfitted burials

Figure 1. (a) Bronze flagon with coral ornament from Basse-Yutz in eastern France. © *The Trustees of the British Museum.*

Figure 1. (b) Detail of the creature represented on the top of the handle. © *The Trustees of the British Museum.*

Figure 1. (c) Detail of the face at the base of the handle. © *The Trustees of the British Museum.*

of the fifth century BC, with their gold rings, imported Greek and Etruscan bronzes, and ornate chariots?

Discussion of the first question has revolved around identifying motifs and forms in the art and design traditions known as Greek, Scythian, and Etruscan that might have provided models for the new style in temperate Europe. Debate on the second question has explored the connections between the appearance of the new style and the decline in power of the centers of the sixth and early fifth centuries BC that were associated with the earlier Hallstatt style. These centers include the Heuneburg in southwest Germany, Mont Lassois in eastern France, Châtillon-sur-Glâne in Switzerland, Závist in Bohemia, and the Hellbrunnerberg in Austria, all of which thrived at the end of the sixth century BC and in the first decades of the fifth, and then fell into decline and abandonment in the middle years of that latter century.

My approach in this book is different. My principal concern with the new style of imagery and ornament is not where it came from or how it was connected to "dynasty change" during the European Iron Age. It is rather what the new style can tell us about how people's ways of seeing, their visual

Figure 2. Map showing sites mentioned in the text.

perception, changed during the fifth century BC. As I argue below, this topic is not only of interest in its own right, but bears directly on our understanding of who we are today and how we got that way.

I began this chapter with this brief discussion of the new style that emerged during the fifth century BC, but my theme is much broader.

WRITTEN HISTORY AND THE ARCHAEOLOGY OF OBJECTS

Our understanding of the immediate past—of the past few weeks or even the past few decades—depends upon our personal experience, including our interactions with other individuals, our reading, and the news that we may watch on TV or on the Internet. Understanding the more distant past—beyond a few decades—depends in large part on "history"; that is, on written (or filmed) accounts of what happened longer ago. But written history can take us back only so far. In North America north of Mexico, written texts take us back only as far as the end of the fifteenth century, when the first Europeans arrived. In Mesoamerica, written texts go back considerably further, at least to the beginnings of Classic Maya civilization in the third century AD. An earlier system of signs was used at Monte Alban (around 500 BC), and perhaps as far back as the Olmec culture, around 1000 BC (there is no consensus as yet as to whether or not the Olmec had writing). In Britain, the earliest writing (in Latin) appeared on local coinage of the latter half of the final century BC. In continental temperate Europe north of the Mediterranean Sea, there is early evidence of writing before the Roman conquest, but it is all in Greek or Latin script, and the inscriptions do not constitute anything that we would call history. In the Mediterranean, the alphabetic scripts of Greece, Etruria, and Rome developed during the first half of the first millennium BC. Linear B script in Greece emerged around the fourteenth century BC. Writing had begun at least by the time of the Shang Bronze Age in China, around the sixteenth century BC, and in the Indus Valley region of southern Asia, around the twenty-sixth century BC. The earliest signs that most scholars accept as writing developed in Mesopotamia and in Egypt, in both cases around the thirty-third century BC. But in both those cases, it was not until about seven centuries later that texts appeared that we might consider actual "history"—accounts of events and of rulers' lives. For much of the world—South America, Africa south of Nubia, northern Asia, North America north of Mexico, the Pacific islands—what we understand as writing was first introduced by merchants and explorers from outside.

While history in this sense of written documents takes us back only a few centuries in most of the world (or at most a few millennia), the techniques of archaeology provide us with ways of learning about human actions, practices, and behaviors all the way back to the time of the earliest datable products of human activity, stone tools manufactured 2.6 million years ago. Just as the earliest texts do not provide much information from which we can write history, the earliest archaeological materials do not allow us to say very much about human behaviors or practices. But from later periods in human development, we often have access to rich sources of information in the form of physical evidence, as from Bronze and Iron Age Europe. I define "archaeological materials" here as any objects shaped or arranged by humans. These include tools made of stone, bone, copper, bronze, and iron; ornaments of shell, silver, and gold; pottery; textiles; wheeled vehicles; walls around settlements; graves; ditches—anything that humans have made.

The aspect of the past that constitutes the focus of this book is visual perception—how people saw in the past, compared to how we see today. "We" is not as simple as it might seem. We tend to assume that everyone perceives things as we do. But already in 1912, the American psychologist William James raised the question, can two different individuals perceive in exactly the same way. And indeed between two individuals raised in very different environments—one in a modern Western city and the other in a Bronze Age house in France, say—differences in perception are likely to be substantial.

UNDERSTANDING THE PAST

There is a general tendency in our society, as in all societies, to interpret objects from the past in terms of objects with which we are familiar. If we see an Early Bronze Age bracelet in a museum, we think about the bracelets that people in our own society wear and assume that the ancient bracelet served the same purpose. We read Caesar's description of the peoples of Gaul as if they were modern newspaper reports or magazine stories about peoples with different customs from our own. We look at a seventeenth-century painting by de Hooch showing the inside of a house, with furniture and people in it, and transpose ourselves into that house and imagine what it would be like to live there. In the case of all of these reactions, we assume that we understand the object, the story, and the scene, because they all seem familiar. They look and read like things that we know about from our daily lives, and we have no reason to suspect that understanding them is any more complicated than understanding how a bracelet that we buy in a jewelry store should be worn, how to read a story in *National Geographic*, or how to interpret a photograph of a living-room setting in an interior design advertisement. But just because things look familiar, we cannot safely assume that we can understand them, without considering the context in which they occur.

But the matter is yet more complicated. People who lived in the Early Bronze Age, who led Roman armies against the inhabitants of France, or who lived in seventeenth-century Holland all inhabited worlds different from ours. A bracelet meant one thing in 1800 BC; a bracelet today can mean something quite different. Caesar saw the Iron Age peoples of Europe through the eyes of a wealthy and powerful member of Roman society. Dutch genre painters of the seventeenth century were conveying specific social and political messages with their paintings of house interiors. In each case, there is a great deal of background information that we need to know about the Early Bronze Age, about elite Roman attitudes toward other peoples, and about ideology and politics in seventeenth-century Holland if we are to understand what these things meant to the people who created them and to those who experienced them.

In order to get some understanding of the past, an appreciation of how people lived and what they experienced, and to better understand objects that survive from the past (paintings, sculpture, buildings, pottery, brooches . . .), we need to take account of how peoples' experience in the past was different from ours today. It is all too easy to visit a reconstructed house at Plimoth Plantation in Massachusetts, for example, or the reconstructed medieval village of West Stow in southern England, and think "they must have been so uncomfortable living in such small houses," or "how could they possibly see with no big glassed windows and no electric lights." In thinking this way, we imagine putting ourselves, with our experiences and our knowledge of our own world, into the physical situation we see before us. But our experience and knowledge are profoundly different from theirs, the peoples who lived in the situation we are imagining.

We know that the experiences of people in ages past were different from ours, but the only intellectual tools that we can bring to examine and study those experiences are our minds of today. In this sense, we can never really experience what things were like in the past. But there are ways that we can get closer to a sense of what they were like. One way is to read what people have written about the worlds they inhabited. From Nathaniel Hawthorne's stories, we get a feel for what life was like in nineteenth-century New England. Samuel Pepys helps us to understand London during the seventeenth century. Pliny the Elder gives us an idea of what the Roman Mediterranean world was like in the first century AD. Of course, their writings express their personal points of view, and they may be consciously representing things in a way favorable to them. Certainly, no individual can ever represent more than the fraction of the society and experience with which he or she is familiar. Even the meanings of words change over time, so that a word that Pepys used may have a different meaning or a different connotation today, and when it comes to translations from another language, matters are of course even more complex. For the most part, texts expose us only to the perspectives of elite members of society. But we can nonetheless learn a great deal about living conditions, the physical realities of life, values, attitudes, beliefs, aspirations, and much else from writers who set their stories in the times in which they lived. Charles Dickens is a prime example, since much of our understanding of life in mid-nineteenth century Britain comes from his descriptions of conditions in his time.

Visual representations are another important source. From paintings, drawings, and photographs, we can glean information about conditions and lifestyles of the past. Jacob Riis's photographs from the late nineteenth and

early twentieth centuries are an important source of information about society and economy in New York City. James Fenton's photographs of mid-
nineteenth-century England provide information about the character of the
English countryside and about architecture, while his photographs from the
Crimea show what the results of war really looked like. Landscape paintings
by Rubens, van Ruisdael, and Constable inform us about agriculture, forestry,
settlement patterns, and economy in early modern Europe. In Egypt and
Mesopotamia we can study scenes going back some five thousand years to see
how painters, sculptors, and other artisans represented the worlds in which
they lived. As with written texts, we need to approach pictorial representations critically if we are to gain real insight into what they can tell us. Paintings
and drawings are artists' creations, not objective representations of reality.
Even photographs have never been as straightforward and objective as some
people think—and this was true even before the possibilities of Photoshop.
Yet despite such shortcomings, these sources of information are important for
understanding the past.

We can also use nonverbal and nonpictorial objects from the past to help
us to understand peoples' perceptions, practices, and experiences. Every
manufactured object embodies essential features of the society that produced
it, and the more complex the object, the more information we should be able
to derive from it. As I shall argue in this book, objects played a much greater
role in communication and expression in societies that do not have writing
than in societies that do. Howard Morphy speaks of the "multidimensional
nature of objects," and the myriad ways in which they can communicate
meanings. As Jan Mukarovsky has argued for art objects in particular (but the
same is true of all crafted items), every object can be viewed as possessing two
essential aspects: the basic physical thing, and the meanings that the object
embodies in the unique cultural context in which it was produced. Chapter 11
treats this topic in some detail.

DIFFERENT VISUAL WORLDS

People who lived in Europe between four thousand and two thousand years
ago inhabited a different world from that of today. Though they were physically very much like us, and presumably psychologically similar as well, and
although the landscape and climate were not very different either, their material culture was unlike ours in fundamental ways. Most importantly, they had
far fewer objects than we have. There simply was not as much stuff around.
Where the typical modern American or European might have a kitchen with

several hundred plates, glasses, and pieces of cutlery, a typical Iron Age European might have had five or ten ceramic containers at any one time. A modern American might have a tool chest containing fifty or a hundred tools, while his or her Iron Age counterpart had perhaps two or three, depending upon whether that individual was a craftsworker or a farmer. A modern American or British individual might own fifty to a hundred pieces of jewelry, an Iron Age person perhaps two or three. And there are many categories of things that we own that did not even exist in the Bronze and Iron Ages—cars, kitchen appliances, sports equipment, "collectibles."

An implication of this difference is that the typical object means less to us today than an individual object would have meant to the person who owned it in late prehistoric Europe. And, as we shall see, objects that we might consider trash were valued by prehistoric people. Moreover, as many investigators have argued, objects had much greater significance to people who did not possess a system of writing, because they were means of communicating a whole range of kinds of information that writing communicates in literate societies.

OBJECTS IN TIMES BEFORE WRITING

This book is a study of a two-thousand-year period in Europe (Figure 3) from which we have vast quantities of material for study and analysis, but with which the great majority of people today are not very familiar. This period, from 2000 BC to the Roman conquests during the last century BC and the first century AD, is known by the terms "Bronze Age" and "Iron Age," names devised by archaeologists during the nineteenth century, when the discipline of archaeology was first becoming systematic in its approaches to understanding the past. From these millennia we have large collections of pottery, jewelry, tools, weapons, metal vessels, wagons, horse harness ornaments, farming implements, and kitchen utensils, as well as rich documentation of settlements, cemeteries, and other places of human activity. Museums all over Europe offer rich and informative displays of objects from local cultures of the period. Reconstructed settlements are accessible to the public as open-air museums, often with costumed performers demonstrating how pottery was made, how bronze was cast, and how food was prepared. Thousands of publications illustrate and discuss material from the Bronze and Iron Ages, ranging from detailed reports on new discoveries and excavations to glossy coffee-table books with photographs of the most stunning prehistoric objects.

Before the Roman conquests, the peoples of temperate Europe had not developed any kind of communication technology that we would consider

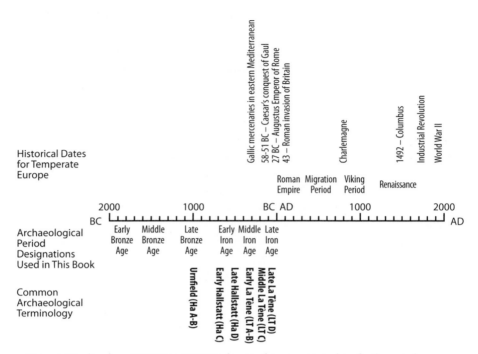

Figure 3. Timeline from 2000 BC to AD 2000, showing the approximate dates for the periods discussed in the text (center), other terms commonly used in the archaeological chronology of prehistoric temperate Europe (bottom), and some historical dates (top).

writing. The many short inscriptions from the second and first century BC, most of them on coins, are names in Greek and Latin characters, not part of any indigenous writing system. Many scholars, Jack Goody and Walter Ong prominently among them, argue that the development of writing has had a profound effect on human history, not only because it enables us to preserve records of the past in a permanent form and allows the circulation of information on a vastly larger than direct person-to-person basis, but because it fundamentally changed the way that humans perceived their world and interacted with others. In the past few decades we have seen much similar discussion about the effects that television has had on perception and thought, and today much the same dialogue critiques the impact of the Internet, Facebook, Twitter, and other media of contemporary communication. If it is true that writing has profoundly affected human perception and thought wherever it has been introduced, then to understand human development more broadly, it is essential that we examine the character of perception and thought *before* the introduction of writing.

The adoption of writing changes the meaning of objects. Temperate Europe in the period between 2000 BC and the Roman conquest is an ideal context in which to investigate this phenomenon, because the database is much richer than that available anywhere else in the world at a comparable period. The results of this investigation will also point the way toward thinking about some of the changes that are taking place in human perception and thought as new communication technologies take their places in human action and perception.

In addition to enabling investigation into this larger, comparative anthropological issue, study of this period in temperate Europe also provides new insight into the development of European civilization, or "the West." Discussions of the "civilization of the West" ordinarily begin with Greece and Rome (sometimes with the Near East), with no serious consideration given to the prehistoric societies of Europe, then move directly into the rise of the early medieval kingdoms of Merovingian Europe and on to Charlemagne, the Holy Roman Empire, the Renaissance, the age of exploration, and modern times. When historians write about the so-called "barbarians" of the Late Roman and early medieval periods, the Franks, Goths, Burgundians, and Saxons, in particular, as well as about other groups, such as the Huns, and their roles in subsequent developments, their discussions depend almost exclusively upon the existing texts of the period, which were of course written largely from a Roman perspective, rather than based upon serious evaluation of the material evidence of these nonliterate peoples. And in all of this discussion, the prehistoric peoples of Europe are all but ignored. I shall argue in this book that the ways of seeing of the Bronze Age and Iron Age peoples of temperate Europe played an integral part in the development of the "ways of seeing" that characterized subsequent Europeans, ways of seeing that were, in fact, quite different from those of the Mediterranean peoples of Greece and Rome.

SEEING AND EXPERIENCE

My approach in this book to understanding the peoples of later prehistoric Europe is through visuality, by which I mean the visual properties of things *as they are perceived by a viewer.* As David Brett writes, "Vision is a form of cognition." My argument is that the people of the European Bronze and Iron Ages saw differently from the way we see today, and that through systematic examination of how they patterned the objects that they made and how they arranged and displayed them, we can develop an understanding of how they perceived and fashioned their worlds.

Numerous studies in the fields of neuroscience, cognitive psychology, and ethnographic anthropology have shown that what we see depends upon what we have seen before—on our experience seeing. What we see is not like a photographic replication of "what is out there." It is a hypothesis based on our personal experience, an interpretation that we *create* from our experience of seeing other things before. As the psychologist Richard Gregory has argued, our visual system develops from a very early age, long before we are able to talk, and in concert with our sense of touch. An infant learns about seeing through the experience of touching its parents, stuffed animals, the edges of its crib, and other things in its environment. The developing sense of sight is calibrated by that of touch. Sight goes on developing and refining throughout our lifetimes, always in concert with the other senses and through the life experiences of the individual.

An infant in modern America or Europe experiences a very different visual and tactile environment from that which an infant in Bronze Age or Iron Age Europe would have experienced. We would therefore expect the modern infant to develop a visual system different from that of infants born three thousand years ago.

Images are an important subcategory of things. Today we are flooded with them—pictures on the Internet, photographs and advertisements in newspapers, billboards along the highways, television, film, magazines. An American typically sees hundreds if not thousands of images every day. Our brain is conditioned to ignore the vast majority of them, paying attention only to those that strike us as having something significant to show us. In the Bronze and Iron Ages, images were rare. The European who lived three thousand years ago probably did not see any on an average day. Bronze figurines, incised scenes on pottery, and other kinds of images were associated with richly equipped burials, ordinarily restricted to a very small portion of society. And because they were so uncommon, images were potent in prehistoric Europe.

Perception is not a passive process but an active one in which our body interacts with our environment. It is the process of physical interaction that enables us to perceive. Several centuries of observation and experiment have taught us that actual perception is accomplished, not by our eyes, ears, nose, tongue, or fingertips, but by our brain. Our sense receptors are the front-line receivers of signals about the nature of the environment around us, but it is our brain that does the actual perceiving, that receives the signals and makes sense out of them, deciding how we should respond to what we sense in the environment.

In the case of seeing, many theorists long believed that the lens at the front of our eyes projects an image of what is in front of us onto the retina at the back of the eyeball, and that it is that image that we see. Since the work of

Helmholtz (1821–1894), however, it has been generally accepted that there is no such projection onto the retina. Rather, the light waves that penetrate the front of the eye stimulate receptors on the retina that send electrical signals to different parts of the brain (as many as thirty different regions are believed to be involved). The brain then interprets those signals on the basis of past experience, and it is this interpretation that we see.

WAYS OF VISUALIZING THINGS IN THE WORLD

While all societies are in a constant process of change, we can identify times when change seems to happen faster than it does at other times. The late eighteenth and early nineteenth centuries, the period we know as the Industrial Revolution, was such a time of rapid transitions. Not only did the way that goods were produced change, but everything else in society was affected as well, from settlement patterns and social structures to subjects and styles of painting and themes in literature. In like manner, today's social scientists are grappling with the on-going and profound changes brought about by twenty-first-century technologies of communication. As I demonstrate in the chapters that follow, two fundamental changes took place during the two millennia at the end of European prehistory, one in the late sixth and early fifth centuries BC, the other during the second century BC. These changes were every bit as sweeping as those brought about by the Industrial Revolution at the end of the eighteenth and start of the nineteenth century. In this book, I shall show how they affected the ways that objects such as everyday pottery and jewelry were made, how high-status items such as swords were decorated, and how rituals were practiced.

A number of important studies in different disciplines have explored ways of seeing in different contexts and have demonstrated that the way that people perceive things visually depends upon the cultural and historical circumstances in which they live. Simon Goldhill shows how the culture of seeing changed in the Greek world, from democratic Athens of the fifth century BC, to Hellenistic Alexandria with its less democratic traditions and more expert testimony of seeing, to the time when Christianity was taking over the Roman Empire. His focus is on institutions and how they fostered different ways of seeing and of thinking about seeing. Peter De Bolla does something similar for the Enlightenment, demonstrating how ideas about vision and visuality during that period were different from those that came before. W. H. Sewell shows how pictorial representations of people working changed between the sixteenth and the seventeenth centuries, when people were represented communicating and interacting against detailed workplace backgrounds, and the middle of the eighteenth century, when figures were represented not interacting, their faces were often not portrayed, and background scenes were bare. For Sewell, these changes in representation reflect the political and ideological changes of the time. In an ethnographic study, Anthony Forge shows how a group in New Guinea has very specific meanings for certain kinds of things that are to be seen and, conversely, how people in that society cannot see some things that we see easily, because of their specific expectations and experiences.

The second part of my argument is that we can learn much about how people who lived in Europe between four thousand and two thousand years ago saw—how they perceived visually—by examining systematically their material culture and the ways in which they patterned the things that they made, decorated, built, and arranged.

VISUAL STRUCTURES AND DIAGRAMS

"Every morning, Frl. Schroeder arranges [her knicknacks] very carefully in certain unvarying positions: there they stand, like an uncompromising statement of her views on Capital and Society, Religion and Sex." This sentence from Christopher Isherwood's *Goodbye to Berlin* illustrates an important point about material culture that is central to the argument of this book: The way that people make things and the way that they arrange them are determined by their basic beliefs and attitudes. As Daniel Miller puts it, "A . . . society elaborates its cultural practices through an underlying pattern which is manifested in a multitude of diverse forms." Every product of a society—religious rituals, kinship systems, marriage practices, myths, burial customs, decorative patterns applied to pottery—encapsulates the whole of the society. Thus cultural anthropologists can use a single ritual to elucidate the social, economic, and political workings of a society, as Glifford Geertz did in his classic analysis of the Balinese cockfight. From songs and stories, folklorists can derive rich information about the basic structures and beliefs of the societies that sing and tell them. Art historians can use paintings to explore in detail the complexities of life in a society, as Simon Schama demonstrates in the case of seventeenth-century Holland.

In my exploration of the societies of Bronze and Iron Age Europe, I apply this principle to investigate how people arranged things in media that survive for us to examine, four thousand or two thousand years later. The way that a potter shaped and decorated a ceramic jar, the style and ornament that a jeweler applied to a bronze brooch, and the way that performers of a funerary ritual arranged objects in the grave of a deceased woman—all of these were determined by the values and beliefs of the communities whose members fashioned the pottery and brooch and arranged the grave goods. As we would anticipate from the studies by Miller, Geertz, and Schama cited above, these patterns are not random but reflect the fundamental character of the societies. The extraordinary richness and high quality of the archaeological evidence from later prehistoric Europe enables us to use these patterns in the material to examine how people perceived and understood the world around them. Most importantly for the argument of this book, these high-quality data enable us to examine changes in these patterns over time and thus to put forward a new model for understanding European societies at the time that they came into intensive contact with the literate Roman world. As we have mentioned, the evidence shows two major shifts in material patterning and visual perception during the course of the Bronze and Iron Age, one during the fifth and the other during the second century BC.

In highly complex, market-driven societies like our own, changing correlations between pattern and perception are difficult to discern, because the very nature of a market economy encourages the proliferation of ever newer products. But in smaller-scale societies with more limited material resources, such patterns can be more readily identified. Howard Morphy's studies of material culture in modern Australia provide many examples.

GREEK AND ROMAN TEXTS

The subject of this book is the peoples of temperate Europe, north of the shores of the Mediterranean Sea. As noted already, these peoples of what we call the Bronze and Iron Ages did not have a system of writing. But from the time of Herodotus in the middle of the fifth century BC on, Greek and Roman writers mention and later describe some of the groups whose material culture we shall consider. Because my focus is on the visual experiences of the peoples of temperate Europe, and not on what others said about them, I shall not say much about these written sources from the Mediterranean world.

Ancient texts have, however, played a very large role in past studies of the Bronze and Iron Age peoples of Europe, and not always a helpful role. Too often the accounts of Greek and Roman writers have been accepted by archaeologists and historians without adequate critical evaluation, and this approach has often led to confusion and even misrepresentation. There is now a substantial critical literature dealing with ways of understanding what these texts tell us about the peoples north of the Mediterranean, and I refer to some of the most useful works in the bibliographic essay at the end of this book.

ON SOCIAL STRUCTURE AND POLITICAL SYSTEMS

Ever since researchers have tried to make sense of archaeological materials as remains of earlier societies, they have grappled with the problem of how to think about and characterize the social systems of prehistoric Europe. This issue came strikingly to the fore with the discovery of graves that were outfitted much more richly, with gold ornaments, elaborate craft products, exotic imports, and larger numbers of objects than was typical in most burials of the period. The problem has always been what to call the apparently elite persons represented in these special graves.

In the continental literature, the common practice is to use the German term *Fürstengräber* (generally translated into English as "princely burials") as a catchword to characterize all graves that are substantially richer in their contents than the majority. Recent debate around the Hochdorf burial and the status of the man in it illustrates the problem. Some argue that the man was a "chieftain." Others use the term "prince" (or *Fürst*). Still others suggest that he was not just a prince, but a prince of interregional importance, perhaps a king. Analogies, explicit or implicit, are drawn with the "tribal leaders" described by Caesar, with early medieval social and political structures, and with "chiefs" described in ethnographically studied societies in other parts of the world.

This approach is loaded with problems, as J. D. Hill and Niall Sharples have argued. We have no idea how the prehistoric Bronze Age and Iron Age communities and societies were organized, and applying such terms as those noted above only masks our lack of understanding. Even when we consider Caesar's descriptions, we need to take into account that he was an outsider, from a very different society, writing about people whose language he probably did not understand. And as a general leading armies of conquest, he is unlikely to have provided the most objective description of his enemies, even if he were in a position to do so.

In the absence of any reasonable system for characterizing the social and political structures of Bronze and Iron Age Europe, I use the more neutral term "elite" to characterize individuals and groups who are marked in their burials by greater "wealth" than the majority in their communities. This term is not ideal either, but it avoids the historically specific and anthropological implications of "chief" and "prince." "Wealth" is also a subjective term, of course. I use it and the concept to characterize graves that have in them more objects than do the majority of graves, especially objects of gold, bronze vessels, weapons, and ornaments of all kinds. One useful way of thinking about grave wealth is in terms of the amount of effort that had to go into procuring objects that were placed in burials, including considerations of the rarity of the raw material, the distance the objects were transported, and the amount of craft effort that went into producing them.

APPROACH AND PRESENTATION

The book is divided into four sections. The first introduces the theme and the approach and includes discussion of techniques for the analysis of visual features that are especially relevant to the world of late prehistoric Europe. The second examines three main categories of objects, ways that people arranged and manipulated objects in the context of communicating with others, and the appearance of two new media in the Late Iron Age; namely, coins and writing. The third section evaluates and interprets the evidence and suggests ways of understanding how and why observed changes came about. The fourth situates the subject of this book in larger historical and contemporary contexts and considers the implications of this study for our experiences in the twenty-first century.

CHAPTER 2

◇◇◇◇◇◇◇◇◇◇◇◇◇◇◇◇◇◇◇

SEEING AND SHAPING OBJECTS

EYE-CATCHING OBJECTS

When you look at David Bailly's *Self Portrait with Vanitas Symbols* (1651), the first thing you see is the human figure, David Bailly, looming large in the left part of the painting, but your eye (your brain, actually) is quickly attracted to the objects on the table in the center and on the right. Why are the objects on the table so fascinating? We are drawn to them, wanting to distinguish each one from the others around it, to identify it in our minds, to feel the weight, texture, and apparent temperature of each. Then we look around, and we see portraits on the wall, and a flowing curtain. (Please see the bibliographic essay for published illustrations of this and other art works mentioned in the text.) The question, why are these objects on the table so fascinating, is one of the central questions of this book. Our concern here is not of course with these particular seventeenth-century objects, but rather with things between four thousand and two thousand years old that people made, looked at, and thought about in ways similar to our reactions to Bailly's charming objects.

So the question remains: why are these objects so enchanting? There are in fact many reasons. The painter has skillfully brought together a whole range of visually attractive objects and arranged them in a special way for just this purpose, to enchant the viewer. Light is an important factor in attracting our attention. Most of the objects are shiny and reflect light, creating visual highlights. Lines play an important part in the picture, leading our eye in specific directions, with the two edges of the table prominent in the left center foreground, as well as the stick Bailly is holding, the long pipe stem on the right, and the vertical lines of the wall in the background. Texture is a prominent visual theme. Note that the surface of the table is covered by different textures, created both by the individual hard objects sitting on it and by the ruffled tablecloth. The drapery in the upper right adds striking texture to the background. The textures of the relief images on the coins are clearly indicated also. And figural images abound—there are nine if we include the painter, and each one is unique.

The appeal of such characteristics as light, line, and texture is universal; as far as we know, all humans are attracted to the same visual features. More specific to the culture of seventeenth-century Holland are themes represented by the objects on the table. The skull, the watch, the roses past their bloom, the hourglass with sand running through it, the extinguished but still smoking candle, and the soap bubbles are all symbols of transience commonly portrayed in Dutch paintings of this period. The knife, goblet, and almost-full beer glass refer to feasting, the flute and palette represent the arts, and the book stands for knowledge. Probably there are yet other messages embedded in the images that are not recognizable to us today. At the time that this painting was completed, 1651, the number of objects that people encountered in their daily lives was much fewer than we experience today, but, in a place like the Netherlands, that number would have been much larger than in the world of the Bronze and Iron Age peoples who form the focus of this book.

Although the scene on the table belongs to the category "still life," the painter in fact represents movement in the scene. The soap bubbles seem to be floating through the air, and the smoke from the snuffed candle twists as it drifts upward.

THE BASIC MECHANICS OF VISION

Current understanding of the basic optical and physiological processes involved in how we see is well explained in a number of recent books on the subject by specialists in cognitive psychology and in the various branches of neuroscience. The bibliographic essay will lead the interested reader into that literature. Here I shall review a few aspects of the topic that are particularly relevant for the subject of this book.

Although in common parlance we speak of seeing with our eyes, in fact we do not see with our eyes, but with our brains. The eyes conduct light, via the retina at the back of the eyeball and the optic nerve, to the various different regions of the brain that are involved in seeing; as many as thirty have been suggested by neuroscientists. Seeing is thus a complex process that takes place in conjunction with other processes in which the brain is involved.

We do not see "what is out there" the way a camera records the scene in front of the lens. Rather, out of literally millions of signals that it receives every second via the optic nerve, our brain selects a tiny fraction that it deems worthy of attention. If the brain attempted to focus consciously on even a substantial fraction of the signals that come its way, it would be overwhelmed with visual information. What the brain sees is determined largely by what the individual has seen before—by what is stored in the memory of the individual and, thus, what the individual expects to see. The psychologist Richard Gregory argues that what the brain sees are hypotheses about the world from which the eyes transmit light signals to the brain and that these hypotheses are based on the individual's past experiences, that is, memories.

Experimental studies have shown that when we devote our visual attention to looking at something, we move our eyes in a series of rapid jumps from place to place, known as "saccades." When we focus more deliberately on an object or a scene, we first look at the edges or frame in order to define the boundaries of our subject, and then look at the interior. Looking at a painting, we examine the frame first, then the details of the picture inside it. When we look at a three-dimensional figure, a marble statue or a bronze horse, we first look at the outline or profile, then at details of the object's form.

Since when we look at something, our eyes move in saccadic jumps, it is easier for us to perceive clearly a moving object than a stationary one. We are all accustomed to looking directly at an object and realizing that we no longer see it well, then looking away, and then turning back to it. With objects in motion, this is not a problem, because we can keep our eyes, and our visual attention, focused on them as they move. We therefore see objects better—we can distinguish their size, color, details of shape, texture, decoration, and so forth—if we see them in motion than if we see them stationary. This is one reason why objects that are manipulated in rituals of different kinds remain much clearer in our memories than things that we have observed in a stationary state. This issue will become important in the discussion of performances in Chapter 9.

WHAT WE ACTUALLY SEE

When we look at something, the light reflected from it transmits only patterns, not actual images of the objects. We recognize the patterns of light as objects—plates, or baseballs, or trees—only on the basis of our experience seeing and touching those objects in the past. As infants we learn the relationship between seeing with our eyes (brain) and touching and feeling with our hands, and it is this calibration of seeing with touching that enables us to develop fully functional vision as we experience it every day. This fundamental relationship between seeing and feeling has been demonstrated in a number of cases of persons who gain sight after an early life spent in blindness. Typically they are able to see only those objects that they have had the experience of touching and handling when they were blind.

Seeing thus involves a person's bodily experience of the world in which he or she lives, a point developed by Mark Johnson. Our direct physical involvement with the world—with our cribs when we are babies; toys when we are children; houses, cars, towns, and landscapes when we are adults—plays a critical role in what and how we see. It is not just knowledge of and familiarity with these different aspects of our living environment that are important, but our active physical participation and interaction in that environment that is so vital to our experience of seeing.

The brain is actually shaped by the process and experience of seeing, changing its physical arrangement as the result of built-up experiences. The most familiar demonstration of this process is the enlarged hippocampus observed in studies of the brains of taxi drivers in London. London taxi drivers famously must pass the test known as "The Knowledge" by demonstrating their familiarity with the streets of London and with the quickest routes between any two points, a test for which drivers spend two to three years preparing. Physical changes in the brain resulting from particular visual experiences are a topic just beginning to attract research attention and one that will surely add significantly to our understanding as studies progress. The extent to which visual experiences of the past several millennia have affected human evolution is unclear at the present, but it is certain that there must have been some measurable effect.

We learn to see through the experience of seeing. What we have seen before greatly affects what we see in any given situation. If when we are infants we regularly see a lot of brown, rough-textured pottery, as infants in Bronze Age Europe did, that experience will strongly affect the way we see things the rest of our lives. If we see forests outside our houses and high mountains in the background, those visual experiences will affect everything we see afterwards. And seeing images affects how we see all images subsequently, a theme familiar from studies of modern populations seeing films, watching television, or playing video games.

Warren Neidich argues that visual art objects can be understood as maps of neurobiological perception. A painting or a drawing or a statue can tell us how people were seeing and otherwise perceiving the world around them at the time when the work of art was created. The same principal applies to all objects shaped by humans—to Middle Paleolithic handaxes, rough-surfaced Early Bronze Age jars, and scenes of seventeenth-century London painted by William Hogarth. Our challenge is to devise means for understanding the visual patterns in terms of the experiences of the people who made and used the objects. We need to bear in mind two fundamental differences between our visual perception of objects from the past and the perception of the people who made them and for whose visual consumption they were crafted. The first is that members of the societies that produced particular objects were much better informed about the meanings of the forms, images, and decorations that are a part of those objects than we much later observers can possibly be. In this sense, our challenge is to decipher their codes, to learn to identify the meanings in their patterns. The second is that objects played a much more important role as media for communication in societies that did not have writing than they do in ours (see Chapter 10).

APPROACHES TO VISUAL PERCEPTION

Several approaches to understanding how human vision works are especially pertinent to the topic explored in this book.

THE VISUAL WORLD

James J. Gibson developed the concept of the "visual world." A visual world is defined as the universe of things that an individual sees in the course of his or her life, the world in which the person lives and experiences daily existence. For studies such as this one, the concept has gained in importance as scientists come to better understand the effect of what the individual has seen on what he or she perceives in the future. Thus, if our goal is to understand how people saw in the past, we need not only to examine the visual attributes of the objects that they created and used, and the ways in which they arranged them in visually significant patterns. We need also to understand as much as possible about the visual characteristics of the world in which they lived—the kinds of landscape features that they saw regularly, the appearance of their settlements, their houses, their everyday pottery, their clothing, and so forth. Everything in their visual world played a part in creating their visual awareness, their cognitive map.

All material culture has a visual aspect. Burial mounds, walls around hilltops, ceramic vessels, bronze pins, iron axes and swords—everything that people create by digging, building, arranging, shaping, casting, engraving, painting, or otherwise fashioning objects become part of that society's visual world. There is little dispute that the principal purpose of much of material culture is visual display. Burial mounds are understood as media for displaying the status of the dead interred underneath them. Ornate clothing pins display status and affiliation. Figural representations convey messages about people, deities, and activities. But even objects that might not be considered first and foremost *visual* objects, such as knives, axes, swords, and plain ceramic bowls, also have important visual aspects and play significant roles in the visual world of the people who use and see them.

ECOLOGICAL PSYCHOLOGY

Gibson's interest in the importance of the environment to visual perception led him to formulate an "ecological psychology" based on the concept that the individual's perception is directly dependent upon the environment (in the widest sense of that word) in which the perception occurs. A close study of the environment in which perception takes place is, therefore, as important as the analysis of the individual doing the perceiving. Other investigators, including George Lakoff and Mark Johnson, emphasize the physicality of perception—the way that the human body in its environment perceives things through direct physical experience, especially through direct interaction with objects. Our perception, including visual perception, is determined in large measure by what we do with objects in the world around us, not just what we look at. We see things by interacting with them—touching them, handling them, carrying them, using them. The same principle pertains to our perception of landscapes, as Christopher Tilley argues. A landscape is understood not just as something to see, as if in a painting, but as something to act in—to walk through, to collect wood in, to harvest cereals in. We become familiar with a thing or a place, we come to recognize and understand it visually, by actively interacting with it.

We cannot fully understand the meaning or structure of any representation or decoration without examining it in relation to its entire visual context. An ornate fibula, a plain Bronze Age pot, a decorated scabbard—all of these objects can tell us much about the visual world and experience of the persons who saw and used them, but we can learn even more if we can examine them in the context in which they were seen and used by the people to whose material culture they belonged.

EXTENDED MIND THEORY

Extended mind theory, as outlined by Andy Clark, provides a useful way of thinking about the visual importance of objects. The essence of the theory is that when we make use of objects in the environment as "mnemonic devices" to extend our recall capabilities, we use those objects as extensions of our brains. Clark uses as an example a bartender who quickly lines up glasses of different kinds to remind himself or herself of the different drinks ordered and their sequence. Another instructive example is stage directions in Shakespearian theater, where specific objects are used as signals to remind the actors when to do something or what to say. We all use objects in our everyday lives to remind ourselves to do things—we place a particular item on a chair by the door to remind us to take something along when we go out or to pick something up at the store.

The value of this theory for studying the prehistoric past is that if we can identify particular objects that consistently occur in specific contexts, or decorative elements that consistently occur on pottery or on metal objects, then we may be able to identify uses to which such objects and ornaments were put as visual cues to action, for example in the course of ritual performances. Such objects remind the performer what to do next, and this function imbues them with an abstract meaning associated with that action. The usefulness of this approach will become clearer in later chapters of this book. For example, when we note the arrangement of objects in graves, we will notice that the placement of each individual object is likely to have been carried out at a specific point in the funerary ritual, and perhaps in the context of a specific oration or song (see Chapter 8).

In Chapters 5 through 12, I argue, on the basis of close analysis of the archaeological material, that fundamental changes in the visual patterning of material culture took place twice in later prehistory, once during the fifth century BC and then again during the second century BC. Both came about in large part as a result of the opening of European societies to ideas, motifs, and styles from outside, and to increasing receptivity on the part of the European societies to those stimuli. Clark's extended mind theory and the closely related "material engagement theory" of Lambros Malafouris and Colin Renfrew, would suggest that as increasing numbers of foreign objects enter a society, and, more importantly, are integrated into the material culture and practices of the society, they will have a significant cognitive effect on the members of that society. People's experience of their material culture, and, concurrently, their perception of their world, will change as a result. I discuss these changes in detail in Chapters 11 and 12, but shall summarize them briefly here.

In the Middle Iron Age (500–200 BC), societies of temperate Europe were for the first time exposed on a broad scale to designs, styles, and lifeways of peoples in other parts of the world—along the shores of the Mediterranean Sea especially, but also further afield in the Near East, Central Asia, and East Asia.

During the second century BC, even more profound changes took place, now as the result of societies in temperate Europe engaging directly with large-scale commercial systems that were expanding in Eurasia and Africa. These changes are apparent in the spread of the practice of coinage (adopted from Greek, and later also from Roman, societies), the limited adoption of writing (using Greek and Latin letters, mainly in the form of legends on coins), the mass production of pottery and iron tools, and increasingly extensive and intensive trade. The archaeological evidence shows substantial changes in life-styles at the great *oppidum* settlements of the final century-and-a-half BC, associated with this new, mass-produced material culture.

Along with the new kinds of objects (imports, coins, mass-produced goods) that constituted changes in their visual worlds, both everyday and spe-cial ritual practices changed as well, including those involving disposal of the dead and those concerned with the worship of supernatural forces.

The details of these changes will be presented in Chapters 11 and 12.

WHAT OBJECTS DO IN THE VISUAL WORLD

Objects that people make and use connect them to all the facets of their envi-ronment: to the natural environment, the social environment, and the ritual and political environments. Tools connect people to the natural world around them, axes for felling trees, plows for cultivating the soil; but these activities also have social aspects. Pottery connects people to their food supply, and at the same time links individuals socially through shared meals and celebratory feasts. Personal ornaments, whether in the form of metal brooches worn on the body or decorations on sword scabbards, connect individuals with others in a community through the social meaning implicit in all ornament. And many objects link people with the supernatural through ritual deposits made in ponds, pits, and other locations.

Objects can directly connect people with events, experiences, and memo-ries, as well as fostering relationships with deceased individuals. For example, a ceramic vessel that was used at everyday meals can acquire a special signifi-cance when a family member dies, as a physical manifestation, or materializa-tion, of the relationship.

Objects also act as agents, causing people to react to them in specific ways. They can evoke particular kinds of feelings, or they can constitute a call to action.

As a number of researchers from different disciplines have argued, deco-rative patterns on objects link people to things in special ways. Alfred Gell has called decoration a component of a social technology. In decorative and abstract art, the relationships between different elements in the patterns are significant. In this sense objects, and even the decorative details on objects, can be understood as media of communication, establishing and fostering relationships between people and between people and things.

SHAPING THE EXPERIENCE OF SEEING

People who want to attract attention to their products, whether they are prehistoric craftsworkers, Renaissance painters, or modern advertisers, use a number of devices to enhance the viewer's experience of seeing what they have fashioned. In this section I highlight some of these devices that are particularly relevant for understanding changes in visual patterning in Bronze and Iron Age Europe. In the discussion of specific archaeological materials in Chapters 5 through 10, it will become apparent how craftworkers who made pottery, metal ornaments, weapons, coins, and other objects employed these devices to achieve the visual effects that they wanted, and how individuals who arranged objects in graves and who performed rituals of different kinds applied these devices to their actions. Of particular importance will be discussion of how the application of these visual devices and practices changed during the final half millennium before the Roman conquests and the introduction of the technology of writing.

LINES

A dictionary definition of "line" is "a thin, continuous mark," and that definition will suffice for the basic concept here. Lines can vary greatly in character, location, and purpose, of course. They can be drawn on paper with a pencil, engraved into metal with a burin, created as a ridge on a ceramic vessel, or fashioned by arranging stones or heaping up soil to form a wall. Lines can be fine or thick, flat or raised, two dimensional or three dimensional, straight or curved, and they can form geometrical figures such as squares and circles, or irregular shapes. For the purposes of this book, lines can be understood to perform two main functions.

One is to form frames. The boundaries between things are frequently lines. Lines are abstract shapes, and those shapes can be expressed in a wide variety of media. Boundaries between agricultural fields can be lines of trees or stones. Boundaries around enclosed parcels of land can be linear ditches, earth walls, or wood fences. The boundary between the shoulder and neck on a ceramic vessel can be a linear ridge of clay. Lines can also be incised or engraved in clay, wood, or metal. They can be painted or drawn, pressed or hammered, as are the lines between the zones on Early Iron Age belt plates. (When lines are wide, we call them "zones.")

The other function of lines is to guide vision. A line leads the eye (actually the brain). When a line serves as part of a frame, it guides vision inward to examine the space within the frame. When a line runs along an object, such as a frieze around the top of a building or of a vessel, the eye follows it along its course. Lines incised on the sides of pots cause the viewer's attention to follow their course, enticing or even forcing the viewer to turn the pot or to walk around it to see where the lines lead.

When lines are grouped together in close parallel formation, they create texture. Designs on prehistoric pottery often include shapes defined by lines, such as triangles, which are then filled with finer incised lines, forming textured spaces. An extreme case is the comb-ornamented pottery of Late Iron Age Europe, where closely and regularly spaced parallel lines, sometimes very fine, sometimes broad and deep, cover the entire surfaces of vessels from the top of the shoulder to just above the base (see Figure 15). In these latter cases, the parallel lines give a very rough and highly visible texture to the pottery.

As Bridget Riley has shown with her work with painted lines, lines can create illusions of movement and energy. Experiments in cognitive psychology have shown that different kinds of lines can encourage different kinds of affective reactions in people who look at them. In their study of paintings by Jackson Pollock, Claude Cernuschi and Andrzej Herczynski note that his special technique of creating lines on canvas enabled him not only to create distinctive patterns of color, but also to show "motion and velocity" in a special way. As we will discover, some early European craftsworkers also achieved effects that suggested that lines were in motion.

In the chapters that follow, we shall see that the use of lines as visual devices was fundamental to the shaping and decorating of a wide variety of objects and to the arranging of objects in visually meaningful patterns.

S-Curves

A great deal has been written about S-shaped curves in art and design, because these forms were used so abundantly in many different traditions around the world, including those of Iron Age Europe.

William Hogarth, who thought a great deal about the shapes that were most pleasing to the human eye of his time, wrote in 1734 of the S-curve that "by its waving and winding at the same time different ways, [it] leads the eye in a pleasing manner along the continuity of its variety." He went on to describe the S-curve, which he called the "serpentine line," as the "line of grace," and suggested that it has the effect of leading the viewer's visual attention along a design. This is an important point to which we shall come back in later chapters. Earlier Albrecht Dürer also concerned himself with seeking out what he considered to be the fundamental shapes in nature, and he, too, arrived at the S-curve, together with the circle and the line. In his study of William Blake, W.J.T. Mitchell notes the artist's fondness for the S-curve, together with the spiral and the circle.

We shall see below that the S-curve was a key visual device in the first of the two major shifts in the designing of objects, during the fifth century BC.

Spirals

The spiral is another form often favored by artists and craftsworkers who have thought deeply about forms and integrated what they understood as natural shapes into their visual representations. It is, in fact, a variation on the line. Instead of twisting in opposite directions as the S-curve does, the spiral twists in upon itself in an increasingly tighter circle. Where the S-curve implies wavy and swaying motion, the spiral implies tightening motion, with increasing speed as the diameter of the circle decreases.

Formlines

In his *Northwest Coast Indian Art: An Analysis of Form* (1965), Bill Holm coined the term "formline" to designate the curvilinear shapes that characterize the art of the northwest coast of North America. The term is useful for describing much of the linear design of Late Iron Age metalwork in Europe, and I adopt it in this book. Formlines are lines that increase and decrease in width along their course, and in the process lead the viewer's eye along. The changing width creates a visual dynamism. The eye tends to follow from the narrow end to the wider, and then to retrace that path. The gradual swelling of the line gives the viewer a sense of growth and of motion.

In the European literature these forms in Late Iron Age ornament have been referred to as "trumpet" shapes, because the swelling of the line is like the widening of a trumpet from the mouthpiece to the bell. Whereas in the traditions of the northwest coast the formline is generally employed in two-dimensional designs on flat surfaces, in the European Iron Age the form was also used in high relief and in three-dimensional objects, such as fibulae. Whether in two or three dimensions, the visual effect is the same. The form-line leads the eye of the viewer from the narrow end to the wider end, and then back again.

STRUCTURES

Edges

When we first look at something, we look for the edges. They tell us where the thing we are looking at ends and something else begins. Only after we have located edges and feel satisfied that they are well established in our minds can we turn to the center, the focus of our visual attention. The edges are our guides in seeing.

A good way of thinking about this principle is in the context of frames around paintings, a theme that will emerge again in the discussion of Iron Age scabbards below. As F. R. Ankersmit observes, the frame guides us in looking at a painting. It plays the vital role of creating a border between it and the rest of the world (the wall of the museum), thus concentrating our gaze intensely on the image in front of us and our response to that image. Studies of paintings and frames have shown that a painting looks very different in different frames. Borders play a major part in our reception of what lies inside of them.

In Chapter 8, we shall see how important the frame of a grave was—the edges of the burial space—to participants' perception of the objects placed in it and of the performance of the funerary ritual.

Surfaces and Textures

James J. Gibson conducted extensive research on the visual perception of surfaces, and his work forms the basis for my approach here. His studies show that smooth surfaces attract little visual attention. We glance at smooth surfaces, and then our attention quickly moves on. But textured surfaces, whatever the nature of the texture might be, are visually more challenging and therefore hold our attention. Our brains want to analyze the texture, to understand exactly what is there. It is the different ways in which differently textured surfaces reflect light that gives them their distinctive visual properties. This principle applies to all surfaces, whether we are comparing a smooth paved road with a field of ripening wheat, or a smooth and highly polished ceramic vessel with one incised with linear ornament.

ARRANGEMENTS

I use the term "arrangements" to designate any combination of visual elements in patterns. One kind of arrangement is the way that incised decorations are situated with respect to one another on a ceramic vessel. Another is the positioning of decorative elements on a scabbard. Yet another example, on a different scale, is the way that pottery and jewelry are placed in the open space of a burial chamber.

Arrangements are a key concept in this study, because from the way that people arranged things, we can learn how they viewed and understood the relations between things. Arrangements provide the principal key for our understanding of how people saw in the past (as well as how people see today).

Especially important in the final chapters of this book will be our examination of how the character of arrangements of decorative details and of objects in visual spaces changed during the final half millennium of European prehistory.

IMAGES

Images are representations that the viewer can recognize and identify as signifying other things—humans, animals, plants, houses, pots, swords. They are what we commonly call "pictures," though they include both two-dimensional drawings and incisings and three-dimensional sculpture and reliefs. Decoration can contain images, but it need not. Conversely, images can occur as a part of decoration or as separate entities, as in the case of statues and paintings.

Images are intended to be recognizable by other members of the society in which they were produced and to refer to the thing that they resemble.

Frequently we encounter designs or decorations that we *think* may contain images, but we cannot be certain that they do. What we see as an image might not be recognized as such by a member of the society that produced it, whereas the latter may see an image where none appears to us. This problem of ambiguous images is a complex one and one that is especially important in Middle Iron Age decoration.

Faces

Faces play a special role in visual reception. Numerous studies in the field of cognitive psychology have shown that faces are the most compelling thing to look at in any given scene. The reason is probably that faces are the most social of all parts of the body. They are the principal visible indicators of identity, for although all human faces are similar, every individual has a distinctive face. Facial expressions are, moreover, key media of communication in all societies; speech emanates from faces, and the social activity of eating is centered on the face.

As we shall see in the chapters below, representations of faces were relatively rare before the beginning of the Iron Age. During the Early Iron Age representations of human faces were fashioned in one style, and then with the fundamental changes in seeing that took place during the fifth century BC, a radically different style came into fashion. At the end of the Iron Age, yet another style became dominant. These stylistic changes were part of the broader transformations in ways of seeing that accompanied the major cultural shifts brought about with the opening of Europe to styles, themes, and ideas from other parts of the world.

Animals

Animals play important roles in all human mythology and in thinking about relationships between humans and the rest of the world. They have some qualities that are human-like, but also many that are different. This complex and ambiguous link between the human and the animal fascinates us, as do animals' behaviors and abilities.

As with faces, changes in the ways that animals were represented during the Bronze and Iron Ages help us to understand the major changes in ways of seeing that took place during the final half millennium of European prehistory. And, as with faces, these changes resulted in large part from the increased participation of European societies in the major economic, political, and cultural transformations that were taking place throughout Eurasia and Africa.

Phatic Characters

Many objects were crafted specifically to catch the eye. Paul Virilio has coined the term "phatic" to designate such images, whose primary purpose is to attract attention—to force the viewer to look—rather than to convey information. Alfred Gell uses the expression "technology of enchantment" to mean something similar: a visual image that is so fascinating that it "enchants" the viewer. The viewer is spellbound by the appearance of something and loses his or her ability to turn away. Advertisers are the primary users of phatic images today, their goal being to attract your attention to a particular product so that they can get on with transmitting the message. In later prehistoric Europe, many gold ornaments and some bronze and stone sculptures can be considered phatic, or enchanting, in this sense.

AFFORDANCES

An "affordance," in James J. Gibson's formulation, is a space that allows for a possibility of action, for filling in with decoration, texture, or imagery. It is a space that "affords" an organism (a human, an animal, or a plant) the possibility of adding something, of decorating, or of moving through. It is an important concept the development of which has revolutionized thinking about space and human action and perception.

In earlier analyses of objects such as sword scabbards, attention was devoted to those parts that bore complex ornament, such as the figural or design decoration at the top of the scabbard and on the chape at the bottom. Little attention was given to the flat surfaces between them. In the study of burials, the main focus has traditionally been on the grave goods *per se*. When attention was given to the arrangement of objects in the grave, it focused on the placing of pottery, bronze vessels, vehicles, and so forth in the grave, but very little was said about the open spaces—the spaces left unoccupied by body or grave goods. In the study of enclosed sites, whether settlements or "sanctuaries," discussion again focused on ditches, walls, postholes, storage pits, and other structures, and little notice was taken of the open spaces.

But as Gibson's discussion of affordances makes clear, the open spaces *are* important—the blank surfaces on scabbards, undecorated places on pottery, unoccupied spaces in graves, and open areas on settlement sites. A similar point is made in reference to illustrations in Diderot's *Encyclopédie* by John Bender and Michael Marrinan: the white spaces in the illustrations are important. "When diagrams are treated as material objects, their entire surface plays a role and whiteness is never a void." These spaces on objects, in graves, and on sites are major constituent parts of the objects and places, like the spaces that show ornament and features, they too were acted upon. As Mark Johnson observes, the same object or landscape can offer different possibilities—different affordances—at different times, depending upon the individual, the environment, and the action at hand.

In the discussion that follows, affordances will play a key role in our analysis of perception and action.

PATTERNS, CONNECTIONS, AND DIAGRAMS

All objects, whether portable or earthbound, as well as all other aspects of cultural life—including kinship systems, folksongs, and religious beliefs and practices—are linked by common cultural elements and themes. David Brett uses the term "visual ideology" to refer to the ways that visual elements interrelate in expressing the worldview or essence of a community's culture. These connections are clear in some cases, as with Early Iron Age belt plates, pottery, and personal ornaments, which all show a similar organization of decoration and similar visual themes. We can see the same common patterns of decoration recurring in the different categories of objects. Less obvious are connections between the designs on these portable objects and the architectural styles of houses, the shapes of burial chambers, and the layout of the so-called "sanctuary" sites of Western Europe. Theoretically, all of these things are interrelated in their visual features, and in the following chapters I shall demonstrate the nature of these interrelations.

Any complex crafted or arranged object can be understood as a "diagram," in the sense that Bender and Marrinan use the term. Diagrams are multimedia visual representations of how things work. Elaborately decorated pottery, ornate sword scabbards, arranged burial chambers, and sanctuary sites can all be understood as diagrams of the way that the members of the societies that fashioned them believed that their societies worked and the way that they related to the world in which they lived.

In David Bailly's painting with which I began this chapter, the artist has represented on the table and on the walls an entire complex of themes important to the Dutch in the seventeenth century. One could write a detailed account of the culture, beliefs, and practices of that society on the basis of the objects that Bailly has arranged and represented for the viewer.

This concept of the diagram will be useful in our examination of complex objects and arrangements in the chapters that follow, and it will help us to see the fundamental differences in ways of seeing that developed as European societies became ever more actively involved in the commercial and cultural affairs of greater Eurasia.

CHAPTER 3

<><><><><><><><><><><><><><><><><><>

THE VISUAL WORLDS OF EARLY EUROPE

VISUAL ECOLOGY BEFORE ELECTRIC LIGHTS

Except in broad daylight, everything looked different to the people who lived in Europe three thousand years ago from how it looks to us, and all because we live with electric lights. Our interiors are illuminated day and night. Only when we experience power outages, go camping, or otherwise intentionally limit ourselves to a few small light sources, can we begin to imagine what the visual world must be like for people who have no ready access to modern electric lighting.

Some idea of what things looked like can be gained from paintings that show interior scenes in pre-electric contexts. David Teniers the Younger's *Two Men Playing Cards in the Kitchen of an Inn*, painted sometime between 1635 and 1640 and now in the National Gallery in London, gives an idea of what the inside of buildings looked like before electric lighting. I use this example because of the representation of pottery and of how it reflects light. It is clear from the locations in which Teniers situated the different vessels that he felt that they were important components of the visual world of this scene. In a recent examination of the painting, I counted twenty-eight vessels, nineteen of them ceramic, five of glass, two of wood, and two of metal (these numbers do not include three pipes and the candleholder). Six pottery vessels are clearly shown in the front room, and their importance to the artist's intention is readily apparent from their locations. The tall cylindrical vessel on the table in the middle of the four principal figures is the center of attention. We can see its complete form, and there is space left around and above it, so that it stands out as framed by the surrounding human figures. The large jugs on the lower left and lower right serve to frame the central part of the painting. In the back room, an entire row of vessels lines the shelf at the right side of the picture, and through the window we see part of a high shelf with a row of pots on it.

The pottery vessels play special roles in the overall visual character of the image. Teniers emphasizes their three dimensionality with his use of reflected light and shadow. In contrast to the furniture, they are formed not of straight lines, but of complex in-curving and out-curving profiles. Even the central cylindrical vessel, which looks at first straight with parallel sides, has details of profile that make the base flare out, and the rim has an outset shape. The shapes of several other objects echo those of the pottery—most notably the wooden bucket in the left foreground, the round object in the right foreground, and the metal vessel that the woman in the back room is holding over the fire. Even the round seat of the stool refers to the opening of the wide-mouthed pots. The two most prominent vessels in the foreground, both jugs, have shapes that recall, and may refer to, the human body, with wider middle portions, shoulders that constrict inward at the top, and a discrete neck. These two jugs are brightly lit, much more than seems realistic in a dark tavern interior. Teniers shows us their entire forms in full color, and both have patches of glinting reflection, suggesting a shiny glaze. Even the vessels positioned further back in the picture are highlighted with patches of reflected light.

THE VISUAL WORLD OF BRONZE AND IRON AGE EUROPE

Teniers's painting gives us hints as to how we might think about the way pottery appeared to Europeans a couple of thousand years ago, but we need now to expand the discussion to develop a general picture of the whole of the visual world of late prehistoric Europe.

LANDSCAPE

The Character of the Landscape

On the crudest scale, the landscape of temperate Europe has not changed a great deal in the past four thousand years. By ten thousand years ago, the earth's climate had warmed substantially following the most recent glacial maximum of the Pleistocene, and by about nine thousand years ago, the mixed oak forest that has characterized the natural environment of most of temperate Europe in recent times had established itself as far north as Scotland and central Sweden. Sea levels continued to rise in some coastal regions, but the basic character of the hills, valleys, and plains, the mountains and the rivers, has not changed drastically during the past four thousand years. If we were to travel back over those years we would find the rural landscapes of temperate Europe looking much as they do today, except for the absence of the infrastructure that has been built since the time of the Romans and especially since the Industrial Revolution, including roads and bridges. (There was nothing in prehistoric Europe that would compare with modern cities, suburbs, or large buildings.)

Rome introduced paved roads to temperate Europe, stone bridges, and large-scale stone and brick architecture. In the millennia that are the subject of this book—between four and two thousand years ago—there were no paved roads, practically no buildings built of stone (except in a few stone-rich and tree-poor environments, such as the Alps and northern Scotland), and no settlements that might be called urban, with the possible exception of the *oppida* of the final century-and-a-half BC (see Chapters 10–12).

The character of the landscape differed somewhat in the different regions of Europe, just as it does today. What I describe here is a typical landscape in the middle of temperate Europe. By the Early Bronze Age, some of the most fertile land had been cleared of forest cover. The first farming communities appeared in the central parts of temperate Europe around 5500 BC. Practices of forest clearance varied. In some areas, sizeable stands of forest remained; in others, only small wooded areas. Communities probably always maintained some woodland in their neighborhoods as sources of building timber, firewood, pitch, and tar, and as places to gather berries, honey, and other natural woodland products. The principal trees that grew in the central parts of Europe were oak, alder, beech, hazel, and pine, offering a variety of woods for different purposes. When forested areas were cleared of trees, they regenerated, unless the farmers made efforts to keep them at bay. The experience of clearing forests and seeing the trees grow back was itself visually striking and memorable.

The cleared land bore crops seasonally and provided grazing for livestock. During the growing season, wheat, barley, and millet were the primary cereals, and garden crops such as peas and lentils were grown in smaller plots near the houses.

The basic character of the agricultural and pastoral economy changed only gradually during the Bronze and Iron Ages, with the development of new production technologies—bronze sickles during the Bronze Age, for example, and iron scythes and plowshares during the Late Iron Age—and with the introduction of new cultivated plants.

Seasonality

Both the forested land and the cleared land changed in appearance over the course of the year, and this regular variety and cyclicality of change was important to the way that the inhabitants saw and understood their world. The

foliage on deciduous trees changed color throughout the year, and in the au-
tumn, those trees lost their leaves and remained bare of greenery until the
following spring. In summer, they were again in full foliage and thus visually
"closed in." After the harvest in the fall, the fields would have been covered
with matted cereal stalks; in the winter, the ground would have been uneven,
dark brown, often covered with snow. After planting, the light green shoots
would emerge from the ground to develop into densely growing fields of grain
during the summer. Fields would have had a much more variegated appearance than modern fields do, because there was greater mixing of seed grains
then, and weeds were much more abundant (they are well represented in soil
samples from excavated Bronze Age and Iron Age settlements).

Bodily Interaction in the Landscape

The Europeans of the period we are examining did not just see the landscape,
they lived in it and as parts of it, and through their interaction with its components they changed both the landscape and themselves. The vast majority of
people—probably between 95 and 98%, depending upon the location—were
full-time farmers and livestock-tenders, intimately linked to the land. It was
where they spent their waking hours and what they saw in the course of their
daily routines. And they depended upon it for their livelihood. When we look
at rural landscapes today, most of us view them from highways or country
roads as we pass by. Unless we are directly involved in working the land, our
connection with it, and our view of it is very different. We have been taught
our way of looking at the landforms, vegetation, animals, and people in landscapes through media other than our own direct experience.

Ann Jensen Adams argues that modern Westerners' understanding of
landscape is heavily affected by seventeenth-century landscape painting, that
the images created by the Dutch landscape painters such as van Ruisdael, Rubens, and their successors have taught us what to see in a landscape. Even if we
as individuals have not seen Dutch landscape paintings, most of us have seen
some kind of landscape paintings and photographs, and, Adams argues, all
such representations since the seventeenth-century have referenced, whether
explicitly or not, that earlier landscape tradition.

The physical involvement of Bronze Age people in the landscape—their
plowing, digging, cultivating, harvesting, threshing, storing, herding livestock, collecting firewood, cutting down trees, making fences, and con-
structing buildings—all these forms of work meant that they perceived their
physical world with a directness and intensity that most of us can only try
to imagine. When we look over the countryside from the vantage point of
a pull-off on the highway or a pause at a hilltop along a country road, what

we see (depending upon where exactly we might be) are pretty hedgerows, fields full of grains of different colors (depending upon the season), against a background of villages and church spires. It all looks pretty, neat, ordered, and well tended. The same view would have looked very different to a Bronze Age person. He or she would have seen each feature of the landscape—the fields, trees, fences, and hedges—as a product of intensive labor, direct bodily engagement, and also as a potential source of the raw materials for sustenance and trade. In our case, viewing Dutch (and other) landscape paintings, photographs in magazines, scenes in films, and the like, has taught us to see landscapes in a radically different way, and when we pause by the side of the road and gaze out at the countryside, we are informed by these visual experiences.

A very modest example from personal experience will illustrate the point. During the summers from 1978 to 1981, I carried out archaeological excavations in a field just north of the city of Landshut in Bavaria, Germany. When my German colleague Rainer Christlein, under whose auspices I conducted the excavations, took me to visit the site in the summer of 1977, what I saw was a muddy field covered with crops on the edge of a terrace overlooking the valley of the Isar River. The land looked like all of the other land along the terrace extending in both directions along the edge of the valley. During the four summer field seasons of excavation, we surveyed the land, marked out 5-by-10-meter trenches, and excavated, layer by layer, through the plowsoil and humus to the underlying loess subsoil, in some places just 35 cm below the modern surface (the depth to which modern plows reach), in some places to a depth of 1.5 meters. I became accustomed to seeing the field as a surface marked by large rectangular trenches extending from the surface down to the subsoil, and to seeing that subsoil as spotted with the dark fill of features (prehistoric ditches and pits) and by the hollows left after the excavation team had completed work on those features. Even after we had filled in the trenches after we had explored the prehistoric features and recovered archaeological materials for study, the field retained the shapes of our trenches (Figure 4). Those open trenches across the field, the exposed prehistoric features, and the appearance of the filled-in trenches, are all still vivid in my mind, because I was bodily involved with excavating, photographing, and mapping them, and later with the close study and analysis of the maps, photographs, and drawings that we produced in order to publish our results. I am reminded of the appearance of these workings of the field every year when I show images—now via PowerPoint rather than the slides that we took during the excavation—in my European archaeology class.

When I drive by the field, what I see is different from what I imagine other people must see. There is now a small parking lot on the far western edge of the field, where we excavated, but the rest of the field is planted with crops every summer, sometimes corn (maize), sometimes wheat, sometimes barley.

FIGURE 4. The field at Hascherkeller on the outskirts of Landshut, Bavaria, Germany, where a Late Bronze and Early Iron Age settlement was situated. In the foreground are excavation trenches that have been refilled, in the background archaeologists work in open trenches.

While the casual passerby sees a small parking lot with a handful of cars in it and a field that looks like all of the other fields in the surrounding landscape, I invariably see in my imagination the open trenches, the subsurface features, and the refilled trenches with which I was so intensively engaged. The important point is not that I *saw* the trenches, it is that I was bodily involved in working that land. That is the experience that truly changes how we see something. I am not implying that this experience of spending parts of four summers excavating in the field is comparable to that of the farmer who works the land all year long for decades, and surely our different goals in working in the field and the different ways in which we were involved with the soil greatly affect how we perceive it as well.

Color and Texture

The color and texture of the landscape of temperate Europe varied in appearance with the seasons. In the summer the fields were green with crops, uncultivated areas grew with grasses and shrubs, trees were in full foliage, and wildflowers dotted the edges. In winter, fields were brown and gray, sometimes white with snow, and deciduous trees were bare of leaves. The colors varied, even with the time of day.

The texture of the landscape also varied significantly. In winter and spring, when the fields were bare, the cultivated areas were rough, uneven, and hard-looking. Clumps of dirt froze in the winter and became like rocks. Gazing out across the fields one would see a rough, coarse surface, sometimes softened by snow. As the spring shoots grew into summer grains, the fields took on a very different texture, soft and yielding to the breeze and to rain showers. These different visual aspects of the fields were important, seasonally changing features of the landscape.

The Visual Past in the Landscape

In most parts of temperate Europe, communities of the Bronze and Iron Ages lived in landscapes that had been substantially shaped by their forebears in other ways besides the clearing of some of the forest to create fields and pastures. They also left structures that were visual reminders of past inhabitants and their activities in the landscape. These included burial mounds (Figure 5), megalithic tombs (Figure 6), stone circles (Figure 7), standing stones, walls (Figure 8), and ditches. Often these structures can be understood as parts of complex shaped landscapes, in which different kinds of monuments were arranged in particular ways that remained in place for millennia, as in the recently studied "Catholme Ceremonial Complex" in central England. When local histories began to be recorded during the later Middle Ages and in early modern times, local populations had stories about the monuments in their landscapes that linked the earthworks with the devil, with nature spirits, and with other imaginary forces. Traces of these stories can be seen on modern maps in place names such as the Devil's Dyke in England and *Teufelsmauer* in Germany. In modern times, these landscape features have often served as guideposts for travelers, while earlier they were regarded as significant links with communities of the past. Their existence as part of the visible landscape was an important factor in how people saw and understood the world around them.

Eternal Wilderness

It needs to be noted that parts of the landscapes of temperate Europe were never brought under cultivation and never inhabited. Within the central upland regions of Europe, between the North European Plain and the Alps, are numerous hills and small mountain ranges, where steep slopes and rocky terrain never encouraged settlement. On a recent train ride through the Eifel in western Germany, I was struck by the relative inaccessibility, even in 2010, of many of the narrow valleys just a few tens of kilometers from the great centers of Cologne, Frankfurt, and Trier.

FIGURE 5. Bronze Age burial mounds at Västra Karaby, Scania, Sweden.

SETTLEMENT

The settlement in which the individual lived was a part of the landscape, but it also occupied a special place in daily experience and in the mind, because it was the domesticated part of the landscape, the place separated from fields and meadows and woodlands. What people did in the settlement was different from what they did outside it, and the settlement looked different. The significance of this difference is apparent in the important role played by the boundaries around settlements in Bronze and Iron Age Europe. Especially from the Late Bronze Age on, settlements in many regions of Europe were surrounded by ditches and palisades that marked the the settled area off from the rest of the landscape. Whether the primary purpose of such barriers was to keep unwanted animals and humans out, to keep livestock from straying, or to mark the boundary between inside and outside for other reasons, the result for the visual landscape was the same. The boundary created a distinct divide between the area of the settlement and the rest of the environment.

Visually, the settlement was distinguished primarily by the presence of houses. They were typically post-built, with either vertical timbers sunk into the ground (leaving postholes, their clearest archaeological trace) or with horizontal sleeper-beams laid on the ground or set into shallow trenches, and with walls of wattle-and-daub, and roofs of thatch. The average settlement had two or three houses, along with smaller outbuildings. During the Iron Age, some larger settlements developed with tens and, in the case of the *oppida*, hundreds of houses.

FIGURE 6. Megalithic tomb complex at Lindeskov, Fyn, Denmark.

While the basic technology of house architecture and the size of settlements were similar on the continent and in Britain, house shapes were different on either side of the English Channel. On the continent houses were consistently rectangular, in Britain they were round.

For our purposes here, the most important visual aspects of the settlement are the different texture of the settlement compared to the fields, and the colors and textures of the houses. Also of importance is the visual relationship between settlements and places for the burial and commemoration of the dead. Archaeologists recently have investigated these relationships on Bronze Age sites in the Netherlands, for example at Elp and at Weelde. In these instances, the burial monuments were a constant component of the visual world of the inhabitants of the farms and villages.

HOUSES

The geometric regularity of the houses distinguished them from anything else in the landscape. Continental houses with their rectangular form and slanting roofs, and the conical round houses of Britain, were visually completely different from the fields, meadows, and trees. Up close, the daub walls were unlike anything in the outside world—vertical, smooth, tan in color, and sometimes

FIGURE 7. Stonehenge, an exceptionally complex Neolithic stone circle on Salisbury Plain, southern England. On the far left is the circle of standing stones with lintels on top, to the right of that is the heelstone, and in the foreground and on the right is the circular ditch that surrounds the central part of the site.

painted. Traces of paint have been found on daub at some sites, but it is not clear how common the use of paint was. The thatched roofs had a different character—roughly textured—that contrasted with the smooth and hard daub walls.

In the central regions of the continent, Bronze Age and Iron Age houses were smaller than modern houses in Europe and North America. The recently excavated settlement of the late sixth and fifth centuries BC at Allaines Mervilliers in France is a good example of the central continental type, with small, mostly single-roomed, almost square buildings. On the North European Plain, houses were different in character, as extensive archaeological research in the Netherlands, northern Germany, and Denmark makes clear. They took the shape of long, thin rectangles, incorporating living quarters for humans at one end and byres for livestock at the other. Well-documented examples include the Late Bronze Age houses at Elp in the Netherlands and at Gørding in Denmark. In both central and northern Europe, houses were more uniform in structure and in appearance than are houses in modern times.

One of the most important differences was in the lack of electric light. When we enter a dark house or apartment, we immediately illuminate our spaces with a flick of a switch. We can change the level of illumination by turning on more or fewer lamps, by using bulbs of higher wattage, or by buying

FIGURE 8. Grass-covered remains of the earth, timber, and stone wall at the *oppidum* at Altenburg, southern Baden-Württemberg, Germany (originally published in Wells 1993:4, fig. 1.2).

more lamps. For prehistoric Europeans, house interiors were usually dark, and even the wealthiest had no easy way to increase illumination beyond a certain point. This was more-or-less the case until the late eighteenth century for the great majority of Europeans.

Window glass does not appear in the archaeological record until Roman times. Hence, during the colder months, house interiors were dark even during the daytime. At night, the majority of people had only the hearth-fire for illumination. Although we may think of roaring fires casting considerable light around a room, our modern familiarity with these derives mainly from the fires we kindle on special occasions, for holidays and parties. For most people in earlier times, the supply of wood for burning was limited, and fires had to be kept low most of the time. Oil lamps burning animal fat may have added some illumination, but these were never bright by our standards, and animal fat was a valuable commodity.

Although in most of temperate Europe, the living floors have been destroyed by millennia of plowing, we have enough information from special circumstances of preservation to get a fairly good idea of what the interiors of houses looked like. Lakeshore settlements such as Wasserburg Buchau provide useful information, since they were inundated, and the boggy soil was not subsequently plowed. A number of houses in Iron Age Denmark also yield good evidence for the situation of hearths and pottery arranged on the floor.

The evidence suggests that the interior of houses was dominated by the highly rectilinear forms of furniture and shelves, which corresponded with the linear patterning of the interior structure—the posts, ceiling beams, and thatch. During the Bronze Age folding stools were part of the accouterments of many wealthier burials, and it is reasonable to assume that they were used in furnishing houses of the elites as well. Wooden boards set on top of earth banks arranged along the walls seem to be characteristic of Iron Age houses. The bronze couch in the Hochdorf burial is unique, but it fits into this pattern of rectilinear furniture and was probably used in an elite household during the life of the buried individual. The shape of the Hochdorf couch has been compared to some of the furniture represented in Situla Art of the sixth through the fourth centuries BC, where we see scenes of such furniture in use in social contexts represented on the figural-ornamented pails in Austria, Slovenia, and northeastern Italy (see for example Figure 37, page 160). The presence of remains of furniture in the Grafenbühl grave indicates that furniture was probably not unusual in either the dwellings or the burials of elites during the late sixth and early fifth centuries. Remains of a table in a Late Iron Age grave at Wederath provide additional evidence for furniture that is consistent with the rectilinear pattern suggested above.

Finally, we need to consider the visuality of house interiors with regard to the movement of people within them. Drawings of reconstructed house interiors and reconstructed interiors in open-air museums provide us with a static view of what things looked like inside houses. But for the inhabitants, the way that things looked to people as they moved about in the house was important. A pottery vessel sitting on a shelf or a table viewed from a single vantage point provides one kind of visual interaction, but when the observer approaches the vessel and walks around it, the visual experience is different and much richer.

The important point here is that when people looked at objects inside their houses—pottery, bronze jewelry, iron tools—they saw them very differently from the way we see objects in our houses, and very differently from the way that we see Bronze Age pottery and Iron Age jewelry and tools in museum cases or spread out on laboratory tables. We need to take careful account of these differences if we are to hope to understand their visual worlds.

CHANGES IN THE VISUAL WORLD

During the two millennia between the beginning of the Early Bronze Age and the end of the Iron Age, changes in the landscape, in the character of settlements, houses, and in other aspects of the visual environment were most often (but not always) gradual. A number of significant trends are recognizable in the environmental evidence pertaining to changes in the landscape; and there is archaeological evidence pertaining to changes in tool use, the digging of ditches, the building of walls, and the construction of settlements and houses.

As a rule, more and more land was cleared over time for creating farmland and pasturage. This process did not happen in the same way or at the same pace everywhere, however, and in some cases, farmland even reverted to woodland. A major phase of clearance took place in the Late Bronze Age (1200–800 BC), when new lands were cleared higher on slopes and in regions that had previously been sparsely settled. A pollen diagram from Scania in southern Sweden shows this trend especially clearly. From around 4000 BC, when agriculture was first introduced to the region, until around 1000 BC, the very gradual increase in pollen indicative of cultivated land at the expense of pollen indicative of forest shows the very gradual expansion of the farmed lands. Then, between 1000 and 900 BC, the amounts of pollen associated with agriculture suddenly increases. Similar changes are evident elsewhere in Europe.

During the Early Iron Age and the Middle Iron Age (800–200 BC), the trend toward greater land clearance persisted, but without the great jump evident in the Late Bronze Age. In many of the central regions of temperate Europe, settlement centers developed during the sixth century BC, with populations in the hundreds and in a few cases in the thousands, and evidence of active manufacturing and both regional and long-distance trade, as well as local food production. The considerably larger populations at these centers, of which Mont Lassois in France, the Heuneburg in Germany, and Závist in Bohemia are among the best known, led to the increasingly intensive use of the agricultural potential of the lands around them and increasing exploitation as well of a range of resources, but these changes were largely limited to the regions around these towns. The many often large flat-grave cemeteries of the Middle Iron Age documented throughout continental temperate Europe during the fourth and third centuries BC attest to substantial populations, but there are no signs of the regional centers of the preceding centuries.

A notable change in landscapes that did occur was the cutting down of substantial woodlands for the production of fuel for ironworking. While iron began to replace bronze as the principal metal for tools and weapons during the eighth century BC, it was not until the fourth century BC that its production reached a significant level in many parts of the continent. From that point on, the smelting of iron ore and the forging of iron implements required substantial supplies of fuel in the form of wood charcoal. The large numbers of iron weapons that are recovered in burials of these centuries, along with tools and ornaments from graves and from settlements, indicates that iron production was being carried out on an ever-larger scale, and that a great deal of wood was needed to fuel this process.

With the establishment during the second and first centuries BC of the large enclosed settlements known as *oppida*, the production of iron, as well as that of a range of other materials, reached what we might call an "industrial" stage. But there were other processes at work that also greatly altered the landscape during the final two centuries BC.

The *oppida* were settlements enclosed by walls built of earth, timber, and stone (Figure 8). (The word *oppidum* comes from Julius Caesar's use of that term in reference to the major fortified centers that he encountered in Gaul. It is now generally applied by archaeologists to all of the large fortified centers of Late Iron Age temperate Europe.) The settlement at Manching in Bavaria, the most thoroughly investigated *oppidum* site in Europe, was 380 ha in area, enclosed by a roughly circular wall about seven thousand meters in length. Estimates suggest that some sixty thousand trees were felled for the wooden structure of the wall alone, with thousands more needed for the superstructure that is believed to have been built on top of the wall. A supply of wood of this magnitude would have required the clearing of several hundred hectares of forest. The bottom wooden structure of the wall was held in place by iron spikes, around seventy-five hundred kilograms of which were required. The smelting of iron ore to produce these would have required additional wood from what forests remained. And we have not even begun to consider the wood needed for building houses and making tools, for smelting iron for tools and weapons, or for cooking and heating. The upshot is that the landscapes around the *oppida*, some 150 of which have been identified throughout the central regions of Europe, were profoundly altered through the extensive harvesting of timber for smelting, construction, and manufacturing.

Other changes in the landscape were effected by increasingly intensive techniques of food production. Iron-tipped plows came into general use during the Late Iron Age, enabling the efficient cultivation of rich valley bottom soils. The manufacture of scythes enabled the more efficient harvesting of hay for winter fodder. These new agricultural techniques made possible the larger harvests that would accommodate greater populations, and the sum of all these factors contributed to changing the appearance of the landscapes of temperate Europe. What confronted a viewer in 100 BC was substantially different from what a viewer would have seen five centuries earlier. Except for their surrounding walls and their size, the settlements of this period probably did not look very different from those of earlier times. Houses still were built with post frames and wattle-and-daub walls, and they were of about the same size as those of the Bronze Age and earlier phases of the Iron Age.

In marked contrast to contemporary urban centers in the Mediterranean world, the *oppida* give no indication of large-scale public architecture of any type—there are no recognizable temples, palaces, or administrative buildings that stand out from the houses by virtue of their monumentality. There has been discussion as to whether the *oppida* were similar in character to cities of the Mediterranean world, or whether they were more like groups of villages settled within the great enclosing walls. The lack any kind of apparent central monumental architecture would support the second model. In general, the *oppida* seem not to have had centralized production facilities for making pottery, forging iron, or casting bronze. Instead, excavations have shown that these production activities were carried out in different parts of the sites, in the context of what would be independent villages if they were not within the *oppidum* walls, as at Manching in Bavaria, Staré Hradisko in Moravia, and Stradonice in Bohemia.

The main demonstrable difference between house interiors of this later period and those of the Bronze Age is the presence of larger implements in the kitchen—large bronze-and-iron cauldrons, iron tripod stands with chains for suspending the cauldrons over a fire, and large iron andirons (firedogs).

LIGHT

With Teniers's painting of the interior of an inn at the start of this chapter, I introduced the topic of light as an important issue in any consideration of seeing in times previous to the ready availability of electric light. To close this chapter on the visual world of early Europe, I return to the topic of light, because all of the visual elements and practices that I discuss in later chapters depend directly upon the character of the available light.

SOURCES

In later prehistoric Europe, the only source of indoor light, aside from what natural daylight could enter through doors and windows, was fire. The main hearth provided most of the illumination inside a house. In most households, the fire must have been maintained at a low level, except when cooking food, as the fuel supply was limited. Our main concern with fire in this book is as a source of light, but other aspects must also be considered. Fire played an essential role in the preparation of foods of many different kinds. It provided heat during the long, wet, and cold winters of temperate Europe. And as the primary source of light, of energy for cooking, and of heat for the house, it was an important medium of sociality as well. People gathered around the fire so that they could see what they were working on, for warmth, to eat, and to be with the other members of their household. All of these behaviors affected how fire was perceived and understood. We get some sense of its vital role in the minds and imaginations of people in times before the widespread availability of electricity from the rich body of folklore and superstition that surrounds fire in traditions all over the world.

Finally, fires must be supplied. Even when kept low, they constantly consume wood. A major household responsibility was the collecting of firewood, especially the winter supply. The chore of gathering firewood brought people into direct interaction with those parts of the landscape where wood was available and thus with the experience of seeing stands of trees in the different seasons of the year.

As anyone who has experienced a fireplace in a modern house knows, the light from a hearth fire is not bright compared to that of electric lights, and it flickers rather than providing steady light. Whereas we usually have multiple lamps in a room, creating diffuse light in the space, a fireplace is a single source of light and the room that it illuminates is consequently full of shadows. With the flickering of the fire, the shadows appear to move.

Other sources of illumination, such as tapers (as at Hallstatt) and candles, were available to households that commanded more resources than most, and perhaps to many households on special occasions. When we consider feasts and other special events, we need to reckon with the possibility that these additional sources of lighting were available.

THE MOVEMENT OF LIGHT AND SHADOW

Many of the objects from Bronze and Iron Age Europe that we see today in well-lighted display cases in museums or in photographs in books were crafted to be viewed in the flickering and ever-changing light provided by the flames of fireplaces, lamps, or tapers. Much of the jewelry with figural ornamentation, including gold neckrings like those from Hochdorf and Vix, Erstfeld and Reinheim, bronze fibulae such as the examples from Parsberg and the Glauberg, and belt-hooks like those from Weiskirchen and the Glauberg, was probably designed with this light effect in mind. We can get some sense of the visual effects of firelight on such objects by examining them closely while moving the focused beam of a flashlight across their surfaces. This technique is not an exact replication of a hearth fire in an Iron Age house, nor are our sensibilities those of Iron Age Europeans, but even this simple demonstration shows that moving (flickering) light creates patterns of illumination and shadows that give objects decorated with zoomorphic ornament a lifelike character, almost as if the creatures are moving with the light.

Bronze vessels would have been similarly affected by light. But while the ornate jewelry gave meaning and essence to the individual who wore it, bronze vessels (also highly valued articles of material culture) probably served their principal functions in feasting rituals. And like much of the jewelry in the richer graves, they, especially vessels of non-usual character, bear elaborate figural ornament strikingly similar in character to the decoration that we find on ornate jewelry. The jugs from Kleinaspergle, the Glauberg, Reinheim, Waldalgesheim, and Maloměřice are examples. We need to envision them sitting on tables in front of participants at feasts, illuminated with ever-changing patterns of firelight and shadow, and periodically picked up by hosts or participants as they filled the cups of waiting celebrants.

LIGHT AND SOCIAL INTERACTION

As we consider the effects of different kinds of light on how objects look to people, we need to bear in mind also the important role played by light in social interaction. Before the advent of electric light, people in Europe and elsewhere in the world gathered around fireplaces for the light as much as for the heat. The light of the fireplace enabled people to see one another and thus to communicate by facial expression and gesture as well as by speech. This function is frequently depicted in paintings and described in stories. This social role of light is in fact critical to our understanding of how people responded to the light that illuminated different kinds of objects.

LIGHT'S SPECIAL EFFECTS ON PARTICULAR SHAPES

Spheroid objects, such as pottery vessels, produce special visual effects under light. When light falls on flat or squarish surfaces, the illumination tends to be quite consistent. One surface is in direct or oblique light, while another is in shadow, as we can see in many of Edward Hopper's paintings. With spheroids, what happens is much more complex. Just as there are no edges to the body of the spheroid, so there are no sharp lines dividing light from shadow. And when the shape of a spheroid is more complex than that of a simple sphere, the distribution of light over its surface becomes more complex as well. Many pottery vessels produced in prehistoric Europe have complex

S-profiles, with a narrow base, an outward-swelling body, a constricted neck, and an out-flaring rim, as we shall see in Chapter 5. Light falling on these vessels from any angle results in immensely complex and fascinating patterns of light and shadow that have the potential to utterly captivate the viewer. Even in photographs of Teniers's painting, we get some sense of their power to mesmerize.

CHAPTER 4

<><><><><><><><><><><><><><><><><><><>

FRAME, FOCUS, VISUALIZATION

DIRECTING VISION

Figure 9 shows a cup made during the Early Bronze Age, around 1800 BC. It has a spheroid body with a small flat base, a constricted neck, and a flaring rim, and a single handle on one side. It is a relatively simple object visually, except for its elegant S-shaped profile and four deeply incised lines that run horizontally around the vessel at the top of the shoulder, stopping and ending in little holes at the handle. As an experiment, cover the lines with your finger and look at the vessel. It will appear much plainer and less striking. The lines do a number of things that attract our visual attention and make us look at the object longer than we otherwise would.

Most importantly, they form a border or frame. They divide the lower portion of the vessel, where its contents would have been situated, from the neck, through which the contents would have been poured. They divide the object in a meaningful way into two distinct, and functionally specific parts. They also add texture to the object. Without them, the surface of the vessel would be smooth and undifferentiated, of a character that, as Gibson teaches us, we would not look at for long. Our eyes would glance over it and then move on. Originally, the incised lines probably contained an inlay, most likely of ground limestone, which would have added an important color distinction to the object, with the four white lines sharply defined against the grayish-brown body.

A substantial proportion of the objects that people create are crafted, like this Early Bronze Age cup, with the intention of making them visually attractive. In the modern world, cars, fashion clothing, kitchen appliances, even book covers are carefully designed to be as attractive as possible to potential buyers. In the field of advertising, a science has developed around ways

FIGURE 9. Early Bronze Age ceramic vessel from Hascherkeller, Landshut, Bavaria, Germany. Height 11.7 cm.

to make people look, keep looking, and then respond. But this practice of fashioning objects and images to attract attention and create positive reactions is by no means an exclusively modern phenomenon, nor it is limited to industrial societies, as Alfred Gell demonstrated in a number of his studies. Some have argued that Lower Paleolithic handaxes, made some five hundred thousand years ago, were intended to be aesthetically pleasing.

Our second example is a drawing of a sword scabbard from the site of La Tène in western Switzerland (Figure 10). The drawing shows a foreshortened view, with the undecorated portion of the scabbard unrepresented. When the drawing was made, in the middle of the nineteenth century, it did not occur to the illustrator that the undecorated part would be of interest. But now, mindful of Gibson's theory of affordances, we appreciate that those parts of the object that do not bear decoration are as important to the visual experience of the viewer as the decorated parts. The surface of the scabbard is framed in highly visible fashion by the substantial rim of metal attached to both sides to hold the two pieces together. The visual focus is the relief ornament at the top—the part of the scabbard that would have been closest to the eye level of observers. This ornament is a lively

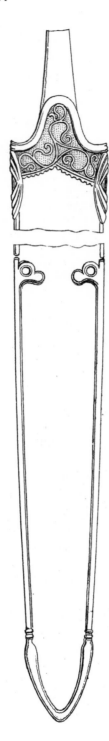

FIGURE 10. Drawing of a scabbard from La Tène, Switzerland. From
    Keller 1866, pl. 74, 4.

composition of S-curves and spirals against a stippled and textured background. On both sides of this decoration are relief formlines that recall vegetal ornament. The top of the decorated portion is framed by the upper end of the scabbard, the bottom part by a relief zigzag line. About two-thirds of the way down the scabbard are two bird heads in relief, attached to the top of the chape, which serve to draw the viewer's attention down to the full length of the scabbard.

The third example is an arrangement rather than an object. In early Europe it was the custom to place objects in graves along with the dead. Some of the objects recovered by archaeologists excavating burials are items of the clothing and personal ornaments of the deceased, others are objects placed in the grave next to the buried individual. In cremation burials, grave goods and ashes were often deposited together following the cremation fire, and we cannot see a systematic arrangement. But in inhumation graves, we can often get a valuable view into how those conducting the burial ceremony arranged objects in the grave, and from this arrangement we can learn about how they set things up to be seen.

Funerary ceremonies are important events for the communities in which they take place. If the grave is a large one containing substantial quantities of grave goods, we can assume that substantial numbers of people participated in the ceremony. In January 1992, a richly outfitted grave was discovered at Boiroux in the commune of Saint Augustin in Corrèze in south-central France. In the roughly rectangular grave was a chamber formed by walls of dry stone, and in the chamber was an assemblage of pottery, consisting of three Roman amphorae of type Dressel IB, twenty-four other ceramic vessels, a set of weapons (a shield, a lance, and a knife), and an iron fibula (Figure 11). Remains of a wooden coffin were also found. The arrangement of objects in the grave provides us with a view into the organizing principles of this visual display from the end of the first century BC.

As the authors of the excavation report note, each of the twenty-four ceramic vessels placed on the floor of the coffin was set in a specific place. Fineware vessels, including an elegant high-footed and high-necked jar with bands of decoration on the widest part of the body, a finely crafted bowl, and a tureen were placed at the head end of the grave, and the lance was arranged along the south wall in such a way that its point was at the head. The other ceramic vessels were all positioned around the deceased's lower legs and feet, and the three Roman amphorae were set just outside the foot end of the coffin, still within the grave. The fineware vessels at the head can be understood as those associated with feasting, while the other vessels, many of them handmade and either undecorated or decorated simply, represent more everyday meals.

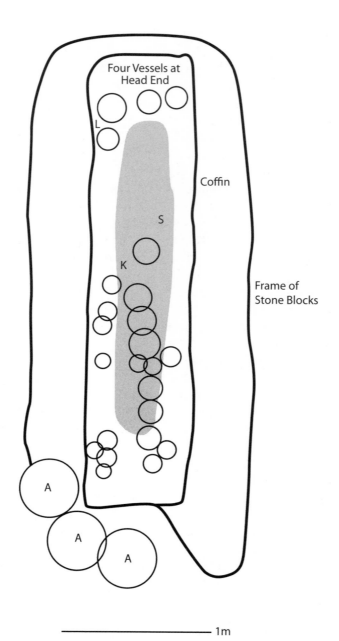

Four Vessels at
Head End

L

Coffin

S

K

Frame of
Stone Blocks

A

A

A

1m

Figure 11. Schematic plan of the Late Iron Age grave at Boiroux in south-central France. The buried
individual was framed by three different highly visible structures. Outermost was a rectangular
border formed by walls of substantial stones on the sides and by smaller stones at the ends.
Within that was a rectangular wooden coffin. Inside the coffin was the corpse of the individual,
framed at the head end by a set of four special feasting vessels and at the foot end by three
imported Roman amphorae. These three frames served to focus the attention of participants at
the funerary ceremony on the individual in the grave and on the objects arranged on and around
him (Dussot et al. 1992). Shading: body space. A: Roman amphorae. K: iron knife. L: iron lance
point. S: iron shield parts.

FRAME AND FOCUS

It will be useful to begin by considering the concept of the frame and how it helps us to understand the visual patterning of space in late prehistoric Europe. Frames, whether they are wooden picture frames that hold paintings on museum walls or boundary ditches around prehistoric sites, perform the important function of establishing for the viewer the boundaries of that which is to be viewed. The frame tells the viewer what is inside and therefore to be considered and what is outside and therefore can be ignored. The frame directs the viewer's attention and focuses it. We are so accustomed to seeing paintings framed, whether in simple plain frames or elaborate baroque versions, that it is difficult to even imagine seeing a Rembrandt or Picasso painting unframed, as simply a painted canvas stretched on a wooden support. The frame is an essential part of the visual structure. To appreciate the importance of frames, try to imagine a painting without clear edges, one in which the painted scene simply fades gradually into the wall on all four sides. Such a painting would be very disorienting to look at.

The three examples noted above all involve the framing of visual space. From a visual point of view, the visible part of a ceramic vessel is framed by its profile, or outline. The edges of the scabbard form the frame for the design on the scabbard surface. In the grave at Boiroux, three different frames play a role, the coffin on the inside, the arrangement of stones in the middle surrounding the coffin, and the edges of the grave pit on the outside. As the discussion below will show, a wide range of objects and arrangements in late prehistoric Europe can be helpfully analyzed in terms of frames, from rectangular bronze belt plates of the Early Iron Age to enclosures defined by ditches in the Late Iron Age.

In an important paper, Meyer Shapiro points out that frames, and in particular the rectangular frames that we are accustomed to seeing today (and using unthinkingly—the edges of rectangular sheets of paper, for example, and of the page that you are reading), are not natural objects. Rectangular outlines do not occur commonly in nature. They were created by humans at some time in the past. This observation is worth bearing in mind as we examine the ways that people in late prehistoric Europe used frames as devices for guiding visual attention.

Whatever it is that is inside the frame—the painting, the surface of the ceramic vessel, the incised decoration on the surface of the scabbard, the objects laid out on the floor of the grave, the spaces enclosed by ditches or burial mounds—is the focus of attention. The frame directs the eye to that focus and keeps it engaged there. Just as in an art museum we tend not to look at the museum wall outside the frame of the painting—and the museum is accommodating in leaving the wall blank, a kind of affordance—so too we would not look outside of a rectangular ditch or wall that encloses a burial mound. The focus would draw and hold our attention.

But there are other kinds of focus that are not clearly centered by frames but rather attract our visual attention through other means. Three kinds stand out and will be discussed below. One is three-dimensional sculpture. Statues and figures can be framed, but they are often recovered without any sign of what their framing (if any) may have been. Even without a frame, however, three-dimensional objects have a special way of attracting and holding our attention, in part because of the binocular vision with which we have been equipped through evolution and in part because of the way that light plays off three-dimensional objects.

A second kind of focus that does not necessarily entail a frame is fire. Humans are drawn to fire. Even today, a fire in a fireplace, or candles burning on a mantelpiece, have a special attraction and powerful meanings for us. We can only imagine how strong the allure of fire would have been before the spread of electric lighting. Paintings from early modern times give us a good idea of how "magical" controlled fire was.

The third kind of focus is another of the primal "elements," namely water. Like fire, water still holds a powerful attraction for us. We are fascinated by water in all its forms—as oceans, springs, and fountains, and this fascination is ageless. Rituals associated with natural bodies of water have long been performed all over the world, and today in the West people pay considerably more for a "water view," whether it is a room with a window overlooking the ocean or a condominium with a narrow view, between buildings, of the Hudson River.

DIAGRAMS

The things that prehistoric Europeans placed within frames, their foci of attention, can be understood as diagrams, in the sense developed by John Bender and Michael Marrinan. These diagrams, whether incised patterns on the surface of pottery, arrangements of vessels and metal objects on the floor of a grave, or broken weapons deposited in the ditches at Gournay (see Chapter 9), all embody information about the communities that made and arranged them. Members of those communities understood how those arrangements conveyed information and feelings about relationships in their societies, and it is our challenge to try to uncover something of the meanings that they conveyed. These objects in the context of their arrangements allow us to see the prehistoric European world to some extent in the way that prehistoric Europeans saw it, and, ideally, to begin to understand some of the meanings and messages that they conveyed through their visual technologies. Warren Neidich suggests that an artistic representation (he is talking about paintings in particular) provides "a map of neurobiological visual perception." I argue in this book that what Neidich says of artistic representations can be applied to all crafted and arranged objects. They all embody information that we can use to begin to understand how people in the past saw things and, consequently, why they fashioned things in the ways that they did.

MODES OF VISUALIZATION

Bender and Marrinan's concept of modes of visualization provides a useful model for examining changes in the way that visuality was structured during the two-thousand-year period under consideration. The basic premise that people who lived at different times and under different circumstances "saw" differently has been well demonstrated and developed by many investigators working in a variety of different fields. Examples include John Berger and his now-famous book *Ways of Seeing*, Michael Baxandall in his work on fifteenth-century Italy, J. B. Deregowski's investigations of different perceptions of visual space, Tom Rasmussen and Nigel Spivey's volume on Greek vase painting, Simon Goldhill's study of different ways of seeing in three periods in Greece's past, Richard Gregory's discussion of cultural differences, Georgia Frank's study of seeing by religious pilgrims, the essays in Robert Nelson's *Visuality Before and Beyond the Renaissance: Seeing as Others Saw*, and Jaś Elsner's work on visuality in the Roman world.

The concept of modes of visualization includes what we refer to when we speak of "style" in art, but it takes in the much broader consideration of the *context* in which things occur than the word "style" usually does. Modes of visualization need to be considered in tandem with the concept of ecological psychology, discussed above in Chapter 2.

A modern example will help to illustrate the nature of differences in the modes of visualization of different periods, and how important a role the larger context plays. In the National Gallery in London there are portraits of two Queens Elizabeth. One is of Elizabeth I (1533–1603), attributed to George Gower. The other is a silk-screen print of Elizabeth II, by Andy Warhol. Both queens are shown in three-quarter view from the left, both have distinctive coverings on their heads, and both wear necklaces. Thus the subjects are very similar, right down to details of angle and personal accouterments. But the mode of representation is completely different, and no one with the faintest familiarity with styles of representation would confuse the sixteenth-century and late-twentieth-century portraits. I use this modern example to emphasize the point that similar things can be represented in very different modes at different times, and that modes of representation—which are in essence the same as modes of visualization—are characteristic of their times.

WAYS OF VISUALIZING IN EARLY EUROPE

CONSISTENT VISUAL PATTERNS, 2000–50 BC

Before I turn to a discussion of the character of the changes that took place in ways of seeing in later prehistoric Europe, it will be useful to consider some of the patterns that persist throughout this entire period of time, from the Early Bronze Age through the Late Iron Age.

Pottery was ubiquitous in most parts of Europe throughout the Bronze and Iron Ages. During the Bronze Age and the Early Iron Age, it was most often brown or tan in color, but sometimes light or dark gray. During the Late Iron Age, it was commonly gray, but also often tan or brown. Until the very end of the Late Iron Age, almost all pottery was handmade. During the final two centuries BC, the potter's wheel came into general use, and this change had a major impact on both the production and the appearance of pottery. As a highly malleable material, the clay from which pottery vessels were formed could be shaped in a variety of ways, and, as we shall see in Chapter 5, many different decorative techniques and styles are evident during the two millennia under consideration here.

Personal ornaments designed to attract attention were worn on the front of the body—either directly on the body, in the case of bracelets, neckrings, and finger rings, or attached to clothing, as in the case of fibulae (Chapter 6), pendants, and belt decorations. Ornaments were usually shiny (of new metal, glass, or polished amber) and they often bore incised decoration or were inlaid or inset with colorful materials, such as coral and glass.

Of the weapons used in Bronze Age and Iron Age Europe, swords played a special role in visual display from the end of the Bronze Age to the end of the Iron Age. The character of the decoration on swords and scabbards changed over time, and it is among the highly informative visual aspects of late prehistoric material culture (Chapter 7).

Throughout the Bronze and Iron Ages, people in Europe deposited objects in places and in situations that suggest the purposeful positioning of objects with no intention of retrieving them (Chapter 9). In common archaeological practice such deposits are referred to as "ritual" and compared to ancient Greek, medieval, and modern "votive offerings." Caution is called for in interpreting these deposits, however, because we do not know the specific intentions of the people who did the depositing. I prefer to use the expression "structured deposition" for such contexts, indicating that the deposits were purposefully arranged (not just rubbish), but withholding judgment as to the intention with which the deposit was made. Among objects so deposited were pottery, bronze and iron weapons and jewelry, and elaborate and ornate objects, such as the Battersea and Witham shields from the Thames and Witham Rivers in Britain and the Gundestrup Cauldron recovered from a bog in northern Denmark. During the final phases of the Iron Age, coins were buried in the ground, tossed into water, and occasionally placed in graves (Chapter 10). Deposits were made in pits in the ground, in water, and in places of unusual natural rock formations.

Throughout the Bronze and Iron Ages, people created visual features in the landscape that often served as places where objects were deposited in one way or another. Burial mounds were erected over graves, ditches were dug to enclose spaces, and walls were constructed around settlements and elsewhere in the environment. Especially in the Late Iron Age, objects were often deposited in the ditches that surrounded rectangular spaces. These objects included weapons, ornaments, and imported Roman amphorae.

Many of these practices survive today, in Europe and elsewhere in the world. We still accord ceramic vessels (as well as glass and metal vessels) special visual roles in our homes and elsewhere. Ornamental vessels adorn mantelpieces and serve as vases to hold flowers. Sports trophies are vessels—the shape of the vessel is what matters, even if the vessel is empty. And vessels adorn much traditional architecture, as well as gravestones in many cemeteries.

We wear jewelry very much the way people in Bronze and Iron Age Europe did—rings on wrists and fingers, necklaces of beads, pins, and pendants on the chest, and (sometimes) large ornate belt buckles.

Swords are no longer a common item of accouterment, but ornate swords still have a significant place in formal military uniforms, in coats of arms, and in a great many insignia of various kinds.

We still deposit objects in the ground and in water. People bury objects in order to achieve particular objectives, and they toss coins into fountains. It is striking to see the large numbers of coins that end up in the fountains at shopping malls, the consummate twenty-first-century context for consumption.

Changing Ways of Visualizing

Within the broadly consistent pattern that I have outlined above, there were important changes over the course of the final two millennia BC in modes of visualization, and it is these that form the principal topic of this book. Two points need to emphasized here.

None of the changes happened overnight. We are examining processes that took place over long periods of time. Change was gradual, and it happened in different ways and at different times in different places. This book presents an overview of the changes and cannot go into detail on regional variations.

We need to be aware that different individuals in late prehistoric European communities experienced these changes in different ways. Inevitably in archaeology (as in history), our richest evidence comes from contexts associated with "elite" individuals; that is, people who had more material goods than the average member of a community. In some periods these differences may have played bigger roles than in others. It is during the late sixth, the fifth, and the early fourth centuries BC, for example, that we see the greatest disparity in the quantity and quality of objects placed with individuals in graves. During the Early Bronze Age and during the latter part of the Middle Iron Age and the beginning of the Late Iron Age, such differences do not show up as sharply.

The Bronze Age and Early Iron Age (2000–500 BC)

The starting date here—2000 BC—is arbitrary. It will serve for our purposes here. During the millennium-and-a-half from that date to 500 BC, which includes what are traditionally known as the Bronze Age and the Early Iron Age, the dominant organizational principle in decoration and arrangement was geometric patterning. Pottery tended to be decorated along strictly geometric lines. Throughout the Bronze Age, pottery was decorated most often with linear patterns, horizontal in character, sometimes accompanied by vertical linear configurations. In the Late Bronze Age some of the finest pottery was ornamented with curving designs such as garlands. In the Early Iron Age, pottery decoration became zonal, with horizontal, vertical, and oblique lines defining zones of ornament that were often filled with different elements in neighboring spaces.

Shades of brown were the dominant colors for pottery, with some graphite used to produce a shiny black coating from the Middle Bronze Age on, and "cherry red" paint during the Early Iron Age.

Personal ornaments also tended to be very geometric in form and decoration. Most common throughout the millennium-and-a-half were bronze pins that were both decorative and served to fasten garments together. Early, straight pins were most common, later fibulae (brooches) assumed special importance. The straight pins were fundamentally linear in shape, while the fibulae ranged from rectangular to arc-shaped to, toward the end of this phase, objects shaped in rudimentary S-curves. Especially in the Early Bronze Age, the flat heads of pins often bore linear ornament similar to that on the pottery of the time.

Bracelets, neckrings, legrings, and finger rings, were circular in shape and often ornamented with incised patterns of straight lines. Sheet-bronze belt plates were relatively common, and they exhibit the geometric pattern of ornament very clearly. By the Early Iron Age, they were strictly rectangular in form, with rectangular patterns on their surfaces, which were divided by vertical and horizontal lines into zones containing distinct ornament, much like the pottery of the period.

Swords and scabbards, objects of special craftsmanship and distinction, also bear geometrical ornament. Earlier Bronze Age scabbards have strictly linear ornament, most often long vertical lines down the length of the scabbard. In the Late Bronze Age, many of the cast-hilted swords have incised decoration on their hilts, consisting of geometrical patterns such as circles, spirals, and triangles. Hilts from the first part of the Early Iron Age sometimes are inlaid with exotic materials, such as ivory, amber, and gold. The sheaths of the daggers of the second part of the Early Iron Age are decorated in strictly linear geometric fashion, while the ends of the hilts sometimes have a colorful inlay of coral that was originally pink and now is usually white.

Figural representations, which were common but not abundant during these centuries, tend to be naturalistic, in the sense that figurines of humans can be seen to clearly represent humans, and figurines of bulls clearly represent bulls. In the earlier part of the period, a water-bird was the favored animal theme, most often represented in profile rather than three dimensionally. In the latter part, the bull and stag became common, most often as three-dimensional figures. It is rare to find a figurine the character of which is not immediately clear upon quick visual inspection.

In the later phases of this period, representations of ornaments and of weapons, as well as of animals and of humans, are increasingly found on other objects. Examples include the dagger, neckring, and belt indicated on the Hirschlanden statue, and the scenes of sword fighters and fighting wagon riders on the Hochdorf couch.

Also in the later phase, scenes of likely narrative significance begin to appear. These are important in that they show us people doing things with objects, and yield clues as to how people, objects, and the environment interacted. The situlae, such as the one found at Kuffarn in Austria (see Figure 37, page 160), are prime examples. The Strettweg cart and the Sopron burial pottery are other relevant objects in this regard.

In the arranging and outfitting of graves, we see a gradual change over the millennium-and-a-half (Chapter 8). In the Early Bronze Age, burial was typically in irregularly shaped grave pits, and few objects were included other than the personal ornaments that adorned the deceased. In the Middle Bronze Age, more structured spaces were created, and larger numbers of objects were placed in the grave chamber, and in some cases arranged in relation to the body. In the Late Bronze Age and Early Iron Age, when inhumation was practiced, the layouts of graves were often quite elaborate, with finely crafted wooden chambers and more lavish and carefully placed contents that might include four-wheeled wagons, sets of feasting equipment, and sets of weapons.

THE MIDDLE IRON AGE (500–200 BC)

During the fifth century BC, a new and generally more curvilinear way of marking and decorating objects replaced the geometric linear and zonal patterns that had been characteristic for the preceding millennium and a half. This new way of decorating was part of a wide-ranging change in modes of visualization—in the way that people saw and understood the world around them, the objects that they used and displayed, and their relationships with other people and with the natural and supernatural worlds.

Contrary to what some accounts suggest, the change did not happen suddenly. Elements of the new style can be identified at least as far back as the Late Bronze Age, and many curvilinear forms and S-curves were present in the latter part of the Early Iron Age. Nor did geometric patterning disappear. But the fifth century BC was indeed a time of profound, if gradual, innovation.

Three main changes best represent the transformation in the mode of visualization. These were the adoption of the S-curve as the basic structure of ornament, the development of a repertoire of hybrid creatures represented in three-dimensional fashion on ornaments of various kinds, and the creation of large-scale open-air spaces for the performance of public ceremonies.

The S-curve (see Chapter 2 for discussion of the form in general) was already used to a limited extent on decorated pottery of the Late Bronze Age and on metalwork during the Early Iron Age. But after about 500 BC, it became the main organizing principle of design. It formed the basic structure of ornament for fibulae, neckrings, bracelets, pendants, bronze vessels, scabbards, and sometimes even pottery. The S-curve occurred in the form of tendrils or palmettes, and it could also be developed into a spiral and used to decorate bronze animal and hybrid figurines. Formlines, lines that widen and narrow along their courses, are a striking characteristic of this kind of ornament. In some expressions of the S-curve, as on the Hochscheid scabbard (Figure 29), the S-curve served as the basis for the creation of animal forms that grew directly out of it. Especially later in this new period, decoration was often asymmetrical, something that never (or extremely rarely) happened with the geometric ornament of the preceding phase.

In this new mode, a large proportion of the creatures represented three dimensionally on jewelry, bronze vessels, and elsewhere, were hybrids—creatures that combine elements of different real animals to form "monsters" that did not actually exist in nature. These creatures, as seen on the Erstfeld neckrings, the Weiskirchen belt-hook, the Parsberg fibula, and many other objects represent a phenomenon very different from the naturalistic representations of the preceding period, where there is almost never any doubt what animal a figure represents.

The one striking exception to this general pattern is in birds. While mammals (or what look like mammals) are shown as unnatural hybrids, birds are realistically depicted. Good examples are on the gold neckrings from Erstfeld and Reinheim. In contrast to the water-birds with their long necks and flattish, upturned beaks, the birds now are birds of prey, with sharply pointed, down-turned beaks.

Both of these new features—the S-curves and their derivative forms in linear ornaments, and the ambiguous hybrid creatures—were designed specifically to serve visual purposes—to make people look, to attract and hold their attention, to engage them in fascination and puzzle-solving (Chapter 2). The patterns and modes of representation of the earlier period did not share these particular properties (although many objects were certainly charming and enchanting in their own ways). The changes represent a major departure from what went before, and they require explanation as well as identification and description.

The third major change in the visual landscape of temperate Europe during this time was the creation of large spaces at which performances of ceremonies could be carried out before a sizable public. As we shall see in Chapter 9, there is no lack of evidence for the performance of a range of ritual ceremonies in earlier times. What is different now is the scale of the performances. Much bigger constructed spaces were created, and much larger quantities of manufactured goods were displayed and dispatched, than ever before. Among the outstanding examples of these sites is Gournay-sur-Aronde in northern France, with its thousands of purposefully broken and bent weapons arranged in a perimeter ditch enclosing a rectangular space in which cattle were killed and their remains deposited in pits near the center of the enclosure. Similar practices were being carried out in a different kind of environment on the shore of Lake Neuchâ-tel in Switzerland at the site of La Tène, where deposits were made into water rather than into ditches. A third example, in yet a third kind of environmental context, is the site of Wartau-Ochsenberg in the Swiss Alps. There objects were consumed or otherwise destroyed in a large fire that would have been visible for tens of miles in all directions. What all three sites have in common, and what makes them different from earlier sites, are the substantial quantities of valuable objects that were ceremonially altered—-broken, bent, dumped into muddy lake beds, or burned; and, at least as important, the fact that these sites were large enough to accommodate hundreds of potential participants.

Finally, in the Middle Iron Age, we find the first pictorial representations of people engaged in activities (not just posed, as on the Strettweg vehicle). The figural scenes on the scabbard from Hallstatt Grave 994 and on the bronze situlae from Austria and Slovenia will be discussed in Chapter 9.

THE LATE IRON AGE (200–50 BC)

At the end of the third and start of the second centuries BC, another impor-tant series of changes in visual material culture becomes apparent, all part of a new mode of visualization that will dominate the two final centuries be-fore the Roman conquests. Material culture is now both more abundant and more diverse. Large-scale iron production is in evidence at many locations throughout temperate Europe and it results in the manufacture of much larger quantities of tools of various kinds. The introduction and later proliferation of coinage yields enormous numbers of coins, a new category of visual object.

The potter's wheel comes into regular use, so that the majority of the pot-tery on many sites, such as Manching, is wheelmade. In addition to being more efficient, wheel manufacture has important effects on the visual char-acter of pottery, especially on its shape and surface texture. New vessel forms are introduced, and the overall pottery assemblage is broader and more di-verse than previously, a point explored for southern Britain by J. D. Hill. On the continent, vertical comb decoration is now common on a wide range of pottery vessels, from large, heavy graphite-clay "cooking pots" (as they are known) to thin-walled, delicate jars. The range of fabric colors also expands from the browns and grays that were dominant earlier. Those colors continue to be used, but the graphite-clay pots, with their gleaming, sparkling surfaces are visually new, as are beige fineware vessels, sometimes painted with red and white bands and other decoration. In south-central France, the practice of painting elaborate ornament on tall jars, including stylized horses and other La Tène-style designs represents a regional development.

Fibulae of this phase are different from those of the two previous phases in their visual simplicity. They no longer commonly bear heads or bodies of creatures, nor do they have wide ornate bows (see Chapter 6). They are made instead of simple wire, sometimes partially flattened to form a small flat surface at the front. Experiments have demonstrated that one of the most common types—the Nauheim fibula—was designed specifically for mass production.

Figurines of animals cast of bronze are relatively common. Unlike those of the preceding phase, but in common with those of the earliest, these figurines are generally simple and straightforward, and the animal they represent is immediately recognizable. A wide range of different animals are depicted, including stags, bulls, and birds of prey.

The richly patterned plant-based ornament of the preceding phase declined in use during this period, except in the British Isles, where a distinctive metalworking tradition further developed the general European themes and forms. In Britain, scabbards continued to be ornamented with motifs that employ the S-curves and floral patterns, while on the continent scabbards tend to be plainer.

A new visual element appears both on the continent and in Britain: openwork in metal. On the continent a series of sword scabbards was decorated with openwork plaques that were attached to the upper ends of the scabbards and that bore sometimes complex patterns of decoration, incorporating S-curves and floral forms (e.g., Figure 32, page 129). Both on the continent and in Britain, some types of fibulae were fashioned with openwork patterns on the foot (e.g., Figure 25, page 111). Similar openwork patterns in metal appear on some other kinds of objects as well, including the handles of tankards and mirrors in Britain and on the feet of some bronze vessels.

Two new visual media make their appearance. The first coins produced in temperate Europe during this phase, were based on Mediterranean prototypes (Chapter 10). The earliest were gold coins of around the start of the third century BC, which were based on those minted by Philip of Macedon. The first silver and bronze coins, modeled after prototypes from Roman Italy, appeared around the middle of the second century. As visual objects, coins were especially important because of their quantity, their ubiquity, and their uniformity.

Writing first began to appear with some frequency in temperate Europe at about the end of the third century BC (Chapter 10). Much earlier examples, such as the controversial piece of amber apparently with Linear B signs carved into it from Bernstorf in southern Germany, are infrequent and do not seem to have had any effect that needs to concern us here. From the end of the third century on, Greek inscriptions, then Latin inscriptions, appear in temperate Europe, and by the time of the Roman conquests, objects bearing writing, such as the KORISIOS sword, the Greek-incised sherds from Manching, and the Negau helmets are a fairly regular occurrence. These inscriptions became then a significant part of the visual world of late prehistoric Europe. Other indications of writing before the Roman conquest include parts of bronze frames for wooden writing tablets and bronze and iron *stili* of Roman type (pointed implements used to incise letters into the wax surface of the wooden tablets) found on some of the major Late Iron Age settlements.

In much of temperate Europe, the practice of burying the dead waned during this period, giving way to other methods of disposing of bodies, most of which leave no recognizable archaeological trace. There are a few exceptions, most notably in the region between the confluence of the Main and the Rhine and the English Channel, where the traditional practice of burial was maintained. At the large cemetery of Wederath in the valley of the Moselle River in western Germany, most graves of this period contain cremations, with grave goods arranged in small rectangular pits along with the ashes and burned bones. At Clemency and Goeblingen-Nospelt, both in Luxembourg, sizable wooden chambers allowed for the arrangement of many objects in the burials. Similarly, across the Channel in Britain, graves like those at Welwyn Garden City were inside wooden chambers and showed complex arrangements of objects (Chapter 8).

These changes in the final two centuries BC created a profoundly different visual world from what went before and one that was in some significant respects increasingly like the world of Roman Italy. As we shall see in Chapters 11 and 12, these changes in the material culture of societies in temperate Europe came about as they became increasingly involved in the expanding commercial world of Eurasia and Africa. The mass production of objects that had in earlier times been handcrafted, notably pottery, fibulae, and metal tools, changed people's relationships with these objects, both in terms of how they were made and obtained by others, and as regards their visual appearance. A wheel-thrown pot looks very different form a hand-shaped one, and a mass-produced Nauheim fibula looks mass-produced, not individually crafted as earlier fibulae had been. Thus the Europeans' entire experience of their visual world changed as their societies joined into the larger commercial networks.

THE DYNAMICS OF CREATING THE VISUAL ENVIRONMENT

MAKING

In the preceding three sections, I have outlined the salient visual features of the material culture of temperate European societies between 2000 BC and the Roman conquest. The rest of the book will develop this discussion and present specific evidence from a wide range of sites all over temperate Europe. Two further topics need to be considered at this stage.

One is the making of things. Changes in technology had a major effect on the visual aspects of material culture. For example, the regular use of the potter's wheel in the final phase of the Iron Age meant that pottery would look different from earlier pottery, almost all of which had been made by hand-building. Also, in the third phase, mass-production techniques were developed for the manufacture of fibulae, and the fibulae so made look different from those that were individually crafted by metalsmiths.

Acquiring

The second topic is the acquisition of things. I use this very general term instead of "trade," or "gift-giving," or "interaction," so as to encompass all instances of interaction that resulted in objects collected or crafted elsewhere being recovered in temperate Europe. Trade and interaction have long been major themes of interest and research in European archaeology, in large part because they are so readily apparent in the material evidence. A ceramic wine cup made in Athens stands in sharp contrast to everything else in an Early Iron Age grave in eastern France. We are coming to appreciate that there was a great deal more trade and interaction than direct evidence suggests throughout the period covered in this book. What is not clear is the impact interaction had on local communities at various times and in various places. Debate has raged, for example, on the role of the interaction systems that bought "southern imports," such as Greek and Etruscan ceramic and bronze vessels, to the large settlements of the latter part of the Early Iron Age—to Mont Lassois, the Heuneburg, the Hohenasperg, and the rest. Do these imports indicate commercial and political relations that made possible the emergence of powerful princes or kings and allowed them to maintain their control over more than half a century? Or were the imports merely "frills" that powerful groups were able to command to enhance their elite lifestyles? This topic will be addressed in Chapter 12.

The same applies to the final period. But from the second century BC on, the evidence for intensive interaction between the societies of temperate Europe and those of the Mediterranean world—now especially Rome—is much more abundant and even supplemented by textual sources. Again, the question I pose is not "what influence did Rome have on the societies of the final two centuries BC," but rather "how did the rich and diverse interactions between groups throughout temperate Europe and the Mediterranean world affect the visual worlds of temperate Europe?"

POTTERY, FIBULAE, AND SWORDS: IDEAL
MATERIALS FOR ANALYSIS

The next three chapters apply the theories and principles set forth in the preceding three chapters to crafted objects in Bronze Age and Iron Age Europe. I have selected three categories to examine in detail. Pottery is by far the most abundant material that survives from later prehistoric Europe, and it was one of the categories of objects that people saw, touched, and used the most. Fibulae, most often made of bronze or iron, but sometimes of gold or silver, constitute the most visually informative item of personal ornamentation. Swords and their scabbards played special roles in the expression of status and identity among elite men. I will use these three categories of material to development my arguments about the visual worlds of the Bronze and Iron Ages.

In studying societies of the past, whether through the methods that we call "archaeology" or those we describe as "history," we depend upon what survives in the present. Another category of material that was much a part of people's daily visual experience, along with pottery, was textiles. But because the quantity of textiles that survives from the Bronze and Iron Ages is so small compared to pottery and metal objects, the analyses that I carry out in this book would be impossible to apply to textiles—or at least, given our present state of knowledge, would yield extremely incomplete results.

During the Bronze and Iron Ages, wool and linen were the most common textile fibers. By the Iron Age imported silk was to be found in some elite contexts. From the surviving textile remains, scholars have learned much about the types of weaves used in different contexts, about the kinds of garments worn, and about the colors of different fabrics. Waterlogged and slightly acidic conditions are favorable to the preservation of textiles, and much of the research conducted on prehistoric textiles in Europe is consequently based on garments recovered from such contexts. Sizeable assemblages have been recovered from bog environments in Denmark, such as at Huldremose; from the meticulously excavated and very well preserved Early Iron Age grave of Hochdorf near Stuttgart; and from a number of burial sites in Ukraine, including Chortomlyk and Velyka Ryzhanivka, and in southern Russia, where silk from China has been reported at the Semibratniy site.

Small fragments of textiles frequently survive when in contact with bronze, because the corrosion products create a chemical environment that preserves the organic fibers. Thus in many graves, pieces of textile are recovered in contact with sword scabbards, bronze vessels, and other substantial pieces of the metal, as, for example, those published in Martin Schönfelder's study of textile fragments from Iron Age graves in the Champagne region of France. Textiles also survive in some other special environments, such as in the salt mines at Hallstatt and at the Dürrnberg in Austria.

Finds from these and a few other sites have enabled informative reconstructions of the visual character of the clothing that Bronze and Iron Age people wore, but from the vast majority of sites in Europe, we have no textile remains to work with. This situation contrasts markedly with pottery, which survives at almost every site, and with fibulae and swords and scabbards, which are found well preserved in most environments.

CHAPTER 5

∞∞∞∞∞∞∞∞∞∞∞∞∞∞∞∞

POTTERY

The Visual Ecology of the Everyday

THE VISUAL ECOLOGY OF A JAR

The object in Figure 12 is a portion of the wall of an Early Bronze Age jar. The two sherds of pottery glued together here were recovered in a pit, along with 523 other Early Bronze Age sherds, at the site of Hascherkeller on the outskirts of Landshut in Lower Bavaria, Germany. The object may not look like much to the uninitiated observer, but it can provide a wealth of information about the community that made, used, and deposited it.

The pottery is darkish gray, with some patches of brown. What we see in this photograph is part of the exterior of the upper half of the jar. At the top is the rim, the edge around the opening through which the jar's contents were poured in and poured, or ladled, out. Along the rim are a series of little indentations, just visible in this photograph, made by the potter gently pressing his or her (we do not know whether the potter was a man or a woman) fingertip into the drying and hardening, but not yet fired, clay. The rim would have worked just as well without these added impressions, yet the potter made the decision, and took the time, to make them.

A little over halfway down the length of the piece is a row of what look like rough circles. They are not just pressed into the fabric of the jar's wall, but are indented into a little ridge of clay that was added to the jar to accommodate these impressions. These are also fingertip impressions made by the potter, but this time we see them as full circles and not just as wide grooves in the thin rim. They were part of a complete ring of such circles that once ran around the entire jar. This ring is situated at a particular place on the side

FIGURE 12. Rejoined sherds of an Early Bronze Age jar from Hascherkeller, Landshut, Bavaria, Germany. Height 13.7 cm.

of the jar; namely at the top of the shoulder where the body bulges out to accommodate the load of material to be kept inside of it. Thus this row of circles marks an important boundary: between the widest portion of the vessel and the narrowing of the neck; or in other words, between the place where the contents were stored and the place through which they were poured to extract them. We see this arrangement repeatedly on storage jars of the Early and Middle Bronze Age—a ridge added to the top of the shoulder, and a ring of little circles made by fingertips marking that ridge as the boundary between these two functional parts of the vessel.

Finally, look at the light particles that appear scattered throughout the surface of the object. These are little pieces of quartz and other stones that were added to the fabric of the clay as temper, foreign material that would help to bind the clay molecules together during the firing process. Not only are these tiny stones visible on the surface, but when you handle the sherd, you can feel the stones; they protrude from the surface and give it a rough exterior texture.

Having had a close look at this object to absorb its principal visual properties, we turn now to its ecology. Why was the object made, and what do the visual aspects we have observed have to do with its place in the community that used it?

Jars—vessels with broad bulbous bodies, narrowed necks, and wide mouths—were used during the Bronze Age primarily for storing grain, often in cellar holes underneath houses, where they are sometimes found with grain still inside them. They were vital repositories of the basic foodstuff of Early Bronze Age communities, storing it between the harvesting and winnowing of the grain and its preparation for consumption. Thus these vessels played a fundamental role in the ecological cycle of the community. The vessel as a container could represent a range of different ideas to the people who kept it and others like it under their houses; it denoted nourishment, security against hunger, and the sociality that is associated with meals.

Finally we come to the connection between the visual characteristics and the physical role that the jar played in the household. Jars are one of the three main categories of pottery vessels that were in use in the Early Bronze Age in temperate Europe. The others were bowls and cups. As we shall see below, bowls and cups were decorated differently from jars, and their surfaces were finished differently. Jars are the only category that had a purposely roughened surface. Bowls and cups were polished smooth. And jars are the only category within which each individual vessel was distinguished from every other by the pattern of its ornament. From the latter fact, I argue that jars in the Early and Middle Bronze Age were individualized in a way that bowls and cups were not; each was deliberately made different from all others in order that the household that owned it could mark it as its own, and perhaps even use it to display to others in the community that it had abundant stores of grain. The purposeful roughening of the exterior surface linked the vessel visually with the fields—rough, uneven, and dark grayish-brown during much of the year. The jar "referenced" the fields through its visual features, to borrow a term from Andrew Jones.

In a world in which everything was linked together in complex and mutually affective ways, there were good reasons for fashioning objects to refer to the other aspects of existence with which they were closely linked. The more tightly bound together all of the aspects were—the production of food, social interaction, obeisance to supernatural forces, and visual interreferencing—the more smoothly one might expect everything to work.

POTTERY IN EARLY EUROPE

From the Neolithic Period (beginning around 5500 BC in temperate Europe) on, when people first began making and using pottery, it constituted a principal component of the visual world of temperate Europe. During the

Bronze and Iron Ages, every household had some pottery, and ceramic vessels were used for a variety of purposes. Among these were the storage, preparation, and serving of food; the outfitting of graves; and the arranging of deposits in pits in the ground. Good potting clay is available in most parts of the continent, allowing most communities easy access to the raw material for making vessels.

Pottery was a fundamental part of people's visual world. As something that children saw from infancy on and that all individuals saw and handled throughout their lives, the visual character of pottery played an essential role in teaching people how to see. The role that it played in the storage, preparation, and consumption of food, and in the sociality associated with meals, meant that pottery was a vital part of people's conceptual life as well.

Pottery is also, as we noted, by far the most abundant cultural material recovered on Bronze and Iron Age settlement sites. At the Late Bronze and Early Iron Age settlement at Hascherkeller, on the outskirts of Landshut in Lower Bavaria, our excavations recovered 14,853 sherds of pottery, as against eighteen bronze objects, seventeen ceramic loom weights, four iron objects, four glass beads, a sandstone mold, a hammerstone, and a few pieces of worked antler and bone. These numbers are typical of the relative quantities of pottery and other materials recovered from prehistoric settlements.

THE USES OF POTTERY

In the Everyday

We know the uses to which prehistoric Europeans put pottery from the contexts in which it is recovered. Pottery was vital for the processing of food and drink. Large vessels served as storage containers for grain and other foodstuffs. Sometimes such vessels were set into cellar pits under the floors of houses, sometimes they were kept above ground on floors or shelves. Ceramic vessels were used in the preparation of food—for mixing, stirring, cooking, and otherwise processing foods. Large bowls or cauldrons were used for serving foods, and jugs for pouring beverages. And pottery was used as well for the consumption of meals, with individual bowls and cups serving as the containers from which individual people ate and drank. In some contexts, we can identify through residue analysis or through pictorial representation the specific purpose for which certain kinds of vessels were used. In general, small, hand-sized cups were used for drinking liquids, larger pitchers for serving liquids, bowls for eating foods, and large jars for storing grains and other subsistence items. The fact that the main purpose of pottery was the storage, preparation, serving, and consumption of food does not exclude its use for storing other things, such as materials for craftwork or ornaments.

Ceramic amphorae with characteristically long necks and small mouths that could be sealed with plugs were brought into temperate Europe from the Mediterranean shores, usually with wine as the principal contents. Amphorae from the Greek world are recovered especially from late sixth- and early fifth-century BC settlements in eastern France, southern Germany, and Switzerland. During the second and final centuries BC, much larger quantities of Roman wine amphorae were being transported to sites throughout western and central temperate Europe, and across the England Channel to Britain. Roman amphorae were sometimes reshaped by breaking and put to secondary uses.

In Burials

Pottery vessels were often placed in graves as part of burial assemblages. Such vessels could be plain and undecorated, or they could be fine and ornate. Some graves contained no vessels, some had one or two, and some had several tens of vessels. Sometimes the vessels in graves were arranged empty, at other times they contained foods such as joints of meat and grains. Pottery was sometimes positioned in elaborate displays, along with other objects, as for example in the richly outfitted Early Iron Age wagon burials of Hradenín in Bohemia and in the Late Iron Age grave at Welwyn Garden City, north of London.

In cremation contexts, the burned bone fragments and ashes of the dead were often placed in a ceramic vessel serving as an urn. But there are instances when, even though a vessel was present, cremated remains were placed in a pile in the burial or scattered throughout the chamber.

In Deposits

Pottery vessels were often arranged in pits in the ground that are not associated with graves. Examples include a Middle Bronze Age pit deposit at Minoritenhof in Bavaria and a row of fine pottery vessels set into a pit at Late Iron Age Gournay-sur-Aronde in northern France. In France during the Late Iron Age, it was common practice to deposit imported amphorae in ditches that defined rectangular enclosures, as at Braine and Mirebeau. In other cases, pottery was deposited in wells, as at the Late Bronze Age site of Berlin-Lichterfelde, and at striking natural features in the landscape, as at the cliff outcrop at Schellnecker Wänd in Bavaria.

A Medium for Relations

Social Relations

Pottery was the principal material medium for people's interactions with their environment in all its aspects—social, natural, and probably spiritual. In its role in the storage and serving of food produced in the local fields, pottery connected the natural world of the soil with the sustenance of the individual's life. Since meals were social occasions, pottery played a role in the social interaction that took place during meals, as family members and other participants passed vessels containing food around the group.

Spiritual/Supernatural

Pottery was also important in human interactions with the spiritual world. The placing of pottery in graves indicates that it was part of funerary ritual, and the deposits noted above are believed to have involved interactions with supernatural powers.

Ubiquity

Pottery was a material ever-present in the lives of the people with whom this book is concerned. Today we use pottery every day, and most of us see it regularly on our tables and kitchen shelves. But our material lives are so vastly more complex that pieces of pottery hold nowhere near the same importance and significance for most of us that they held for people who lived three thousand years ago. (There may of course be exceptions in the case of vessels that remind us of a special relationship or event.)

In Bronze and Iron Age Europe, pottery was the one durable material that was ever-present in people's lives, from birth till death, and beyond. Not only did pottery play vital roles in nutrition, social relations, and interactions with supernatural beings, but it also taught people how to see. In their first weeks and months, as they were becoming familiar with the world into which they had been born, infants saw and touched pottery. The experience of touching the surface of vessels with their variously smooth and rough textures, at the same time as their eyesight and brains were developing, played an essential role in the infant's learning how to see. And the continuing presence and use of pottery throughout the individual's life meant that this material continued to play a major role in the development, practice, and refinement of vision.

THE VISUAL CHARACTERISTICS OF POTTERY

The Materiality of Pottery

Pottery was made locally in small communities, as we know from the frequent discovery of kilns at settlements sites. Hence it is safe to say that everyone was familiar with how pottery was made, with the raw material involved and with the process of shaping and firing vessels. Pottery was a form of earth, transformed into to a solid material of permanent shape through the application of water mixed with clay, and fire for baking the vessel. The fact that the four "elements" of ancient thinking—earth, water, air (to dry the shaped vessel before firing), and fire—were necessary to the production of pottery may have imbued it with a special aura in the minds of the people who used it.

Pottery in its moist condition is highly malleable. Potters could make vessels of differing sizes and shapes, they could include various details of rim form and handles, they could add different kinds of decoration, and they could determine the final color by using different firing techniques and by the application of graphite or paint. Every society has defined rules and limits regarding what artisans and craftworkers could do, but within those limits, was a wide range of possibilities. This fact will be important as we consider the specifics of the visual features of pottery from Bronze Age and Iron Age Europe.

Shapes and Sizes

Most of the pottery vessels that were made and used in late prehistoric Europe were spheroidal in shape—roughly like a sphere or a hemisphere. Cups were sometimes almost spherical (e.g., Figure 9), bowls often almost hemispherical. Most jars, and some cups, had spherical, bulbous bodies, and narrow necks. Flat forms that we might call plates were rare, as were any kind of rectangular vessels.

Pottery was the most three-dimensional, globular category of material culture that was commonly used in temperate Europe during later prehistoric times. (Bronze vessels shared the basic morphological features of pottery, but they were never in common use but always restricted to a small elite.) In houses and in burials, pottery took up more visual space and, in their three-dimensionality had more of a visual presence than any other portable objects, a point that becomes apparent when we look at reconstructions of Bronze and Iron Age house interiors.

Lines

As we have seen, decoration on late prehistoric European pottery is most commonly linear. It can take the form of a circular line of fingertip impressions along the rim of the vessel, or it can be a ridge running horizontally around the top of the shoulder, usually with some kind of impressed ornament at intervals along it. Lines can be incised—horizontally, vertically, or obliquely—on the surface of a vessel; or they can be painted. During the final centuries of the prehistoric Iron Age, a distinctive pattern of "comb-made" vertical lines, often very fine and tightly-spaced, is the dominant mode of decoration.

Surfaces and Textures

The surfaces of ceramic vessels are especially important to how they are perceived visually and of course tactilely as well. Both texture and color are fundamental. In prehistoric Europe, vessels' surfaces range from the highly polished and very fine-grained, to the very coarse, with sizeable chunks of pebbles actually protruding from the surface.

Light Effects

Its three-dimensional quality, the complex profiles of many vessels, and the kinds of decoration applied meant that special lighting effects played on pottery in ways that light did not on other objects, an observation that is well demonstrated in the paintings discussed at the beginnings of Chapters 2 and 3. As noted in Chapter 3, in most houses, light came in through doors and windows during the day and was provided by a single fireplace at night. The patterns of light and shadow that were created on pottery were much more complex than those that fell on other kinds of objects. This would have been particularly striking at night, when vessels were only dimly lit by the flickering flames of the hearth or, in the wealthiest households perhaps, by the flame from an oil lamp.

Pottery was often polished with a stone or some other object in order to create a hard, smooth, and shiny surface. Such a surface would gleam in the light of a fire or an open door. From the Late Bronze Age on, graphite was sometimes added to the exterior of vessels to create a further kind of shine in the light. In the Late La Tène period, a mixture of graphite and clay produced shiny, metallic-looking vessels of the shape known as "cooking pots" (*Kochtöpfe*).

POTTERY IN THE VISUAL WORLD

POTTERY AND VISUAL ECOLOGY

Of all of the categories of material culture that we can examine in order to study visual structures in Bronze and Iron Age Europe, pottery is unique in its direct physical connections to landscape, dwelling, sustenance, and sociability.

Pottery is made of the earth and thus directly connected with the earth and with the landscape. J. D. Hill, Andrew Jones, and others have noted similarities between the appearance of pottery and the visual character of the landscape in which it was produced and used. In the earlier half of our period, these similarities are particularly striking, as will be seen below.

Pottery provides also a physical means for people to interact with their environment in order to sustain themselves and their families. Since this was a principal purpose of ceramic vessels, the vessels themselves, when placed in a grave or in a deposit, could stand for, or reference, the theme of sustenance. The visible presence of pottery could signify nutrition, nurturing, and all of the themes that revolve around those topics.

POTTERY AND SOCIAL ECOLOGY

Meals are not just occasions for replenishing nutrients, they are also social occasions in the course of which existing bonds are reaffirmed and new ones created. Everyday meals are shared occasions in which members of families interact, and parents pass behaviors and values on to their children. At meals, people engage in conversation to exchange information and share feelings. Special meals—feasts, banquets, celebrations—at which groups larger than families participate, magnify the interpersonal function of the meal and its importance in creating and strengthening social bonds.

We get a good view into the social and political dynamics that can be associated with feasting from such varied literary sources as Xenophon's description of a *symposium*, Petronius's account of Trimalchio's banquet in the *Satyricon,* and the depiction of warriors dining in the great mead-hall in *Beowulf.* Paintings from early modern times also provide insight into the ways that feasts and banquets were media for social interaction, ranging from scenes of peasant "kirmis" celebrations to the formal banquets of royalty. The ceramic vessels that are so abundantly represented in the former, and the silver and gold vessels of the latter, can themselves stand for the social relations that are nurtured and negotiated in the process of those events.

The presence of pottery or of metal vessels in a grave or an arranged deposit can evoke meanings of nutrition and sustenance on the one hand, and of social interaction on the other.

POTTERY AND THE BODY

Pottery had a different relationship to the human body from that of any other material employed by late prehistoric Europeans. Like all craftspeople in pre-industrial economic situations, the potter used his or her body actively in making pottery. The clay must be dug, mixed with water, kneaded, and then shaped into the pot, and any desired decoration added. Making symmetrical and smooth vessels from clay requires considerable skill and experience. While the crafting of most materials in late prehistoric Europe required a great deal of physical, bodily involvement on the part of the craftsworker, pottery is different in that clearly visible traces of the potter remain on the pot. A bronze pin does not show any trace of the bronzesmith, nor does an iron sword bear any direct signs of the blacksmith. But pottery, especially in the Bronze Age, was often decorated with the potter's fingertip impressions, sometimes along the rim of the vessel, sometimes around the shoulder—both very visible locations. On many jars from the Middle Bronze Age, the potter drew his or her fingers down the exterior wall of the vessel, leaving finger-wide shallow rills. In such cases, the potter's body is directly represented by the permanent impressions on the pot. The finished pot literally embodies the potter. Even today, four thousand years after an Early Bronze Age jar was crafted, we still see on it the marks left by the potter's actions.

A number of researchers have argued that ceramic vessels—in particular, tall vessels with narrow bases, wide shoulders, narrow necks, and flaring rims—served as metaphors for the human body and were treated accordingly. Incised or impressed decoration around the base of the neck has been interpreted as necklaces. Matthieu Poux has argued that Roman amphorae, which occur as imports in the Late La Tène Period, are the closest in shape to a human body of any pottery known in late prehistoric Europe.

POTTERY AND THE DEVELOPMENT OF WAYS OF VISUALIZING

As discussed in Chapter 2, people learn how to see through the experience of seeing. This process begins at birth, and the first weeks and months of life are particularly critical. What an infant sees at that very early stage plays a disproportionate role in the child's development of ways of seeing, because more synapses in the brain are available to make connections than at any later stage. Since pottery was present in all households of Bronze and Iron Age Europe, and since it was among the most visible and spatially striking of all objects in those households, it played a major role in the development of seeing and visual perception.

Two reconstructions give an idea of the prominence of pottery in the visual environment of the Bronze and Iron Age house interior. A drawing of an Early Bronze Age house interior at Feudvar in the Vojvodina in Serbia illustrates how visually striking pottery was. A photograph of reenactors in an Iron Age house at Lejre in Denmark similarly shows the dominant role of pottery in that setting.

Pottery was a part of every mealtime, but it was visible to the infant and child at almost any other time as well, arranged on shelves, on tables, or on the floor. It played a much greater role in the child's visual development than metal tools or personal ornaments, or in fact any other category of material culture.

POTTERY IN THE VISUAL ECOLOGY
OF LATE PREHISTORIC EUROPE

Overview

It would be impossible to deal with the pottery of all of temperate Europe in any practicable way, so my strategy here will be to focus on the pottery of one region—southern Bavaria, an area of roughly 30,000 square kilometers. The aim of this section is to examine in some detail changes in the visual characteristics of the pottery produced there between 2000 BC and the Roman conquests, and to suggest how those characteristics relate to other aspects of peoples' visual experience. I select southern Bavaria for three reasons. First, the region is situated in the center of the European continent and thus likely to be more representative than other regions might be. Second, the database of well-excavated, well-documented, and well-published pottery from late prehistoric contexts is exceptionally good in Bavaria. And third, it is a region with which I am closely familiar, having directed excavations at three settlement sites in Lower Bavaria: Hascherkeller and Altdorf, both on the outskirts of Landshut, and Kelheim on the Danube.

The great majority of pottery vessels belong to one of three main categories: cups, bowls, and jars.

Cups are more or less globular vessels of a size that fit conveniently in the palm of an adult's hand. They generally have small flat bases, rounded or cylindrical sides, and small band handles. Sometimes the neck is constricted and the rim flares outward, forming a profile in the shape of an S-curve. In the case of cylindrical or conical forms, the rim does not flare. Cups are often decorated with incised patterns.

Bowls are low, relatively flat vessels, sometimes with wide bases and upward-sloping, convex sides and with the greatest diameter at the rim. Some are relatively deep and roughly hemispherical in shape, others are flatter. Small bowls fit conveniently in the adult hand, larger ones require two hands to hold. Bowls sometimes have handles. In the earlier part of the period, bowls are generally not decorated, in the later part they sometimes are.

Jars are the largest vessels, in both height and diameter. They often have broad bases and, particularly in the earlier part of the period, widely flaring, bulbous sides. In the Bronze Age, they had shoulders that constrict to a narrower neck and flaring rims. In the Iron Age, they are less bulbous in shape, the neck is less constricted, and the rim is thickened rather than flaring.

THE BRONZE AGE AND EARLY IRON AGE (2000–500 BC)

The Early Bronze Age (2000-1600 BC)

Early Bronze Age cups are globular, almost spherical in shape. They are typically 10 to 12 cm tall and gray in color, with patches of brown and tan. The exterior surface is relatively smooth, but not as highly polished as that of many of the bowls of the same period. The profile is S-shaped. Decoration consists of linear patterns at the top of the shoulder. On some cups, three or four deeply incised horizontal lines circle the vessel, stopping on either side of the small band handle, as in Figure 9. On others, incised triangles drop down from a horizontal line, and the triangles are filled with small holes. On many cups, the incised lines and the small holes are filled with a white substance, probably ground limestone.

Bowls are low and flat, most often tan in color, and have smooth, often highly polished surfaces. In contrast to cups, they are rarely decorated; when they do have decoration, it consists of patterns of small straight lines incised into the rim. Bowls sometimes have small handles, but more often do not.

Jars have bulbous shapes, but they are much larger than cups and have a less constricted mouth. They often have two or three handles at the top of the shoulder. Jars are generally tan in color, like bowls. Their exterior surfaces are coarse in texture compared to those of cups and bowls, with large pebbles often visible. Around the top of the shoulder is a raised band decorated with marks. These can be fingertip impressions, pairs of "half moons," thin slits set obliquely, grooves of different shapes, small round holes, or other impressed ornament. The variety of these motifs is striking. In addition to this decorated band, some jars have marks on the rim, either fingertip impressions or grooves.

The three forms of pottery vessels—cups, bowls, and jars—are distinct from one another, and within each category there is also some variation in size, shape, surface finish, and decoration. Decoration characteristic of each never occurs on other categories. This exclusivity of decoration with respect to vessel form indicates that the three forms were distinct in the minds of the people who made and used them, and that the decorative patterns were directly connected to the specific vessel types on which we find them. Size, form, surface texture, and decoration were interrelated elements in the visual character of each vessel.

Both cups and bowls are of sizes appropriate for the serving and consumption of individual portions, of beverage in the case of cups and of food in the case of bowls. The fact that cups are decorated ordinarily in just one of two patterns suggests that the users of the cups were individuals belonging to a particular category of person (we know from cemetery evidence that specific kinds of objects are associated with specific genders and statuses), but that in the village communities there were a number of individuals who shared membership in those categories. Decoration on bronze ornaments such as pins that were placed in graves was structured in similar ways, around lines and triangles.

The decoration encountered on Early Bronze Age cups represents a substantial change from that found on Bell Beakers, the drinking cups of the immediately preceding centuries. Bell Beakers typically bear incised linear ornament that covers most of their exterior surfaces. The ornament on Beakers is also horizontal in its basic structure, and each beaker is unique in its specific patterning. The lines and triangles on Early Bronze Age cups thus represent a marked reduction and simplification of ornament compared to these earlier drinking vessels.

With bowls, the situation is different. Usually bearing no decoration, bowls have none of the markers of special status that the cups possess. In the preceding Beaker period, bowls also tended to be plain and undecorated, as they would be in succeeding periods as well. This general (but not complete) lack of ornament on bowls throughout the Bronze Age is a significant aspect of the pottery assemblage.

Jars are unique in Early Bronze Age assemblages in two respects. First, each vessel is distinguished from the others in its assemblage by the specific pattern of ornament on its ridge and rim. Each jar is thus clearly and visibly marked as a distinct individual object. To judge by the evidence from sites such as Zuchering-Ost, where jars were found set in pits under house floors, they were the storage containers of households. The uniqueness of each jar with respect to its decoration suggests that the identity of each household, marked by its material possessions, was being highlighted.

Jars, as we have remarked, also differ from cups and bowls in having very coarse exterior surfaces compared to those of cups and bowls. Following the ideas of J. D. Hill and Andrew Jones, I argue that the potters who made the jars intentionally created surfaces that referenced the fields on which the grain that was to be stored in the jars grew. In the Beaker period, vessels comparable in size to Early Bronze Age jars were unusual, and those that have been identified lack the decorative details that characterize Bronze Age jars.

These two aspects of the jars in Early Bronze Age contexts suggest important and interrelated changes that were taking place in ecological relationships during this period. The connection between crafted material culture (the jars) and the landscape in which food was produced was becoming increasingly intimate, as human communities grew more confident in their ability to control the forces of nature to produce their crops. The imitation of the visual aspect of the fields in the pottery used to store the produce of the fields marks an intensification of the relationship between people, their food supply, and the landscape in which it grew. As this relationship intensified, divisions within the community became more pronounced and group identities more significant with respect to the economic processes of food production and storage—hence the new emphasis on marking each individual jar to make clear its connection to a the specific household.

Archaeologists have shown that the Early Bronze Age was a time of profound change in Europe. Agricultural activity was expanding in much of the continent, and new settlements were established. The building of defensive walls around hilltops indicates a need for protection, as well as a need to create visible boundaries, which may have resulted from the accumulation of greater stores of food surpluses and perhaps also the acquisition of ever-increasing quantities of such valuables as bronze, amber, and gold. Both the accumulation of valuables and the differential outfitting of graves suggests that status differences were increasing. The ability to organize the manpower necessary to build hillfort defenses and to coordinate relationships with different groups so as to facilitate the flow of valued goods also implies the development of larger and more complex political entities.

The character of the cups, bowls, and jars can be understood in terms of these large-scale evolving changes in relationships between communities, with their food sources, and with the larger world in which they lived. The specific visual features of the pottery—the common decorative themes of the cups, the plain but highly polished character of the bowls, the distinctive and ecology-referring surfaces of the jars—can be understood in terms of the social, political, and ecological (in the widest sense) changes of the time. The visual character of the vessels was first and foremost a means whereby people, as individuals, households, and communities, could negotiate the social and ecological relationships in their ever-changing world.

A large proportion of the pottery of Early Bronze Age Europe comes from deposits in pits. At one time, such pits were interpreted as "trash pits," but that idea was sensibly dismissed decades ago. Instead, extensive study of pit deposits all over Europe has resulted in our current understanding that many of these are "structured deposits"—intentional deposits of pottery (and often other materials as well) made at particular places, sometimes within settlements and even under house floors, but sometimes with no apparent link to any settlement. There has been a tendency to consider such deposits as "ritual" and to regard their contents as "offerings" to deities or other supernatural beings. But as Joanna Brück has persuasively shown, the notion that prehistoric peoples distinguished between ritual and secular activities in the way that we do is probably wrong. The "ritual" vs. "secular" opposition as we understand it today is a creation of the Enlightenment of the eighteenth century and not a distinction that all societies make. Deposits such as those of Early Bronze Age pottery in pits in the ground may well have been made in the context of activities that the participants felt would effect a desired outcome—a better harvest, a healthier community, protection from raids by neighbors—but they most likely did not conduct the "ceremony" (if we may call it that) in a way that we would consider "ritual." It was simply the way things were done.

The Middle Bronze Age (1600-1200 BC)

During the Middle Bronze Age, the category of cups became more diverse. Vessels similar in shape, texture, and color to the globular cups of the preceding period continued in use, but they tended not to have the distinctive S-shaped profiles of the earlier cups, and the number of incised horizontal lines varies more widely.

A new form of handled cup was developed. This does not have the globular shape of the Early Bronze Age cups, but rather a slightly rounded or even almost straight-sided shape, with a broad band handle that extends from the shoulder to the rim. The handle opening is large enough to easily fit an adult index finger, in contrast to the small hole of the Early Bronze Age cups. These cups lack the horizontal incised lines of the earlier cups, but some have a row of little dots or impressed circles around the vessel at the top of the shoulder. The color is light gray rather than the dark gray of earlier cups.

Also new are smaller and more ornate cups with flat bottoms and complex ornament comprised of vertical incised lines, rows of deep dots, and incised

FIGURE 13. Middle Bronze Age cup from Kelheim, Bavaria, Germany. Height 7.1 cm.

zigzag lines from top to bottom. A vessel from Kelheim will serve as a good example (Figure 13). This is shaped like a squat cylinder, with a broad flat bottom and a slightly incurving rim. The body is divided into a series of zones by shallow incised vertical lines. In some zones there are vertical rows of impressed holes or dots, in other zones incised zigzag lines.

These small cups are part of a phenomenon of much wider geographical significance than were the globular cups of the Early Bronze Age. Small cups of roughly this shape occur in contexts throughout much of the continent, and they are well represented also in the British Isles. Their geographic range is reminiscent of the Bell Beakers, which were widely distributed across Europe at an earlier time. The ornamentation on these Middle Bronze Age cups, with their deep holes and zigzag lines, distinguishes them from other pottery and draws special attention to them.

Bowls of the Middle Bronze Age are similar to those of the preceding period, though they are sometimes larger in mouth diameter and often have handles. Graphite applied to the rims of some bowls represents a decorative innovation.

Another distinctive new feature of Middle Bronze Age pottery is decoration consisting of parallel horizontal lines incised around jars with groups of short vertical lines between them, sometimes filled with a white substance.

This distinctive pattern occurs on thick and medium wares, and on vessels of different colors.

Jars differ in the details of their shape from those of the preceding period, but fundamentally they are similar. The decoration of large fingertip impressions is much more consistent than the varied patterns of ornament on Early Bronze Age jars. Sometimes there are two rows of bands with fingertip impressions. A distinctive feature of some jars are rough vertical strokes made by fingertips down the sides of the jars, creating smooth channels separated by little ridges. With fingertip impressions on the rim and shoulder ridge, and finger strokes on the sides, Middle Bronze Age jars show the embodiment of the maker to a greater extent than do the jars of the preceding period.

The increasing diversity of cup forms can be related to growing social complexity, reflecting a greater number of discrete categories of people in the communities. The small, highly decorated cups are of special interest. Each one is unique, in contrast to the situation in the Early Bronze Age, when the universe of cups consisted of only two major variants. Whereas in the Early Bronze Age decorated cups are largely restricted to a limited region of southern Germany, small and highly decorated cups of the Middle Bronze Age are a Europe-wide phenomenon of this period. These Middle Bronze Age cups provide strong evidence that communities throughout Europe were in contact and that this special kind of vessel was in fashion among those elites.

Many investigators have argued that the Middle Bronze Age was a time of great economic and social change, with the expansion of settled farmland and clearing of forests, the establishment of ever-longer-term settlements, and the development of stronger bonds between communities and their lands. The Europe-wide distribution of the distinctive small cups accords with this heightened economic and social change around the middle of the second millennium BC, as does the practice of tumulus burial, which became more common in this period. Involving the construction of highly visible monuments in the landscape (where flat grave inhumation had been the dominant practice over much of the continent previously), it can be viewed as a visual representation of closer and more permanent connections between people and the land they inhabited and a heightened concern with marking one's land with "tombs of the ancestors" so as to lay permanent claim to it.

The Late Bronze Age / Early Iron Age (1200-500 BC)

The reason for including both the Late Bronze Age and the Early Iron Age in one category here is that there is no apparent break between these named periods. When he created his typological/chronological system at the start of

FIGURE 14. Sherd of a Late Bronze Age cup from Altdorf, Bavaria, Germany. Width 6.5 cm.

the twentieth century, Paul Reinecke allowed for this fact in his designation of what he considered the final phases of the Bronze Age as Hallstatt A and Hallstatt B, and the phases of the Early Iron Age as Hallstatt C and Hallstatt D. Although the phases A and B have often been treated separately from C and D, typologically there is no break in development in the metalwork, and recent studies have confirmed complete continuity in the pottery as well.

Cups from this period are closer in size to those of the Middle Bronze Age than to those of the Early Bronze Age. While size is consistent, shapes vary. Some have sides curving gradually up from the base to a wide open mouth. Others have a bulbous lower half and a constricted neck. Some have flaring rims, others do not. Some are plain, others carry complex incised or impressed decoration. Of the many decorated cups, each has a unique combination of lines, dots, circles, strokes, and garlands (Figure 14). Many were coated with graphite that gave them a shiny appearance.

In common with bowls from the Early and Middle Bronze Age, those of this period are generally not decorated, and they have very smooth surfaces, both inside and out.

Jars are the largest category of vessels, and have the thickest walls. In this period, they often are as tall as 50 cm and have mouth diameters of 30 cm. They have the roughest and most textured surfaces, frequently with sizeable pebbles protruding. As in the earlier periods, the rims are often decorated with fingertip impressions, and fingertip impressions sometimes occur on a raised band around the shoulder as well.

Large jars are often recovered in pits beneath houses, as at Straubing-Öberau and at Altdorf-Römerfeld, where they served as storage containers for grain and other foodstuffs.

Cups stand out from other categories of vessels by nature of their color. They are usually dark gray, while other pottery tends to be brown or tan. They are also by far the most elaborately decorated pottery of this phase and are also more ornate than those of the earlier phases. Even more than in the Middle Bronze Age, each of these decorated cups is markedly different from every other, an important indication of the developing practice of marking individual identities through the medium of objects. We see the same phenomenon at this time in the decoration of hilts and pommels on cast-hilted swords (see Chapter 7).

During the eighth century BC, a new pattern of decoration on pottery (and on some other categories of objects) became dominant in much of temperate Europe. It involved the use of lines—most often incised but sometimes painted—to define zones that were filled with different kinds of ornament, each zone having a different ornament than that of its neighbors. Zones can be rectangular, diamond-shaped, triangular, or circular. The ornament inside them can consist of incised parallel lines, dots-and-circles, fine points, hatched squares, and other elements. The radical departure from earlier patterns of decoration consists here in the creation of bounded spaces and the filling of neighboring spaces with different ornament. These themes of fashioning boundaries on the pottery, and marking differences between neighboring units, are key elements of the structuring of visual experience during this period. They are not common in either the preceding phases of the Bronze Age or in succeeding phases of the La Tène period, but highly distinctive of this specific time. Among the best examples are vessels from the cemeteries at Riedenburg and Geiselhöring. Similar patterns of ornament can be seen on the sheet-bronze belt plates of this time.

The Middle Iron Age (500–200 BC)

In the course of the fifth century BC, the strict geometrical and the zonal emphasis in pottery ornament waned, and new shapes and motifs appeared. Especially noteworthy is the increasing use of curvilinear forms such as S-curves, spirals, and formlines, frequently forming vegetal motifs such as tendrils and petals.

The basic categories of cups, bowls, and jars continue to dominate assemblages, but a new form is introduced, the bottle. Although there is variation, the dominant color of pottery in this period is light gray, a color that was less common in earlier periods. Another change is the lack of decoration on cups, the category of pottery that was most highly decorated in earlier times. A third is the prevalence of the S-shaped profile, a shape noted earlier in cups of the Bronze Age phases, but now common on bowls and bottles as well as cups.

The handled cups that were such an important visual component from the Early Bronze Age to the Early Iron Age are rare now, and cups generally take the form of small bowls, generally without decoration, but often with a characteristic sharp angle in the sides.

Bowls tend to be undecorated, like those of earlier periods, but they often bear two new visual features. One is the S-shaped profile comprised of a curved upward-sloping side that curves inward slightly just below an outcurving rim. This shape is distinctly different from the profiles of bowls earlier. The other is an omphalos, a "pushed up" circular bottom, which creates a visual focus in the center of the bowl. The omphalos is often ornamented, with incised decoration concentric to it and with linear patterns, such as S-curves and dot-and-circle motifs, on the circular bulge.

Jars tend to have broad flat bases, often coarse exteriors, little profiling at the shoulder and neck, and sometimes horizontal lines incised around the top of the shoulder.

Bottles have broad but low bodies (often described as lens-shaped) and funnel-shaped necks that widen toward the opening at the top, where the rim often curves outward. The base commonly has an omphalos, and the top of the shoulder frequently bears ornament. The decoration can be simply a horizontal ridge running around the shoulder, or it can consist of incised or impressed patterns. A vessel from a grave at Mittelburg has at this location a band defined by two sets of incised lines and filled with incised S-curves and impressed dots-and-circles. One from a grave at Drosendorf has a ring of dots-and-circles impressed around the top of the shoulder next to the base of the neck, and triangles formed by dots-and-circles on the shoulder just below the ring. The famous bottle from Matzhausen has an incised frieze of four-legged animals, including deer and hares, as well as a wavy line and patterns of little S-curves. Other pottery is ornamented with incised floral patterns, including blossoms and palmettes.

Another form that played a visual role was the ceramic jug modeled on the Etruscan bronze *Schnabelkanne*. Whereas there are no clear cases of locally manufactured imitations of Attic pottery, these Etruscan bronze jugs, which are well represented in Early La Tène graves in temperate Europe, served as models not only for ceramic jugs, but also for locally made bronze vessels.

Attic Pottery

Pottery made at Athens in Greece was the first major category of pottery from a distant location to appear in noteworthy amounts in temperate Europe, beginning around 530 BC. Until a couple of decades ago, Attic pottery was known only from a small number of archaeological sites in the region, most notably at the settlements at the Heuneburg in southern Germany, Mont Lassois in eastern France, and Châtillon-sur-Glâne in Switzerland, and from richly outfitted burials such as those at Vix, Kleinaspergle, and several Early La Tène sites in the Middle Rhineland. Since then, sherds of Attic pottery have been reported from many more sites in eastern France, from the Ipf and other places in southern Germany, and from Bohemia. While Attic pottery still needs to be regarded as an "exotic" material associated with elites, it is now clear that it was not restricted to a few major centers and was apparently used by many more people than at first supposed. It was a much more significant part of the visual world of late sixth and fifth century BC temperate Europe than was thought three decades ago.

Even if the evidence of future excavations continues to suggest that the possession and use of Attic pottery was restricted *largely* to elites, we nonetheless need to assess its impact on the visual world and visual imagination of Iron Age Europeans. As sponsors of craftsworkers who produced pottery and metal ornaments, elites played a disproportionate role in the shaping of the visual world. We also need to reckon with these elites playing the roles of hosts at socially and politically significant feasts (see Chapter 9).

Several kinds of evidence show the ways in which Attic pottery affected the visual world of Iron Age Europeans. It replaced locally made pottery in feasting sets. This is most evident in contexts such as the Vix burial, where two Attic *kylikes* were included as drinking cups, a function that otherwise would have been performed by local vessels, such as the drinking horns in the Hochdorf grave. The quantities of Attic sherds on the Heuneburg and at the settlement of Mont Lassois also suggest that Attic vessels were substituting for local vessels, but in settlement deposits we do not of course have the same kinds of closed contexts that we have in the burials. At the Heuneburg, the presence of Attic vessels associated with the Greek symposium—the *kylix* and the *krater*—suggests that these vessels were parts of an entire feasting set, as the two *kylikes* in the Vix grave were, together with the bronze *krater*, jug, and basins in that grave.

The special treatment accorded the two *kylikes* from the Kleinaspergle grave is another indication of the role that Attic pottery played in the visual world of temperate Europe. These cups were decorated with thin sheet-gold ornaments in the La Tène style, carefully attached to the pottery with tiny bronze rivets. If craftsworkers went to the trouble of fashioning and attaching these extremely fine and delicate ornaments to the vessels, clearly the cups themselves were considered important.

THE LATE IRON AGE (200–50 BC)

The most striking change in the visual character of pottery is a reduction in complex ornament and an overall simplification of form. The complex S-shaped or angled profiles of the preceding period are no longer much in evidence. But while the variety and complexity of ornament decreased, a new kind of decoration came to dominate the pottery repertoire—vertical comb-made lines. The potter's wheel came into regular use during this phase and had a major effect on the character of the pottery produced.

Handleless beakers, small jars, and small bowls seem now to have served the same purpose as cups did in the earlier period.

Bowls occur in two main variants, both undecorated. One has a slightly inturned rim and ranges in form from low and shallow to high and deep. The other has a sharply angled profile and was wheelmade.

Jars range from the common "cooking pots" (*Kochtöpfe*) of graphite-clay (especially earlier) and plain clay (especially later) to tall thin vessels with broad flat bases, slightly outcurving sides with the greatest diameter two-thirds to three-quarters of the way to the top, and thickened and/or slightly outcurved rims, but no necks. Jars range widely in texture, from coarse to extremely fine. The finest are thin-walled, beige-colored painted wares, most commonly decorated with red and white bands, and sometimes with patterns of wavy lines or crisscross lines. In some parts of Europe, notably central France, painted wares include jars with elaborate stylized figures of horses, along with rich decorative motifs, but such figurally painted wares are unusual elsewhere.

Large jars used for storage have relatively coarse exterior surfaces and thick rounded rims, but lack the types of decoration that were common on Bronze Age jars.

Several general features of pottery in this phase should be stressed. The use of the wheel meant that pottery could be made much faster. It could, essentially, be mass-produced. It also meant that pottery tended to have a smoother surface than the handmade pottery of earlier times, and thus a very different kind of texture. With the use of the wheel, we note the disappearance of any direct marks of the potter on the finished vessels, such as the fingertip impressions so typical of earlier periods.

The fabric of the fine painted wares is light beige in color, similar in color to that of Roman amphorae that were being brought into temperate Europe at this time. Also reminiscent of Roman amphorae are the pedestal urns and tall cylindrical jars that are distinctive new forms of pottery common in some regions, including the Rhineland and southern Britain, at this time. Their shape is similar to that of a Dressel IA amphora with its neck and the top part of its shoulder knocked off (as was commonly done so that amphorae could be reused for secondary purposes).

Especially in the latter part of the period, during the phases known as La Tène D2 and D3, a wide diversity of forms and of decorative techniques came into use, paralleling a new diversity in belt-hooks, fibulae, and other types of decorative metalwork.

Comb decoration and vertical linear incised decoration in general are of special significance (Figure 15). Comb decorated pottery is unusual in temperate Europe before this period. It became common around the end of the third century BC, and it stands out for several reasons. In earlier pottery, decoration tends to be horizontal in orientation, not vertical. And unlike the decorative patterns of earlier periods, the comb decoration of the Late Iron Age was applied to a wide range of pottery shapes and degrees of coarseness, from the finest wares, decorated with very thin and delicate lines, to very course pottery with roughly incised, wide lines. Another contrast with most earlier forms of decoration on pottery, is the tendency for this new ornament to cover almost all of the surface of vessels, with the exception of a narrow neck at the top and a narrow band left free of lines just above the base.

Comb decoration gave a very different visual character to pottery from that produced by the decorative schemes of earlier times. It left very little open space—little affordance, in other words—and it gave the entire vessel a filled, highly textured appearance. This vertical line decoration on pottery appeared at about the time when coins with writing on them were first introduced into temperate Europe (see Chapter 10). We can see from local imitations of early Greek staters that the verticality of the Greek letters was important to the makers of the coin dies, because in place of the Greek letters, straight vertical lines were engraved into the dies. It is not altogether unreasonable to hypothesize that these lines on the coins were the source for the idea of decorating pottery with vertical lines. I have no evidence to support this idea, but I do plan to pursue it further.

Roman amphorae were a significant part of the pottery assemblages in temperate Europe from 150 BC on. The principal forms are those known as Dressel 1A and 1B, dated from roughly 150 BC to the early first century AD.

The Roman amphorae are visually distinct from all forms of locally made pottery. They are tall—usually between 1.1 and 1.2 m in height—and have a

FIGURE 15. Late Iron Age pottery sherds from Kelheim, Bavaria, Germany, showing a variety of different kinds of comb decoration.

distinctive shape with a thick and high rim, a long narrow neck, and a wide cylindrical body with its greatest diameter around 30 cm. The body tapers at the bottom to a rounded point, designed for easy standing in sand or soft soil. Between the top of the neck and the shoulder are two vertical handles. Their shape makes them easily identifiable, as does their hard-fired and generally beige or pinkish color. The Dressel 1A variant is taller and has a higher rim, longer handles, and a longer, more tapered base than the Dressel 1B.

The shape of these vessels is much more suggestive of a human body than is that of any locally made vessels. Their height, their diameter, the narrowing from shoulder to neck, the thick and long rim, especially on the Dressel 1A amphora, and their handles, all make one think of the human form. Matthieu Poux notes that at some sites at which humans were beheaded (Lyon Verbe Incarné, Aulnat, Basel Gasfabrik), amphorae were "beheaded" in the same way, having their top part slashed off at the neck.

The presence of these imported amphorae, often in great quantities, at settlements, at what are interpreted as ritual sites, in graves, and in rivers attests to the eagerness of elites in Late Iron Age Europe to acquire wine from the Mediterranean basin and to the intensity of the wine trade.

POTTERY AND THE VISUAL WORLDS, 2000–50 BC

The Bronze Age and Early Iron Age (2000–500 BC)

From the Early through the Late Bronze Age, the color, texture, and decorative themes on storage jars link them visually with the fields where the grains stored in these vessels were grown. As noted above, during these centuries, communities were in the process of establishing themselves permanently on the land, clearing forests, and creating field systems, as they began to practice a more intensive kind of agriculture than their predecessors had. The making of storage jars with visual characteristics that reference the fields can be understood as part of a process whereby relationships were forged between the human community and the landscape on which that community depended for nutrition.

At the same time, each jar was distinguished from every other by the distinctive pattern of decoration on its shoulder and rim. These distinctions reflect the growing importance of each household's identification with the produce of its fields and its labor. The jars, more than any other category of pottery, embody the individuality of the potter in the fingertip impressions and fingernail impressions that mark the shoulders and rims of the vessels and, in the Middle Bronze Age, in the impressions of the potter's fingers drawn down the sides of the vessels.

Bowls tend to be plain throughout this fifteen-hundred-year period. Their surfaces, both interior and exterior, are polished smooth, unlike those of the jars.

Cups stand out by virtue of their color and their decoration. Whereas jars and bowls tend to be brown or tan, cups tend to be dark or light gray. In the Early Bronze Age, cups were large, suggesting communal use, but in both the Middle and Late Bronze Age, they were small, suggesting that they were designed to hold individual portions. The individuality of cups reaches its apogee in the Late Bronze Age and earliest Iron Age, with the numerous very thin-walled and uniquely decorated cups of the southern Bavarian group known as "Attinger" ware. The unique pattern of ornament on each cup parallels the unique patterns of incised linear decoration on the cast-hilted swords of this period and indicates an emphasis on the personal identity of each individual user of those objects.

In the Early Iron Age, zonal decoration on pottery became important. The zones defined by lines and often filled with contrasting ornament are similar in structure to the zonal decoration on other categories of objects of this period, most notably belt plates, and they are also related visually to the increasing use of enclosure as a means of separating settlements from the surrounding countryside. Zonal decoration is most common on jars and bowls, while cups tend to be undecorated.

Thus, toward the end of this period, the visual emphasis of pottery shifts from relations with the landscape and food-producing fields to relations between persons and groups. The theme of opposition, contrast, and distinction between things occupying neighboring spaces is repeated in the different categories of pottery, in personal ornaments such as belt plates and neckrings, in the enclosing of settlements, and in the arrangement of objects in graves.

The Middle Iron Age (500–200 BC)

During the fifth century BC major changes took place in pottery and in other areas of material culture and life. The zonal patterning of the preceding period decreased in importance. Most importantly, the S-curve that played such a major role in decorative metalwork (see Chapters 6 and 7) also became an equally significant factor in major changes taking place in pottery. A new form, the bottle, was created, and both bottles and bowls had distinctive S-shaped profiles.

Craftsworkers in temperate Europe responded to ideas and imports from outside. Most notably, the Etruscan bronze *Schnabelkanne*, represented in many fifth century BC graves, served as the prototype for local jugs of similar shape, as well as for a series of bronze vessels. Attic pottery imported from the Greek world stimulated response, as we see at Kleinaspergle, where the two Attic cups were transformed by the application of local gold ornaments in the new style.

The pottery of this phase tends to be gray in color to a much greater extent than earlier pottery, and storage jars to have a much less rough exterior. References to the fields in the landscape and to social differences within communities are no longer the visual themes that dominate pottery. Instead, the prevalence of S-curves, both in vessel profiles and as incised patterns in the fabric of pots, suggests that the new features were responses to the widening of the horizons of the inhabitants of temperate Europe and to the ever-increasing availability of goods from distant lands. We will look at this phenomenon in greater detail in Chapters 11 and 12.

The Late Iron Age (200–50 BC)

The pottery of these final centuries further reflects the growing intensity of contacts and interactions with societies in other parts of the eastern hemisphere, especially with the Roman world, but with other regions as well. Four features of pottery now dominate visual aspects:

1. The use of vertical incised lines covering most of the sides of many categories of vessels.
2. The use of the potter's wheel. At many settlements, well over 50% of the pottery is now wheelmade. In visual terms, the most important aspect of wheelmade pottery is the distinctive profiles of vessels made on the wheel. Missing now is any visible trace of the individual potter.
3. Thin-walled, light beige pottery. This color is unusual in prehistoric Europe and may have been adopted in imitation of Roman amphorae.
4. The appearance of new forms. Prominent among them is the pedestal urn and tall cylindrical jar. Many of the painted vessels are of this shape, and the shape is also represented in many unpainted but wheelmade vessels. The shape closely resembles the form of a Roman amphora of Dressel 1A type that has had its neck knocked off, a fate that many Roman amphorae shared.

All four of these new characteristics appear around 200 BC and signal major changes in the visual ecology of prehistoric Europe. Related changes are apparent in the visual character of many other kinds of material culture, such as the fibulae and scabbards that are the subjects of the next two chapters.

CHAPTER 6

∞∞∞∞∞∞∞∞∞∞∞∞∞∞∞

ATTRACTION AND ENCHANTMENT

Fibulae

THE CHARM OF FIBULAE

Fibulae are charming. Of all of the common objects preserved from late prehistoric Europe, they are the most attractive, in the sense that even today people are drawn to them, finding them intriguing to look at. They are especially interesting to see in three dimensions—in museums cases, but even in photographs and drawings, they are usually the visually most interesting objects in an assemblage. Writing about later Iron Age brooches in Britain, E. M. Jope described their "pleasing tectonic ingenuity" and the way their forms "may sometimes serve to please the eye." And, he noted, "brooches may . . . add points of playing reflected light or of colour."

Fibulae were clothing pins that operated on the same principle as the modern safety pin. The pin was slid through textile fabric and its end set into a little catch at what is called the "foot" end that held the pin tight. We know how fibulae were worn, because they are consistently found on the chest or shoulder of buried individuals, sometimes with remains of fabric still adhering to them. Many types of fibulae made during the Bronze Age were structurally very much like modern safety pins, with a bow, a spring at one end (known as the "head" end), a pin, and the catch at the foot end. During the Iron Age, the shapes of fibulae became much more complex and varied. Many fibulae, especially those of the fifth and fourth centuries BC, are among the most complex and visually fascinating objects from prehistoric Europe.

Since the style of fibulae changed relatively rapidly throughout the Bronze and Iron Ages, they have long been used as the principal chronological indicator for a given grave or settlement. Fibulae are much more "time sensi-tive" than most kinds of material culture in early Europe. The rapid changes in the visual aspects of fibulae can be useful for chronological purposes but also, as in this investigation, to explore changes in ways of visualizing.

The reason that they are so appealing to us today is that they embody a number of the visually commanding features outlined in Chapter 2. In their shapes, they are unlike anything in nature—especially the fibulae of Iron Age date—and thus immediately seize our attention. Straight pins, which fibulae largely replaced, are of a form that is common in nature in, for example, the shapes of flower stems. But there is nothing in nature anything like the many different forms of Iron Age fibulae.

Many Iron Age fibulae form three-dimensional S-curves. Many are shaped as formlines, with narrower head and foot ends and widened bows. Some have additional S-curve ornaments incised or in relief on their bows. Those made during the fifth century BC are often ornamented with faces, some hu-man, some animal, and some hybrid. They are among the "classic" objects of what is commonly known as "Early La Tène art" or "early Celtic art."

In addition, fibulae had a unique property among material culture items of late prehistoric Europe. In order to operate a fibula—to attach it to a garment—the user had to apply considerable force with the thumb and forefinger to the pin in order to lift the end out of the catch. Then, after sliding the pin through a textile garment or removing it from one, he or she released the pin to sit in the catch again. No other objects—straight pins, bracelets, finger rings, neckrings, or pendants—required this kind of bodily manipulation in order to serve their intended purposes. This aspect of fibulae imbued them with a property differ-ent from all other personal ornaments. The sight of a fibula, whether attached to a person's garment or in a deposit, brought not only fascination with the shape of the object and the decoration on it, but also fascination with the mechanism, with the physical power embodied in the spring that required the user's bodily involvement to operate. I shall come back to this point below in discussing rep-resentations of fibulae. As Werner Krämer cogently observed, there are many representations—pictures—of fibulae, especially on pottery and on coins, and these representations always show them in their open position.

FIBULAE ARE DIFFERENT FROM POTTERY

Fibulae played a role in the visual world of early Europe that was quite unlike the role played by pottery. Pottery was always visible as a part of the household and "belonged" (whatever that may have meant at the time) to the household

community. Fibulae were worn by individuals, and thus their visual properties accrued to the individual who wore them.

Fibulae were highly portable—they were small, light, comparatively sturdy,
and were worn on garments as the wearer moved about. Their easy portabil-
ity meant that they could be transferred from one community to another easily, through trade, gift exchange, or other mechanisms. The broad distribution
of fibulae of particular types across Europe shows that they did indeed circulate widely, and perhaps also that they were often copied and imitated. Thomas
Völling's study of fibula types dating to the end of the prehistoric Iron Age and
early Roman Period includes many distribution maps that make this point clearly.

Most pottery was portable (except the largest storage jars, which could only
have been lifted with considerable difficulty, and never when full), but was
probably not moved as extensively as fibulae. Dropping a ceramic vessel on any
kind of hard surface would cause it to break. Distributions of particular types
of pottery show that pottery did not circulate nearly as widely as fibulae did.

Pottery was also different from fibulae with respect to its visual references. As I argue in Chapter 5, during the Bronze Age storage jars referenced
landscapes and food production, bowls referenced domesticity, and cups
referenced individuals. Fibulae, as thin, S-curving, visually complex objects,
linked to other domains of life and concern.

FIBULAE IN PREHISTORIC EUROPE

Settlements

Fibulae are frequently recovered on Iron Age settlements, the majority of
them in fragmentary condition. Excavations of small settlements often yield
none, while large-scale excavations at major Iron Age settlements often result
in hundreds being discovered. For example, in his publication of fibulae recovered at the Heuneburg between 1950 and 1970, Günter Mansfeld studied
105 specimens. Rupert Gebhard's 1991 analysis of the fibulae from Manching
examined 1,850, about 20% of them of bronze, 80% of iron, and a few of silver.

Graves

The majority of fibulae are found in burials. From the end of the Early Iron
Age on, they were regularly buried with the dead in most parts of temperate Europe. The numbers found vary, however. Many graves do not contain

fibulae, many contain only one or two, and a few contain larger numbers. A few examples will illustrate the kinds of burial contexts in which they occur.

A recent excavation of the inhumation grave of a seventy-year-old woman at Oberstimm in Upper Bavaria, dated around 300 BC, yielded three fibulae. Two were recovered in the shoulder area, the third beneath the head. A nearby grave of a forty-year-old man contained an iron fibula, found next to the man's left elbow.

The rich grave at Hochdorf (dating to about 525 BC) contained two gold serpentine fibulae, similar in style and form to the common bronze serpentine fibulae, as well as two bronze fibulae. All four were found on the chest of the buried man.

A young woman was buried at Saint-Sulpice in Switzerland around 375 BC with a substantial quantity of personal ornaments, including two bronze fibulae, one of them ornamented with coral.

At Burgweinting near Regensburg in Bavaria, three inhumation graves contained skeletal remains of adults, each with an iron fibula at the left shoulder. Three more richly outfitted inhumations each included three fibulae as well as other personal ornaments. Another grave (nr. 7001) had three bronze fibulae, two on the upper part of the chest and one on the right shoulder. Grave 5635 had in it a bronze fibula and two iron fibulae.

The third-century-BC grave of a warrior at Dubník in Slovakia contained a fibula as well as a long iron sword in a scabbard and an iron lance point.

At Giengen on the Brenz River in southwest Germany, a small cemetery of thirteen graves was completely excavated in 1972. All were cremation burials, and some of the grave goods had been placed in the funeral pyre along with the bodies. Nine of the graves included weapons and are thought therefore to have been the burials of men. They contained iron fibulae. The other graves are thought to be those of women, since they contained personal ornaments commonly associated with women. One had in it the burned remains of bronze fibulae, another had two bronze and two iron fibulae. In another grave, unburned jewelry had been placed in a pit; among the items in it were nineteen bronze fibulae and fragments of two iron fibulae. The date of this grave, and of the cemetery as a whole, is about 200 BC.

A grave at Deal on the east coast of Kent in England, dating to around 135 BC, contained a sword, a shield, and an ornate bronze headring and also an iron fibula with coral insets.

It is clear from the way fibulae were worn that they were important visual objects. In all phases of the Early and Late Iron Age, they are recovered on the chest and shoulder area in burials—most often and most abundantly with women, but sometimes with men as well. Their positioning on the upper part of the torso would ensure that they were the personal ornament that a person approaching the wearer would have seen first. There has been much discussion of fibulae as signaling devices, and some attempts made to associate details of fibula types and decoration with particular categories of individuals.

DEPOSITS

Besides the visual enchantment of the fibula as an object, the contexts in which fibulae are often found provide evidence that they were regarded as special objects, above and beyond their use as items of personal attire. The addition of extra fibulae to burials, as in the woman's grave at Giengen, is an example. Besides burials, locations at which substantial numbers of fibulae were purposefully deposited, mainly from the late sixth century on, include unusual rock formations, springs, streams, lakes, and rectangular enclosures bounded by ditches.

At the site of the "Heidentor" in Egesheim in southwest Germany, a large natural limestone arch formed through erosional processes, a sizeable quantity of ornaments was recovered, including about seventy fibulae of Late Hallstatt and Early La Tène character. Unfortunately, the majority were recovered by looters, but archaeologists were able to establish that the collection came from that site and were able to recover more fibulae in the course of a subsequent systematic excavation. The report notes that in addition to fibulae, glass beads, fine hairpins of both bronze and iron, and iron belt-hooks were found—all important accessories of women's dress during this period. The report observes further that other objects that are characteristic in women's graves, especially bracelets, neckrings, and leg rings, are not represented here, implying that some special selection was made. No settlement remains or burials were reported in the area. The numerous fibulae seem to be part of a special deposit made at this unusual natural rock formation.

Excavations at the source of the Douix River at Châtillon-sur-Seine in eastern France have yielded an assemblage of 210 fibulae, most of them of the fifth century BC. A variety of different types are represented, but the assemblage is quite homogeneous chronologically. About 90% of the fibulae are of iron, 10% of bronze.

At Duchcov in Bohemia, 80 km northwest of Prague, an enormous assemblage of at least 850 fibulae was found in a bronze cauldron on the site of a spring. In 1882, as they were digging in the vicinity of the spring, workers came across the cauldron at a depth of about five meters. In it was a large quantity of bronze objects, mostly fibulae and bracelets. Estimates of the original number of objects vary between twelve hundred and four thousand. A recent study of those that can be traced has concluded that there were at least sixteen hundred and that among them were the 850 fibulae, along with 650 bracelets, and 100 finger rings. Most of the fibulae are of the same basic form, though they vary in details of ornament. The date of the deposit is probably between 300 and 250 BC.

At La Tène in Switzerland, along with the swords and scabbards recovered from the lake deposit (discussed below), 382 fibulae have been reported.

At the site of La Villeneuve-au-Châtelot in northeastern France, sizeable quantities of fibulae, weapons, and other metal objects were deposited over several centuries. In his analysis of the over seventy-five thousand objects recovered during excavations, Gérard Bataille notes that in the first chronological phase (La Tène B2–C2) about 20% of the objects were fibulae. In later phases, fibulae were still present, but in smaller percentages. But in the same region of France, excavations at the site of "Chatelets" at Vendeuil-Caply (Oise) yielded a different result, with the majority of the seventy-eight fibulae recovered being characteristic of the Late Iron Age.

In the Netherlands at the site of Empel, Late Iron Age fibulae were deposited in pre-conquest times, and Roman Period fibulae were deposited in the "Gallo-Roman" temple built on the site after the conquest of the region.

At Hayling Island in south-central England, fibulae were among the objects deposited in what has been interpreted as a Late Iron Age temple dating from the early or middle first century BC that had been transformed into a Roman temple sometime between AD 60 and 80. Details on the fibulae have not yet been published, but investigators report that a substantial number of them are of the Nauheim type (see Figure 24, page 110).

REPRESENTATIONS

Fibulae are shown represented in a number of different media. If we think of them as practical items of everyday clothing, items analogous to our belts or shirt buttons, the idea that they should be pictured on pottery or coins strikes us as unusual. But when we realize that objects during the Bronze and Iron Ages meant different things to the people of those times from what comparable objects mean to us today, we can appreciate that there are also profound and significant differences between the way that we see things and the way that they did.

Werner Krämer published an important study of representations of fibulae in late prehistoric Europe. Pictures of fibulae scratched into the surface of sherds of pottery have been identified at the Late Iron Age settlements of Aulnat and La Cloche in France and at Staré Hradisko in Moravia. A small bowl from Aulnat has no fewer than four fibulae represented on it. Actual fibulae had been pressed into the damp clay of pots that were recovered at the Early Iron Age enclosed site known as Babilonie at Lübbecke in northwestern Germany, and at the Late Iron Age sites at Seuthopolis in Bulgaria and Zimnicea in Romania. The results were impressions of the fibulae that are preserved in the surfaces of the fired vessels.

Fibulae are also represented on coins, for example on a silver coin from Owlesbury, Hampshire in England, and on a gold coin from northern France (see Figure 44, page 181).

Krämer makes the important point that fibulae are consistently represented open, not closed. He argues that as a garment fastener, a fibula was a symbol of holding things together and so could be interpreted in a metaphorical sense as well as a literal one. It may have been this meaning that was being invoked both when fibulae were deposited at the sites noted above and when they were represented by incised pictures on sherds of pottery.

The representations of fibulae that we find on sherds are never across breaks, which suggests that they were incised on the sherds of broken pots rather than on whole pots. In discussing sherds in this context, Krämer refers to *ostraka* in the Greek world, sherds of pottery that were inscribed for purposes of invoking or performing magic. We do not know what people intended with the fibulae that they represented on potsherds in Iron Age Europe, but we can surmise from the fact that they were representing them thus, and offering them in deposits at special places, that these objects had meanings far beyond that of simple clothing pins. If fibulae were indeed powerful devices, then something of their power could be conveyed through their images on other things, whether sherds of pottery or coins. It was not just the physical fibulae themselves, but even the idea of them—represented by the image—that was important.

The representation of fibulae on coins is particularly significant. Unlike sherds of pottery, coins were media that circulated, both within communities and beyond to other communities across Europe (Chapter 10). And with the coins, the images of fibulae circulated as well.

Fibulae are conspicuously missing from the life-size statues of men from Hirschlanden, Vix, and the Glauberg, although those statues do wear neckrings. The neckrings on the statue of the woman at Vix and on that of the man at the Glauberg link them directly to individuals in the associated graves. And those graves have fibulae in them as well. What, then, was the difference between attitudes toward fibulae and neckrings that would account for one category being represented on statues while the other is not? Was it simply a matter of neckrings being easier to represent in rough sandstone sculpture than fibulae were?

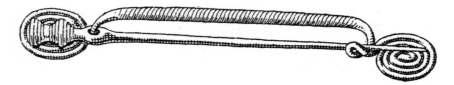

FIGURE 16. Drawing of an Early Bronze Age fibula from Bredsätra, Sweden. From Beltz 1913:668, fig. 4.

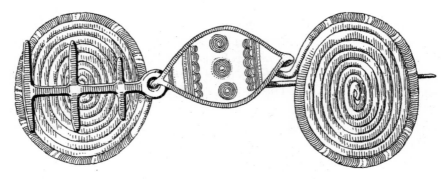

FIGURE 17. Drawing of an Early Bronze Age fibula from Świdnica, southwestern Poland. From Beltz 1913:671, fig. 9.

FIBULAE AS VISUAL OBJECTS

Fibulae gradually replaced straight pins, which were characteristic of well-equipped women's graves throughout the Bronze Age. Straight pins were also highly significant visually, especially when they achieved the enormous lengths of some Middle Bronze Age examples and when the ornaments on the heads of the pins referred to another item of material culture, as in the case of vase-headed pins that referred to specific kinds of Late Bronze Age cups; but fibulae are much more complex in both form and decoration.

The Bronze Age and Early Iron Age

In the earlier Bronze Age in northern Europe, most fibulae were long and thin, with low bows (Figure 16). Sometimes the bow was hammered flat and incised with fine hatching and concentric circle decoration. The forms were linear and geometric. In later phases of the Bronze Age in northern Europe,

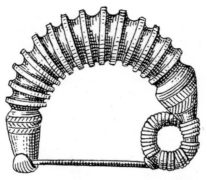

FIGURE 18. Drawing of a Late Bronze Age fibula from Mörigen, Switzerland. From Beltz 1913:685, fig. 32.

FIGURE 19. Drawing of an Early Iron Age fibula from Zirknitz, Austria. From Deschmann 1879, pl. after p. 144, 3.

both the foot and head of the fibula could terminate in wire spirals or flat, semi-oval forms, decorated with incised ornament (Figure 17).

In the final phase of the Bronze Age, or Urnfield Period, fibulae could vary from very thin wire bows and pins, sometimes with flat semi-oval plates at either end, to spectacle brooches consisting of two spirals of wire, to the thick, solid, D-shaped arched bow of the Mörigen type (Figure 18).

The most significant change in the form of fibulae in the course of the Iron Age is the appearance of S-shaped bows. These include the serpentine fibula (Figure 19), sometimes with several S-curves along the bow, and later the drum fibula (*Paukenfibel*) and the foot-decorated fibula (*Fusszierfibel*). The schematic diagram by Mansfeld (1973:4, fig. 1), showing these different forms of Early Iron Age fibulae in the central regions of temperate Europe, makes these shapes particularly clear. In the *Fusszier* fibulae (dP, F, and dZ on Mansfeld's diagram) the S-shape is especially prominent. From the head end at the spring, tracing the line of the bow forms one part of the S, then the down slope of the bow and the upturn of the vertical ornament on the foot forms the second part of the S. This new fibula form was an important factor in the transformation of ways of visualizing during the Middle Iron Age. The addition of ornament such as coral inset onto the foot accentuates the form of the S-curve.

FIGURE 20. Drawing of an Early La Tène fibula from Panenský Týnec, Bohemia, Czech Republic. From Beltz 1911:672, fig. 1.

FIGURE 21. Drawing of an Early La Tène fibula from Beilngries, Bavaria, Germany. From Beltz 1911:677, fig. 13.

THE MIDDLE IRON AGE

In the Early La Tène Period, the S-curve became fundamental to fibula design. It was the classic shape around which all of the ornamental fibulae were structured. Over time the curve became more accentuated than in the preceding period, with the foot no longer standing up vertically but instead curving backward toward the bow in an extension of the S-curve sweep. The curve shape now was often accompanied by figural ornament in the form of human, animal, and hybrid heads, integrated into the fundamental S-structure. It is also at this time that the S-curve becomes predominant on scabbards (Chapter 7).

Fibulae from this period frequently exhibit three-dimensional formlines, the foot and head ends being thin, while the bow widens considerably. As explained in Chapter 2, such formlines offer a visually attractive and enchanting shape, and they also create the impression of movement. Fibulae often bear images of hybrid creatures—animals that combine parts of different real animals to form imaginary beings.

The fibula from Panenský Týnec in Bohemia is an example from this period (Figure 20). Two animals are represented. There is a sheep's head on the foot end and a bird of prey with spread wings at the head. Both representations are three-dimensional, with the sheep's snout and ears projecting outward, as do the bird's head, wings, and tail. Both creatures have decorated collars around their necks. The sheep wears a crown or crest on top of its head and has spiraling forms along its sides, perhaps representing fleece. The bird, which is represented more naturalistically than the sheep, is covered with tiny incised dots, and its wings are decorated with fine incised lines, as

FIGURE 22. Drawing of a Middle La Tène fibula from Duchcov, Bohemia, Czech Republic. From Beltz 1911:677 fig. 15.

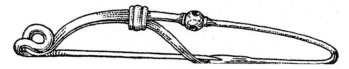

FIGURE 23. Drawing of a Middle La Tène fibula from Münsingen, Switzerland. From Beltz 1911:684, fig. 45.

are the four tufts at the end of its tail. The entire bow of the fibula is a form-line, with the thinner portions near the foot and head, and the thickest in the middle. On the middle a rhomboid is incised, with patterns of hatched lines inside it.

Fibulae of the fourth century BC continued to be structured around the S-curve. On some, the foot curves backward toward the bow (Figure 21), on others it touches the bow (Figure 22). The bow is often broader than previously, and sometimes bears relief ornament. Both the foot and the central part of the bow are sometimes accentuated visually with coral inlay.

THE LATE IRON AGE

Fibulae produced during the late third and second centuries BC tend to be much less elaborate and ornamental and to be built around narrow, wire-style bows and feet. They are often longer and lower in profile than in the preceding periods (Figure 23). The broad bow and inlaid ornament are gone, and the S-curve, while still apparent in some examples, is no longer as pronounced. Three-dimensional formlines are rare.

At the end of the second and during the first century BC, on the majority of fibulae the foot was no longer a distinct part of the fibula, the whole object being cast as a single piece. Among the most common forms is the Nauheim fibula, designed specifically to be mass-produced (Figure 24). Other forms, such as the Beltz J fibula and the *geschweifte* fibula, are similarly simple in design and construction.

FIGURE 24. Drawing of a Late La Tène Nauheim-type fibula, from Stradonice, Bohemia, Czech Republic. From Osborne 1881, pl. 3, 8.

At the end of the Late Iron Age, a new feature is a foot decorated with openwork ornament. This consists of an open space in the foot with one or more small connecting elements that span the opening (Figure 25). This feature is striking, because it is different from anything that was made before. As we shall see in the next chapter, openwork ornament appeared on scabbards at this same time, and in the case of both the fibulae and the scabbards, its use was widely distributed throughout Europe.

PATTERNS OF CHANGE IN THE VISUALITY OF FIBULAE

Fibulae were among the visually most striking and enchanting objects in late prehistoric Europe. As the most decorative object worn by an individual, and worn so prominently on his or her person that they would be seen immediately by others, they were of special importance in communicating information visually about the persons who wore them.

The great change in fibula form and decoration during the fifth century BC, presaged by the creation of the S-shaped fibulae during the Early Iron Age, is an important indication of changing ways of visualizing during that century. The S-curve, the three-dimensional formline, figural ornament, and hybrid creatures, were all major changes in the visual qualities of fibulae, and these changes paralleled changes in other categories of material culture, including bronze vessels, belt-hooks, pendants, and rings of various kinds, as well as sword scabbards, to which we turn in the next chapter.

Another major shift is apparent in the fibulae of the second and first centuries BC. Except for some remaining traces of S-curves and formlines, the fibulae of these centuries are very different from their predecessors. Now fibulae were cast as one piece and then bent into shape, not assembled from separate bow, pin, and spring pieces. These were now industrial products, not products reflecting the small-scale individuality of crafting workshops. They were made for a different world, one in which a large proportion of society's goods were mass-produced—wheelmade pottery, iron tools, and coins among them. People no longer wore objects that distinguished them as individuals. They

FIGURE 25. Drawing of a Late La Tène fibula showing ornate openwork inside the opening on the foot. From Beltz 1911:688, fig. 56.

wore common fibulae, just as they used common forms of pottery and the same coins as their fellows.

Two points deserve special attention. Along with the new mass production processes, the creation of the openwork foot marked a significant departure in the visual appearance of fibulae at the very end of the prehistoric Iron Age. Often within the open space there were one or several small, delicate, and ornate connecting pieces, often with "jags" in them to elaborate the decoration (Figure 25). Examples include a well-known piece from Great Chesterford in southern Britain, and the more recently recovered and highly ornate fibulae from grave 2 at Hörgertshausen in Lower Bavaria. This was a "baroque" touch, and it matched the openwork plaques crafted for decorating the tops of scabbards. In the increasingly mass-produced material culture of this period, these openwork ornaments ensured that their objects would be distinct from others. One way to interpret them, then, is as a form of resistance to the growing dominance of mass production and the gradual assimilation of writing (Chapter 10), an action taken by individuals concerned with maintaining the richer medium of handcrafted objects.

The representations of fibulae on pottery and on coins all show types that date to the final phase of the Iron Age. As noted above, the fibulae represented are invariably shown in an open state, with the pin not engaged in the catch. This quality of being open suggests something of their potential, of affordance in the Gibsonian sense. It contributes to the idea that fibulae have agency, that they are powerful objects that need to be treated and handled in special ways. Fibulae were the only objects that had springs and required this particular kind of bodily interaction to engage. This requirement meant that a different relationship between person and object developed with fibulae than was the case for any other object in prehistoric Europe.

CHAPTER 7

∞∞∞∞∞∞∞∞∞∞∞∞∞∞∞

STATUS AND VIOLENCE

Swords and Scabbards

THE VISUALITY OF SCABBARDS

The Bugthorpe scabbard is 60.8 cm long and between 4.6 and 4.0 cm wide along most of its length (Figure 26). The two plates thus form long, thin rectangles that narrow slightly from the top to the bottom, where the scabbard terminates in a chape. The outer plate is elaborately decorated over its entire surface with ornamental patterns incised with a burin ornament, which is built up of curving elements—S-curves and formlines—observes the edges of the scabbard precisely. Each curve ends just before the edge. There are large S-curves that extend over a third of the length, and small S-curves within them and extending out from them. The lines that form the S-curves widen and narrow, and these formlines are filled with fine-line ornament.

The S-curves and formlines create an effect of motion, similar in some respects to that generated by the linear patterns that are such a major part of the artist Bridget Riley's work (Chapter 2). When we look at the scabbard, we tend to follow the curvilinear pattern along its length from top to bottom, and then back again. The fine-line ornament that fills the formlines accentuates those shapes and thus adds to the effect of motion.

Open circles and other shapes add further complexity to the pattern and serve to accentuate the shading of the formlines. Two of these circles, set next to each other, are actually the tops of the rivets that hold the two plates of the scabbard together.

Along the edges of the design, many of the smaller S-curves end in shapes that suggest bird heads in profile, each with a prominent beak and a large

FIGURE 26. Drawing of the scabbard from Bugthorpe, Yorkshire, England. From Stead 2006:258, fig. 92. © *The Trustees of the British Museum.*

FIGURE 27. Sketch of a wooden scabbard containing a sword from Muldbjerg, Denmark. Based on Müller 1897:223, fig. 108.

open circle for an eye. This merging of bird heads into designs in the Late Iron Age is not unusual. Of special note here is the range in variation in the heads—some look clearly like the heads of birds, others are less obviously bird-like. Were it not for the former, we might not even think of birds in the other cases. But the range from clearly identifiable bird heads to those that only hint at such an identification is the important point here.

Finally, the open spaces on the scabbard are significant. They occupy more of the surface than does the design. The purpose of the spaces is to allow the design to flow, to look as though it is moving. If more of the surface had been filled, the entire pattern would not have the light and dynamic visual quality that it has.

SWORDS AND SCABBARDS IN PREHISTORIC EUROPE

Swords were never as common as pottery or fibulae. Whereas pottery was made from locally available clays, Bronze Age swords were made of the alloy bronze, comprised of copper and tin, each of which had to be mined where deposits were available, and the the two had to be smelted, brought together, and alloyed. In the Iron Age, iron ore was available in most places, but the process of smelting and forging was complex and time-consuming. A sword required a considerable amount of metal as well as a highly skilled smith to fashion it. The evidence from burials suggests that swords were possessed only by a small proportion of the adult men in late prehistoric Europe. Only during the fourth and third centuries BC were swords sometimes placed in more than a very few graves in a community cemetery.

Swords played a special role in representing male status. Almost every richly outfitted man's grave from the Middle Bronze Age on contained a sword (between about 600 and 450 BC the sword was replaced by a dagger in much of temperate Europe). Swords were also significant in the iconography of Iron Age Europe (Chapter 9).

Swords were important visual objects, larger than most other objects in Bronze and Iron Age Europe, and their shape made them visually striking. Two parts of the sword were especially important in this regard. In the Late Bronze Age and Early Iron Age, the hilt and pommel were often the vehicles for elaborate eye-catching ornament. When a sword was in its scabbard, whether worn at the side of the bearer, hanging on a wall, or placed in the burial chamber, the only parts of the weapon that were visible were the handle and its end.

During the Middle and Late Iron Age, the scabbard became especially important as a vehicle for decorative elaboration. Bronze and Early Iron Age scabbards were mostly made of wood (Figure 27), and we do not, therefore have much information about how they were decorated. From the end of the Early La Tène period on, however, swords were long, and scabbards of bronze and iron offered extensive rectangular surfaces for decoration. Since the scabbard was ordinarily the most visible part of the weapon, this decoration played an important role in communicating visual information about the weapon and about its bearer.

WHERE SWORDS ARE FOUND

GRAVES

In inhumation burials, the sword was most often placed next to the corpse on the individual's right side, but there are many exceptions. Sometimes the sword was set on the left side, sometimes it was placed on top of the body. In cremation burials, the sword was commonly positioned on one side of the burial pit. During the later phases of the Iron Age, swords were often bent into U-shapes or even into circles and placed in the grave in that altered form.

From the Middle Bronze Age, when they first became relatively common, swords were a standard accouterment in well-outfitted men's graves; graves, in other words, that contained other special kinds of objects, such as feasting vessels, wheeled vehicles, and gold ornaments. A sword can thus be seen as a standard part of the elite man's outfit from the middle of the second millennium BC until the seventh and eighth centuries AD, when the practice of outfitting graves with goods gradually declined in much of Europe. Swords almost never occur in otherwise "poor" graves, and it is unusual to find a wealthy male's grave that does not have a sword (or, during the sixth and early fifth centuries BC, a dagger).

The arrangement of swords in graves provides important evidence for our understanding of their role in the visual world of late prehistoric Europe. Clearly care was taken to place each sword where it would be visible to the participants at the funerary ceremony. A particularly striking case is that of the cremation grave at Mailleraye-sur-Seine in northern France. There a whole series of objects was arranged in a clearly defined pile, and three swords were placed together across the top, as if sealing the deposit.

In many Late Iron Age graves, the sword and its scabbard were bent before being placed in the burial, sometimes into a circle, sometimes at 180 degrees. This practice has been referred to as "killing the sword," so that it was in a condition to accompany the deceased, but we need to think more broadly about this practice. I would instead emphasize the visual effect on viewers of a sword, the most potent and visually powerful object in the assemblages of later prehistory, being in effect destroyed before their very eyes prior to its placement in the burial.

LANDSCAPE DEPOSITS

Swords occur as parts of deposits that are generally interpreted as ritual in character. They are abundant and well preserved at the big Middle Iron Age "sanctuary" sites in northern France. Gournay-sur-Aronde is the most striking of these. Of twenty-five hundred objects recovered in the course of excavations between 1975 and 1984, more than 700 are parts of sword scabbards, representing at least 180 individual scabbards—the largest collection in Iron Age Europe. The arrangement of the weapons at Gournay shows a dense distribution of swords and scabbards all along the inner ditch, with especially dense concentrations on either side of the entrance. Jean-Louis Brunaux and his colleagues have suggested that the weapons were originally hung on trophy stands, on the palisade wall, and on the gateway to the sanctuary. There is little convincing evidence for such an arrangement, however, and if the weapons had originally been hung on trophy stands and later fell into the ditch, that model would not explain how all of the swords and scabbards came to be bent and broken. A more economical explanation of the arrangement is that they were destroyed in the course of a ceremony and placed in the ditch as part of the boundary of the enclosed area.

The regularity of the occurrence of weapons, especially swords, and other objects in the ditches that surround enclosures during the Middle Iron Age indicates that they were purposely placed in those locations for specific reasons. They were meant to be seen in the ditches that defined the enclosed areas, and they were particularly arranged on either side of the entrance—a key location with respect to the enclosed space. The view of hundreds of iron and bronze weapons, piled up along a stretch of tens of meters in the ditch, most of them showing clear signs of damage by breaking, bending, and hacking, must have had powerful effects that contributed to the experience of approaching and entering the enclosure.

Swords were significant objects in deposits made in bodies of water as well. From the Late Bronze Age on, they have been recovered in substantial numbers from streams, rivers, ponds, lakes, and bogs. The river Saône in France and the Thielle in Switzerland were particularly rich in finds. The site of La Tène on the shore of Lake Neuchâtel in western Switzerland, investigated since the middle of the nineteenth century, is, however, the classic find-place in this connection, with its 166 swords (as well as 269 lance points). Swords were clearly a key element in the water offerings made at the site, and they are well represented at many other water-deposit sites all over Europe. Particularly well-documented examples include Port and Tiefenau in Switzerland, Kessel in the Netherlands, and the Danube River in southern Germany. Swords are common among the objects deposited in ponds and swamps in northern Europe, as well, as at Hjortspring during the prehistoric Iron Age and at the much larger Roman Period deposits such as those at Illerup and Vimose in Denmark. A great many swords have been recovered from rivers in England, especially the Thames and the Witham.

ICONOGRAPHIC REPRESENTATIONS

The significance of swords as visual objects in late prehistoric Europe is clear from the frequency with which they occur in iconography. Scenes of humans doing things are not common in prehistoric Europe, but in the relatively small numbers of representations that are known, swords play a major role. On the back of the bronze couch from the Hochdorf grave, four individuals are rendered in repoussé, each holding aloft a sword, and two figures shown standing on wagons hold swords in their right hands and shields in their left. The life-size sandstone statue of a man from Hirschlanden wears at dagger on his belt, in the same position as the dagger in the Hochdorf burial. The near lifesize sculpted limestone male figure from the enclosure ditch at Vix is shown wearing a short sword on his right hip, as is the statue at the Glauberg tumulus. Swords are important elements in the scene on the scabbard from Hallstatt Grave 994 and on the silver cauldron from Gundestrup in Denmark, both of which will be discussed below (Chapter 9).

SWORDS AND SCABBARDS AS VISUAL OBJECTS

SHAPE AND SIZE

In the central part of temperate Europe, the evolution of sword shapes went something like this: In the Middle Bronze Age, swords were long and thin, with a rapier-like blade sharpened along both of the parallel cutting edges. In the Late Bronze Age, many swords were broader, especially the so-called leaf-shaped swords, which often had the thickest part of their blades closer to the tip than to the hilt. Typical Early Iron Age swords often show traces of the Late Bronze Age leaf shape, though Hallstatt swords were predominantly of iron rather than bronze, and they were often much longer than earlier swords (Figure 28). In the latter part of the Early Iron Age, daggers of long triangular

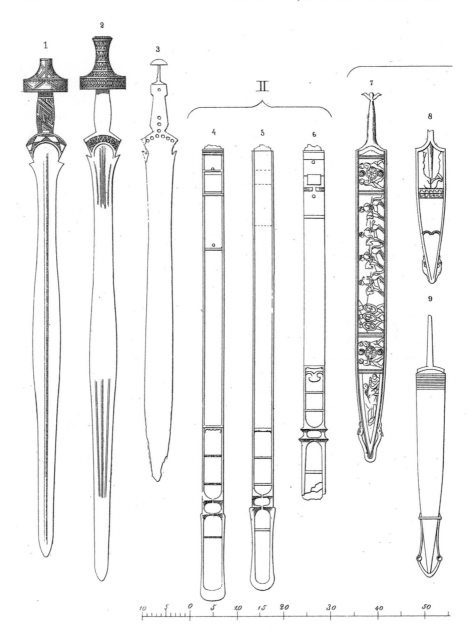

FIGURE 28. Drawing of iron swords in scabbards, from earliest Iron Age (left) to the latest prehistoric Iron Age. From Lindenschmit 1891, pl. 10.

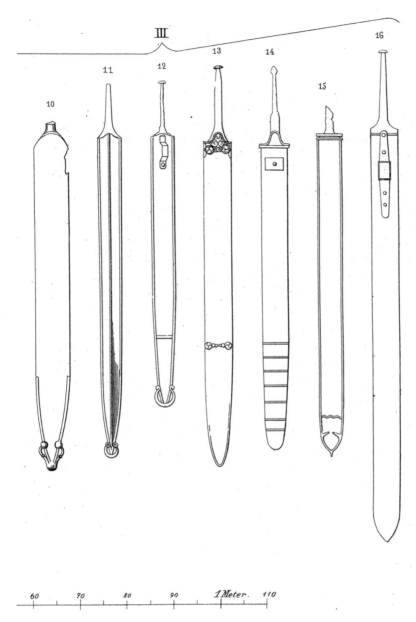

FIGURE 28. (continued)

shape replaced swords in wealthy male burials. Most often the iron dagger was contained in a bronze sheath. The hilt could be of either bronze or iron.

During the Middle and Late Iron Age, the trend was for swords to become longer. In the Early La Tène Period, swords were often short, ranging in length somewhere between the daggers of the preceding century and the long swords of succeeding centuries. During the Middle La Tène Period, sword blades tended to be long and to have parallel edges. In the Late La Tène, swords reached their greatest length, with many blades measuring around a meter. The basic form of the sword was a long, thin rectangle, bounded at either end by a handle and a point. Most types of late prehistoric swords had parallel edges, both of which were blades. (Exceptions are the "leaf-shaped" swords of the Late Bronze and Early Iron Age, in which the sides were not parallel, and one-edged swords, which were common in parts of northern Europe.)

Scabbards have a special relationship with swords, especially as far as visuality is concerned. When a sword is worn on the person, it is generally in its scabbard. The viewer does not see the blade of the sword, unless the bearer withdraws it from its scabbard. When a sword was worn in everyday life, as when the sword-bearer traveled, on ceremonial occasions, and when it was placed in the burial of the individual, the scabbard was the most visible part. Thus from a visual point of view, a scabbard stood for the sword. The observer could see the scabbard but could not see the sword, and yet the observer knew that the scabbard meant that a sword was present, attached to the hilt that extended beyond the scabbard.

The importance of the scabbard in this respect is apparent in the fact that the scabbard was most often the part of the sword-scabbard combination that was decorated.

Although scabbards are common in graves, deposits, and ritual sites during the Late Iron Age, they are much less common than swords during the Bronze Age and the earlier part of the Early Iron Age. During the Bronze Age scabbards were generally made of wood or leather and thus rarely survive (Figure 27). The iron swords characteristic of the earlier part of the Early Iron Age (Hallstatt C) ordinarily also had wooden scabbards. The sheaths for daggers of the later part of the Early Iron Age (Hallstatt D) were commonly made of sheet bronze, sometimes with a textile wrapped around them. During the whole of the La Tène Period, metal scabbards are a major component of the archaeological record and a highly significant vehicle of decoration.

PATTERNS IN THE VISUALITY OF SWORDS AND SCABBARDS

THE BRONZE AGE AND EARLY IRON AGE

The earliest swords in temperate Europe are the Hadjusamson and Apa types, made in eastern Hungary and Transylvania around 1700–1500 BC. It was not until the Middle Bronze Age—after 1500 BC—that swords become relatively common across most of continental Europe. When they did, the similarities between specimens from southern Germany in the west to Romania in the east and to the lands bordering the Baltic Sea in the north indicate that the communities in these regions were in contact and that swords or swordsmiths were circulating between them.

Swords of Middle Bronze Age date were not generally decorated, and scabbards from this period are scarce, as mentioned above.

During the Late Bronze Age Urnfield Period, many of the cast bronze hilts of the so-called *Vollgriffschwerter* were decorated with patterns of fine lines incised into the grip and the pommel. The patterns of linear decoration are geometric, with horizontal lines, circles, spirals, garlands, and rows of fine parallel lines among the most common forms. Significantly, no two hilts bear exactly the same pattern of decoration. Clearly this differentiation between individual swords was intentional. Each individual sword-bearer had his own weapon that was distinctly marked as his alone.

A sword found in the Main River at Untereisenheim has a plain and undecorated blade, but a highly ornate hilt. Across the grip are four bands of incised lines, and between those bands are rows of dots-and-circles running around the grip. Below the bottom of the four bands is a row of smaller dots-and-circles, and below them are larger concentric circles ornamenting the bottom part of the hilt down to the rivets that secure the hilt to the sword. The bottom side of the pommel is covered with twelve groups of four incised concentric semicircles, while the top is covered with eight incised concentric circles. The "busyness" of the hilt and pommel contrasts sharply with the very plain surface of the sword blade.

In the first part of the Early Iron Age (Hallstatt C), the hilt and pommel continue to be the foci of decoration (Figure 28), but the character of the decoration is different now from that of the Urnfield Period. Scabbards are generally of wood. When they survive, if they show any decoration, it is linear and geometric, corresponding to the decoration on pottery of the period. No longer are there many swords decorated with similar patterns of uniquely combined elements, as the earlier cast-hilted swords had been. Only a few of the roughly six hundred specimens known from this period have decorated hilts and pommels. A few have hilts inlaid with rectangular gold pieces arranged in a geometrical pattern. Several pommels are made of ivory, as for example on a sword from Kinding in southern Germany.

The Hallstatt C iron sword from a well-outfitted cremation grave at Gomadingen has a strikingly ornamented hilt and pommel. Both handle and pommel are made of wood and decorated with a geometrical pattern of sheet gold. On the handle are narrow strips arranged in a zigzag pattern, on the pommel is more zigzag together with zones filled with very fine lines forming little squares. An iron sword from a cremation grave at Oss in the Netherlands has its handle ornamented with diamond-shaped gold sheet pieces, and its pommel with zigzag-shaped pieces of sheet gold. In cremation grave 573 at Hallstatt there was an iron sword of exceptional length—1.15 m—with a hilt carved of ivory and a pommel of ivory inlaid with amber. A second iron sword in the same grave had on its grip an inlaid gold band.

The difference in visual patterning between the earlier cast-hilted swords of the Urnfield Period and these of the Early Iron Age is significant. Many of the cast-hilted swords bore similar decoration, though it was always different from sword to sword in its details. In the Hallstatt C context, only a few swords were distinguished by ornament at all (as far as we can judge, given the missing wooden scabbards), but these few all bore ornament that displayed greater craft effort, often involving the addition of precious and exotic material. The use of imported materials, such as gold, amber, and elephant ivory, was especially significant at this time, because it served to draw attention to the far-flung contacts of the elites (however indirect those contacts may have been) and to the elites' ability to command these exotic materials from far away.

In the latter part of the Early Iron Age (Hallstatt D), swords were largely replaced in elite men's graves by daggers—weapons of roughly the same shape as swords, but much shorter. The positioning of daggers in the men's graves suggests that they played the same visual role that swords had played previously and would play again. For example, in the exceptionally well-excavated Hochdorf burial, the dagger was recovered still attached to the man's belt, the same position in which a dagger is shown on the statue from Hirschlanden.

The decoration associated with the daggers—both on the hilts and on the metal sheaths that often accompany them—is geometric in character. Some daggers have "antennas"—projections from the two sides of the end of the hilt. The sheet-bronze sheaths are often decorated with rows of repoussé dots or with incised patterns of lines and triangles. The lines can be in relief or incised.

In a few cases, incised lines on the sheaths are S-curves, as on one from Salem in southwest Germany. An iron dagger from a double inhumation burial at Wolfegg has an H-shaped hilt, with horizontal iron bars at the top of the dagger and at the end of the hilt. The sheet-bronze sheath is ornamented with three rows of six large decorative rivets at the top, nine repoussé lines running vertically from the rivet area to the base, where they converge, and, at the far end of the object, a ball decorated with rills. The overall visual pattern is geometrical, with straight lines, circles, rectangles, and spheres.

The Middle Iron Age

During the fifth century BC, swords again came into common use, taking the place of Hallstatt D daggers as the key weapon in rich men's graves. Swords were most commonly, but not always, placed on the right side of the man's body. On both the Vix and the Glauberg male statues, the sword also is worn on the right side.

The new style of decoration that characterizes the fifth century BC finds one of its most striking expressions on sword scabbards. This decoration is different from anything associated with the swords of the preceding period (Hallstatt C) and different as well from anything seen on the dagger sheaths of Hallstatt D. Only the sheath from Salem mentioned above, with its S-curve-based lines, shows an early expression of this new style.

Characteristic of the scabbards of the late fifth and early fourth centuries BC is fine incised-line decoration that covers the entire surface, and, sometimes, as in the case of the sword in Glauberg Grave 1, most of the back as well. On the Weiskirchen scabbard, this decoration consists of two rows of figure-8s, based on S-curves, that fill the surface.

The scabbard from the grave in mound 2 at Hochscheid is of special interest (Figure 29). Its basic shape is a rectangle that comes to a gradual point at the end. The object is long and thin, with almost parallel edges formed by clearly delineated frames along the two sides. At the top, the surface of the scabbard ends in an incised line that traces the line of the handle; at the bottom is a large and distinct knob at the base of the chape.

The incised decoration covers the surface and does so in precisely mirrored fashion, the patterns to either side of the midrib being mirror images of one another. At the bottom are S-curves in the form of squiggly lines, then begins a series of eight broad S-curves in the shape of formlines; each end of the S is pointed, and the curve becomes thicker toward the middle, then thinner again to the final point. In the center of each S is a pair of lines forming an hourglass shape. At either end of the S is a fan-shaped figure, also of a formline, with three little palmettes inside. These figures are eye-catching in several ways. The S-spirals are enticing. They suggest movement, demanding our attention and concentration. The added incised detailing—inside each S and in front of and behind it—adds to the allure and attention-holding power of these designs.

The seventh pair of S shapes, counting from the bottom, are not decorative abstractions, but rather assume the form of animals. Seen from a distance, or at a quick glance, the difference between these and the other S-curves would likely escape the viewer, but close examination reveals representations of four-legged mammals. They are clearly delineated, with little incised S-spiral lines on their shoulders and with stippling covering their bodies. Are they deer without antlers? Or foxes?

At the top of the scabbard is another pair of S-shapes, more rounded and fuller than those below the two mammals.

This pattern of ornament on the Hochscheid scabbard is a striking example of what V.S. Ramachandran calls a "visual puzzle," and is also reminiscent

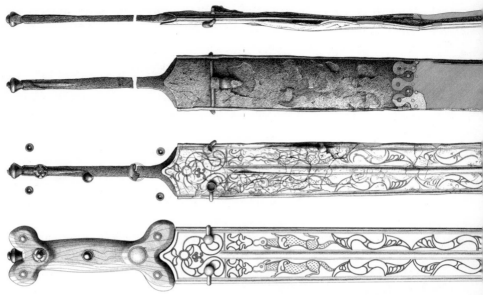

FIGURE 29. Drawings of the scabbard and sword from Hochscheid, tumulus 2, Rhineland-Palatinate, Germany. Bottom: reconstruction of the incised pattern on the scabbard. Second from bottom: scabbard and sword in present condition, front view. Third from bottom: scabbard and sword, back view. Top: profile view. Drawings by L. Dahm. Courtesy of the Rheinisches Landesmuseum, Trier, Germany.

of many of the drawings of M. C. Escher, in which a gradual transition takes place from one form to another. The viewer is captivated by the decoration, seized by a desire to understand the connection between the S-shapes that cover most of the scabbard and the two animals near the top.

While the dominant visual aspect of this object is the incised decoration, the three-dimensional ornament associated with the structure of the scabbard is also visually significant. At the bottom, the chape is attached to the scabbard with a pair of edges that are much thicker than those along the scabbard edges, and the bottom of the chape consists of thick, three-dimensional forms. On the handle were six inlaid knobs, two at the top of the scabbard and five as part of the chape. Haffner suggests that most of these contained coral, but none survives.

Over the course of the fourth century BC, the ornamenting of scabbards gradually changed. Decoration on scabbards made on the continent tended to be restricted to the top of the scabbard, but in Britain scabbards continued to be decorated along their entire length. The basic S-curve motif was retained but transformed into other expressions. One of these is the so-called "dragon pair" motif, consisting of two S-shaped creatures with wide open jaws and round eyes facing each other on either side of the midrib of the scabbard.

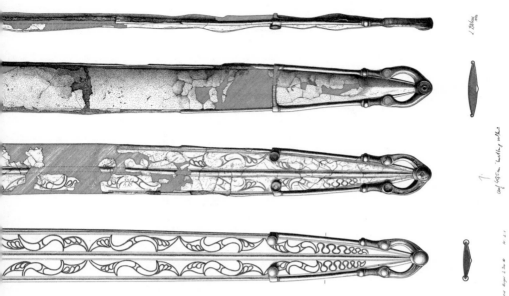

FIGURE 29. (continued).

This motif was used across the whole of temperate Europe. Examples include scabbards from Montigny-Lencoup in France, Münsingen in Switzerland, Taliándörögd in Hungary, and London in England. From the site of La Tène in Switzerland comes a scabbard decorated in a style very similar to that of the dragon pair, but with three horses in relief. Their bodies are composed of S-curves, and tendril-like S-curved incised ornament surrounds them (Figure 30).

During the third century BC, other forms of incised decoration were applied to the tops of scabbards. The decoration was frequently asymmetrical, with S-curves, while still present, often integrated into more complex and intricate patterns in what has been dubbed the "Hungarian Sword Style." Scabbards decorated with these patterns occur across the whole of Europe. Noteworthy examples are from Cernon-sur-Coole in France, Bölcske in Hungary, Batina in Croatia, and, in high relief rather than flat incision, from the River Witham in England.

The Late Iron Age

After 200 BC, fully decorated scabbards are unusual. When there is ornament, it tends to appear only at the top. Two examples will illustrate special features of the scabbards of this period, one from Britain and one from the continent.

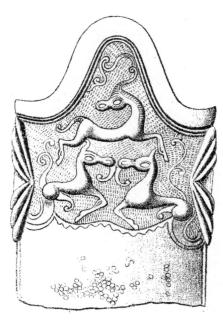

FIGURE 30. Drawing of the top of a scabbard from La Tène, Switzerland. From Keller 1866, pl. 76, 6.

A scabbard from the River Thames at Amerden Lock, near Taplow in Berkshire, is 85.1 cm long and 4.5 cm wide along most of its length (Figure 31). E. M. Jope suggests a date around 125 BC for the object. From the very top of the scabbard to the top of the chape, the scabbard presents an almost perfect rectangle. Visually, this is a particularly striking object, because of the broad areas that are not decorated, anchored by four separate and very different zones of decoration. The greater portion of this object thus offers affordances in Gibson's sense of the word.

The eye is immediately caught by the high-relief crossing ridges and the circular ornament near the top of the scabbard. In most kinds of lighting, this is the part of the object that first jumps out at the viewer. The horizontal ridges set this area off from the rest of the object, telling the viewer that this is where to look, that what matters is inside these bounds. Just below the combination of outer circle, inner oval, and innermost circles of inlaid material provides a clear and sharply defined visual structure. The lines defining the outer circle and the inner near-oval are relatively wide, while those defining the oval are formlines, narrowed at top and bottom, thicker as they approach the inlaid circles. These lines—perhaps better called bands—have very fine incised lines across them, creating a texture of greater solidity and a more imposing aspect than the bands would otherwise have. Similar fine incised lines run across the top and bottom horizontal border bands.

Figure 31. Drawing of the scabbard from Amerden Lock, Berkshire, England. From Stead 2006:235, fig. 69.
© *The Trustees of the British Museum.*

Above these circular ornaments, just beyond the upper band and extending to the top of the scabbard, is an ornament created by incising in a pattern that is more typically Late La Tène in character. This consists of a kind of whirligig with three arms made up of formlines with cross-hatching interfilling the spaces between the arms. This zone of ornament is decidedly subtle compared to the circular zone beneath it and requires much closer examination if one is to make out its details. If the circular zone decoration is the obvious, the straightforward, the call-out part of this object, this zone above it is where the "real" and substantial information is embedded. Only the viewer who is permitted close access and in just the right light will be able to see exactly what that information is.

There is a great distance between these two neighboring ornamental zones and the next interruption of the smooth surface of the scabbard's long affordance, which takes up some 70% of the length of the object. The interruption is a relatively large S-shaped attachment, riveted to the scabbard. Its shape has no direct relation to any of the shapes in the two zones at the upper part of the scabbard, and it is clearly set out as "different." It is an abrupt break in the smooth flow of the main part of the scabbard.

Close to the bottom of the scabbard, at the top of the chape, are two shapes that look very much like bird heads, similar in form to the later bird heads that are so common on scabbards found in bog deposits in Denmark and northern Germany and somewhat similar to other bird heads known from the Late Iron Age, such as the cast bronze head of a vulture from Kelheim. The view is from the top, with the shape of each bird's head with its rounded back portion visible, and its long extended beak reaching out across the scabbard to almost touch the beak of the bird opposite. Two eyes are represented as little holes in the appropriate places. These heads mark the top of the chape, and below them two arms of the chape extend from the edges in rounded curves to meet at a small triangular knob in the center of the scabbard. The rest of the chape is plain, forming a raised outer edge to the bottom of the scabbard.

A scabbard from a grave at Badenheim in the Middle Rhineland is an important representative of a decorative practice that appears at the very end of the prehistoric Iron Age. The grave contained the remains of a cremated individual, seven pottery vessels of different types that can be considered a feasting set, and a sword in its scabbard, both bent into an oval. The scabbard is 92 cm long. The outer side is of thin sheet-bronze and has attached to the top a decorative openwork plaque 15 cm long, cut and shaped with chisels and files (Figure 32).

The shapes of the openwork cut-outs include circles, rectangles, and hexagons, along with forms at the edges that could be seen as human bodies and human heads. At the bottom is a different openwork pattern, with linear

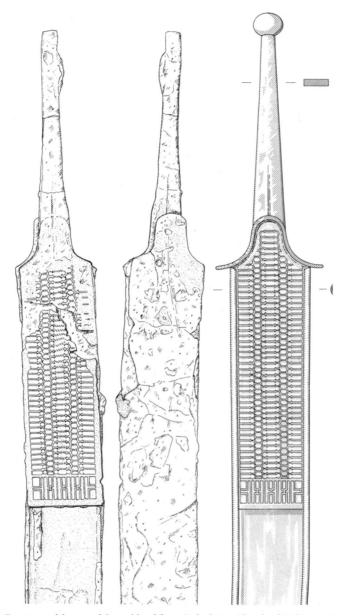

FIGURE 32. Drawings of the top of the scabbard from Badenheim, Rhineland-Palitanate, Germany. From Böhme-Schönberger 1998, folding pl. 1. Left: front of the scabbard. Center: back of the scabbard. Right: reconstruction of the original front of the scabbard.
Used with permission of the Römisch-Germanische Kommission des Deutschen Archäologischen Instituts.

shapes that also suggest human forms, with arms raised and legs apart. The Badenheim plaque is part of a group of some twenty such openwork plaques, each unique, that have been found from Luxembourg in the west to Bulgaria in the east and as far north as Sweden. Their design represents a strikingly different way of structuring decoration. Gone are the S-curves, the dragon pairs, the S-based asymmetrical patterns, the whirligig horses. The symmetry of the plaques is consistent with the uniformity of pottery, iron tools, mass-produced fibulae, and other artifacts of material culture dating to the Late Iron Age. But the Europe-wide distribution of these plaques, though they are few in number, attests to significant links between elites in different parts of the continent. And the unique pattern of the openwork ornament on each indicates a desire on the part of the owners of these swords and scabbards to express some degree of individuality at a time of intensifying cultural homogeneity.

CHAPTER 8

∞∞∞∞∞∞∞∞∞∞∞∞∞∞∞

ARRANGING SPACES

Objects in Graves

EVERYTHING IN ITS PLACE

The objects that were placed in the grave at Hochdorf, near Stuttgart in Germany, in about 525 BC were carefully arranged in a chamber built of hewn oak timbers that was subsequently covered with a large mound of earth. The deceased man was laid out on an elaborate bronze couch that was placed against the west wall of the chamber, its head end close to the south wall. Beyond the man's feet, in the northwest corner of the chamber, was placed a 400-liter bronze cauldron, an import from the Greek world. A four-wheeled wagon, laden with nine sets of bronze bowls and other feasting utensils, was arranged against the east wall, its back wheels close to the north wall and its front facing south. Nine drinking horns hung on the south wall, eight of them were made from auroch's horns mounted with gold bands and a suspension chain, while the ninth—the largest of the group—was of iron and decorated with numerous gold bands.

The man was outfitted with gold jewelry and other accouterments, each object positioned in a specific place. At his head was a conical hat made of birch bark. Around his neck was a decorated gold neckring. On his chest were two gold fibulae. Around his right wrist was a gold bracelet. On the front of his belt was a rectangular gold plate, and attached to the belt was a dagger, its handle and sheath covered with ornate sheet-gold. Gold bands ornamented his leather shoes.

The central area of the grave chamber was left strikingly open and free of objects.

The Hochdorf grave is special because not only was it found in an undisturbed condition, but damp soil conditions meant that the preservation of organic materials was unusually good. Moreover, the excavation and publication of the find were of exceptionally high quality. For these reasons, Hochdorf is a model of what we can learn about how people saw and understood the objects of their world from the ways in which they arranged these objects in their graves. As we shall see, both the absolute position of objects in the grave space and their positions relative to one another are highly significant. We will return to look at this remarkable grave in greater detail later in this chapter.

VISUAL INFORMATION FROM GRAVES

Graves provide us with direct views into how people arranged objects so as to make those objects visually meaningful to them. Arrangements on the floors of graves, in burial chambers, or in other kinds of funeral settings enable us to see those objects in the way that the people who participated in the event saw them—from the same viewpoint, in their relation to one another, and in relation to the overall frame (walls) of the grave. In the same way that a seventeenth-century painting of the interior of a house, with furniture, paintings or maps on the walls, and objects such as vases and flowers in the room provides us with information about how the seventeenth-century Dutch saw their interiors, their possessions, and themselves, we can derive similar understanding from burial arrangements. (With graves of course we need to take account of various possible complicating factors, such as the movement of objects when a burial chamber collapses, disturbances caused by burrowing animals, and soil movement, but as long as we are aware of these potential issues and look for evidence of them, they are not a serious problem.)

In many, if not most, instances, the placement of objects in a burial setting was a critical and dramatic part of the funeral event. It is likely that participants witnessed the placing of each object in the grave chamber, while perhaps a few words were spoken about each and its significance to the occasion. The objects were all meaningful to the participants. They knew the social and political associations of the objects, and the ways in which they were arranged in relation to one another conveyed further specific meanings. Not only the objects themselves, but also the performance involving them, was critical—the bodily involvement of human beings and the movement of the objects from one place to another in the ritual, and, finally, to the floor of the grave. The final arrangement that we see—the tableau—may have been important for the original participants to see as well. Perhaps the grave was left open for a time—an hour, a day?—so that the objects and their arrangement could be seen. But the actual movement of the objects into position is likely to have been more important, to have had a more powerful effect on viewers than the final, static situation of the objects (see Chapter 9).

Graves are only a part of a funerary ceremony. They are of course the part that we can most readily access, because when they are dug down into the ground, they have a chance of surviving into the future for us to study. But usually we do not have good evidence for what happened in the course of the funerary ceremony. In a few instances we have traces of some other aspects of the performance. For example, at Heidetränk near Frankfurt in Germany, archaeologists have been able to identify a site of cremating activity. In her analysis of the materials associated with the rich burial at Folly Lane at St. Albans northwest of London, Rosalind Niblett was able to identify remains of several stages in the process of the funerary ritual. But these cases are much the exception. Usually we have no surviving evidence pertaining to aspects of the ceremony other than the burial itself. We need to bear these facts in mind, but they need not overly trouble us. After all, it could be argued that the process of arranging a still life is the important part, yet what we have to examine and analyze is the painting of the final arrangement.

Finally, it is worth reminding ourselves that subsurface burial—the only kind that ordinarily survives for us to study—is only one way of disposing of dead bodies. Most other means of disposal—depositing bodies in the limbs of trees or on platforms to be consumed by animals, placing them in rivers, or leaving them exposed on the ground surface—leave no trace for us to find two thousand years later. Similarly, if cremation ashes are scattered to the winds or over the surface of a river, nothing will be left for us to uncover.

Even within the category of subsurface burials, there is great variability in the character of graves. They can contain inhumation burials or cremations. They can be round pits or rectangular chambers, or of some other shape. They can be oriented in particular directions. They can include chambers formed of stone or of timbers. Bodies can be buried on their backs, sides, or fronts. Legs can be extended or pulled up. Arms can be positioned in different ways. Cremation remains can be placed in urns or on the grave floor. The range of variation is infinite. I always tell my students that of the millions of graves that have been excavated and published from prehistoric Europe, no two are exactly alike.

GRAVES AS FRAMES AND SPACES

The simplest form of grave in later prehistoric Europe was a hole dug in the ground. For an inhumation burial, the hole was typically either roughly rectangular or a long oval in shape. For a cremation burial, a more-or-less round pit in the ground was usual, though sometimes long graves were used to deposit the ashes from a cremation, as if to suggest that a body were present.

Whatever the shape of the hole dug for a grave, the edges of the hole form the frame of the grave, and those edges enclose a space in which the burial takes place. In temperate Europe, before the Middle Bronze Age (starting around 1600 BC), graves were usually irregular in shape, sometimes more-or-less rectangular but with rounded corners, sometimes more oval. From the Middle Bronze Age on, most graves were dug in the form of rectangles. The edges of many graves were defined by walls of stones, and, especially during the Early Iron Age and again at the end of the Late Iron Age, rectangular wooden chambers were built to house burials, especially burials that included large numbers of grave goods, such as the graves at Hochdorf and at Vix.

In the performance during which objects were placed in graves, the edges of the graves, whether consisting of the dirt on the sides of the grave pit, stones forming an irregular wall, or carefully hewn timbers, form the frame that defines the space in which the action of arranging objects takes place. Just as art historians argue that the character of a frame is critical for the perception and understanding of a painting, so too I would argue that the visual character of the frame of a grave is an essential component of the visual character of the grave as a whole.

GRAVES AS DIAGRAMS

I am going to argue for two points here that diverge from most current interpretations of burials in European archaeology. I am going to argue that the arrangement of a grave, including the selection of objects to be placed in it and the specific arrangement of those objects, relates much more directly to the community than to the individual buried. On one level, most would agree with me on this point. Most archaeologists working in Europe today would not argue that grave goods were intended for the individual's use in the next world, but rather would see grave goods as expressing the connections of the deceased individual to the society of which he or she was part. But burial analysis in European archaeology continues to privilege the buried individual as the focus of the grave and to use the character of the grave goods as media for interpreting the status of the buried individual. Whatever economic model the investigator favors (redistributive, prestige goods, market), the common conclusion is that wealth in grave goods attests to the wealth and power of the individual, and that the grave goods can thus be used as an indicator of the status of the buried individual in the community's social system.

My position is that the character and arrangement of grave goods was of direct meaning and importance to the community and had less significance as regards the individual. In fact, a number of researchers, including Brian Hayden and, in another discipline, John Searle, argue the same point, though not in these same words. The reason that so many of the objects that were placed in graves are so stunning visually, and the reason their arrangement was so carefully attended to, is that the whole frame and structure and content of the burial and the ceremony were calculated to serve the purposes of the community, and not the individual or his or her family. The role of the individual *in the community* was the important point of the funerary rites; they were not intended to honor or celebrate the deceased individual as a separate entity. As Hayden puts it, the death of an individual provides a context, and a pretext, for what is really important, and that is the asserting, negotiating, jockeying, and competing that went on in the (sometimes extravagant) machinations associated with funerary ceremonies and burials. The deceased individual did not care what the objects looked like, nor was their appearance particularly important for that person's surviving family members. But the visuality of the objects and of their arrangement *was* critically important to the community that had to attend to filling the social place vacated by the deceased.

Borrowing a concept from Bender and Marrinan's study of Diderot's *Encyclopédie,* I argue that graves in late prehistoric Europe can be understood as "diagrams." By a diagram here I mean a visual representation of the social world, of "how things work," and one that serves to instruct participants in the ways of the social system in which they live. Rather than seeing objects in graves primarily as attestations to the wealth and power of the buried individual, I am arguing that their main (but not exclusive) purpose was to make a complex statement about the world—more specifically about the social world that was inhabited by members of the community that participated in the funerary event—and about and how it operated. This statement was fashioned by those persons who coordinated the funerary ritual, and hence it was manipulated by them in ways that they believed were advantageous to themselves. In the absence of a tradition of literacy, this statement was made by objects, the visual aspect of which communicated the required information. (No doubt oral declarations were an important part of the process also, but those are lost to us.) I do not mean to oversimplify. Funerary rituals and the display of objects certainly were complex and multifaceted. But it is important here to stress the importance of the visual display of a funeral ceremony for the community, because it is this aspect that has been largely neglected.

Evidence at a number of burial sites indicates that some of the objects buried with individuals were made on site specifically for the occasion of the burial. The cache of goldsmith's tools and scrap buried at the edge of the Hochdorf tumulus is an example.

Anne Villard has made an important contribution to this topic by suggesting and illustrating with a diagram a structural model for the arrangement of objects in graves at the end of the Late Iron Age in northern Gaul. In her model, different categories of objects are arranged concentrically in three zones around the remains of the deceased (commonly cremated) in the grave. In the innermost zone, Villard places on one side weapons, jewelry, coins, and toilet implements; on the other side, objects associated with wine service. Just beyond these are hearth tools. In the second zone are eating and drinking vessels (different from the wine service in the first zone), and beyond these, amphorae. Also in zone 2 are tools and parts of wheeled vehicles. Then, in the outermost zone, there are more parts of wheeled vehicles, and food remains—animal bones and cereal grains. The strength of this model is that it is a relatively simple, straightforward, and visually immediate paradigm that encapsulates the essence of arrangement patterns that in actual practice allow for a wide range of variations. It is, in fact, not unlike the ordering of objects in a still-life painting.

The fact that the objects placed in a grave often include items that were not associated with one another in everyday life can tell us important things about links between ideas in the minds of the members of the community. A set of pottery for eating and drinking, combined in a grave with weapons, for example, suggests thematic connections between these different categories of objects. For us studying these societies, these connections are only evident in the burial setting. It is not only the categories of objects in burials that are important, or even *where* in the grave they were placed, but also the spatial relationships between different objects and between objects and the edges of the grave and open spaces on the grave floor.

We can appreciate the potential amount of information that we can derive from these arrangements of objects in graves if we think of them in terms of Clark's extended mind theory (Chapter 2). As Clark argues and demonstrates with examples, space itself can be understood as a medium in which objects can be arranged in ways such that both the objects and the space in which they are set have meaningful relationships in the minds of the participants. While it might not be obvious to us at first glance why four of the twenty-four ceramic vessels in the grave at Boiroux (Figure 11) should be arranged around the buried individual's head while the other twenty were in two rows parallel to his legs, close analysis of the differences between the vessels in the groups suggests an explanation. The vessels at his head are of four different types, each meant for a different function in feasting. One is a high jar, designed for storing liquid. Another is a large low bowl, suitable for serving dry food. A third is a high, wide-mouthed jar, designed for storing dry food. The fourth is a beaker for consuming liquid. Three of the four are imported and of exceptionally fine ware. Only the beaker is of local manufacture. The specific arrangement of these vessels—beaker at the far left, then the food jar, then the large bowl, and finally the liquid storage jar—is likely to have been intended to remind those officiating at the funerary ceremony of part of the content of the ritual, perhaps of a specific speech to be given or a particular theme to be touched upon in an oration.

GRAVES IN LATE PREHISTORIC EUROPE

The great majority of graves that have been excavated and studied are poorly outfitted in terms both of their structures and of the objects they contain. In many cemeteries, the majority have no surviving objects in them at all, and a great many have no more than one or two objects—a bronze bracelet, perhaps, or a simple ceramic vessel. This fact—that the majority of graves are not distinguished by substantial sets of grave goods—is important to bear in mind. It underscores the special character of those few graves that do contain elaborate sets of objects and bears on questions related to the differential distribution of status and wealth in early European societies. It also underscores the fundamental point that the great majority of people in Bronze Age and Iron Age Europe had, relative to our experience today, very little in the way of material culture.

Since the main topic of this examination is arrangements of objects from a visual point of view, I shall present mainly well-outfitted graves. While these are exceptional, they do allow us to examine patterns of arrangement and visibility, and it is reasonable to think that patterns of visuality—the modes of visualization—were, in their essence, shared by the members of the community.

Burial practices varied by region, and they changed over time. In the earliest of the three phases of late prehistory considered in this book (2000–500 BC), regional differences were substantial, while after 500 BC broader patterns of similarity are evident. In the discussion below, I focus on burials in southern Germany for the early period, then look at examples for the second and third periods that are from different parts of Europe.

GRAVES, BRONZE AGE THROUGH
EARLY IRON AGE: 2000–500 BC

The Early Bronze Age (2000–1600 BC)

Two typical Early Bronze Age graves at Poing in Upper Bavaria are reported by von Quillfeldt (Figure 33). Both are inhumations in small grave pits, and in both the body was positioned on its right side with the legs drawn up slightly. The first, identified as that of a woman between twenty and thirty years of age, contained several sheet-bronze tubes and two spiral wire cones, thought to have been attached to a head covering of some kind. A small awl was found in front of the right thigh. A string of seventy-seven bronze rings had accompanied the burial. They were found underneath and in front of the skull and especially underneath the right forearm.

In the second grave, the skeletal remains were those of an adult, but were not well enough preserved to identify sex. This grave contained two ceramic vessels, a handled cup and a bowl, the first situated just behind the lower back of the individual, the second in front of the stomach. Also in the grave was an enigmatic bone object with dot-and-circle ornament and copper or bronze decorating rivets.

At Mötzing near the city of Regensburg, an Early Bronze Age cemetery was excavated that contained at least sixty-two graves. Grave 18 contained the skeletal remains of a women buried on her right side with her legs drawn up. Objects in the grave consisted of ornaments recovered near the skull and shoulders. They include spiral wire cones, double spirals, a pin, and a number of tubes made of sheet-bronze. A bone ring was around her neck.

A grave excavated at Alteglofsheim, also near the city of Regensburg, was a very roughly rectangular pit with its long axis oriented east-west and the head of the deceased to the east. The skeleton was that of a male, placed on his left side with his legs drawn up. Found on his right shoulder were eight bronze beads. On his right temple was a small ring of gold wire, probably once attached to a hat of some kind or to the hair. On his right wrist was a bronze bracelet. Just behind his skull were a knife and an axe, both of bronze. The skeleton was centered in the grave.

Two of these four Early Bronze Age graves were in very roughly rectangular pits, but with very rounded, not squared, corners; the third was contained in an oval pit, the fourth in an irregularly shaped pit. In all four, the objects in the graves were found close to the skeleton, whether they were personal ornaments that were part of the burial clothing or unattached objects that were added to the grave. In Poing 1 and Mötzing, all of the objects, with the

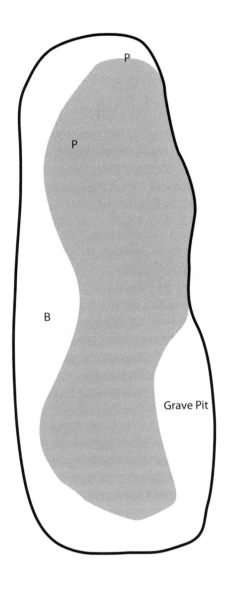

P

P

B

Grave Pit

──────────────────────────── 1m

FigURE 33. Schematic plan of an Early Bronze Age grave at Poing, east of Munich, Bavaria, Germany. The grave pit is in the shape of an irregular oval, just large enough to accommodate the body. The only objects recovered that had been buried with the individual were personal ornaments worn by that person and a small bronze tool, perhaps an awl. Shading: body space. B: bronze object. P: ornaments attached to the person. (Drawing based on von Quillfeldt 1990.)

exception of the awl in Poing 1, were personal ornaments attached to the buried individual; in Poing 2 the objects were placed very close to the body. Alteglofsheim included both personal ornaments and two substantial tools. In both Poing graves there was very little space that was not occupied by the body. In Mötzing there was some space north of the lower legs and some east of the pelvis, but the space was left empty (at least of goods that survived). In Alteglofsheim there was some open space at the head end, in front of the skeleton, and at the foot end, but not much.

The basic arrangement of all four graves was similar and provides us with a good sense of the visual characteristics of grave arranging during this period in central Bavaria. The burial pits were of limited size, just big enough to accommodate the body. Very little open space was left. In all four, the individual was placed on one side with the legs drawn up, in three cases on the right side, commonly (but not exclusively) the position used for women, in the fourth on the left side, as was usual for men. In the three graves that contained personal ornaments, they were concentrated around the head and neck area. The specific kinds of personal ornaments placed in the three graves and the other objects varied considerably, indicating that individual variability in both ornaments and other objects set in burials was not unusual. Some, but not all, of this variability is connected to gender associations.

The Middle Bronze Age (1600–1200 BC)

Characteristic of Middle Bronze Age burials are burial mounds covering the graves, often with circular ditches around their perimeter. At Untermeitingen near Augsburg, a circular ditch enclosed an area 11.6 m in diameter, with, in its center, a burial chamber. The mound no longer existed at the time of the excavation, having been plowed away over the millennia. The chamber was an irregular rectangle in shape, with the long axis oriented north-south, and it was considerably larger than the graves discussed above, 5.7 by 3.5 m. Like most Middle Bronze Age graves, the individual here—a male—was laid flat on his back. Traces of wood were noted by the excavators and interpreted as the remains of some kind of flooring. The skull was not in its natural position but just above the pelvis. No personal ornaments were recovered, but the grave did contain a bronze axe, a dagger, and a pin (possibly for tatooing, suggest the excavators), as well as a ceramic vessel. None of the objects was situated on or very close to the skeleton. Noteworthy is the large amount of space in the burial chamber that was not occupied by the skeletal remains or by the surviving grave goods.

Two graves were found inside a burial mound at Bastheim in Lower Franconia. In both graves, the buried individual was laid out, flat on the back, on a layer of stones. Grave 1 was in the center of the mound and was oriented northeast-southwest, with the head in the southwest. Grave goods included a bronze bracelet on the right wrist, several clasps (probably from a belt), and spiral ornaments found near the feet. Grave 2 contained a pin at the throat, a knife at the hip, a clasp in the waist area, and spirals near the feet.

New in these Middle Bronze Age graves is the creation of a burial space—a frame—with stones.

At Mannsdorf in the county (*Kreis*) of Regensburg, a grave was found inside a chamber formed of piled stones (Figure 34). The top layer of stones had been knocked away by plowing, but beneath it a 2.5 × 1.2 m rectangular space defined by a frame of stones was uncovered. The stones used to construct this frame were slabs of green sandstone and limestone that had to have been brought from at least 25 km away. Outside the main chamber, in what is described as an "antenna-like extension," were found sherds of one or more finely made ceramic vessels. In a small hollow just west of the chamber was a fragment of a bronze bracelet, and just outside the stone setting at the southeast corner was another fragment of bronze. Cremated human remains were found scattered across the stone paving that formed the floor of the burial chamber. Inside the grave, in addition to the vessel or vessels represented by sherds in the extension, six pottery vessels were positioned, five set in the northern end of the chamber and one placed on the eastern edge of the pit just north of the centerline. The vessels were a basin, three bowls of different sizes, a jug, and a beaker. The bowls were undecorated (typical for this period, see Chapter 5), but the basin, jug, and beaker were all decorated with incised line patterns. The jug and basin share motifs of finely incised filled triangles.

Especially noteworthy in this grave of the period Bronze Age D (1300–1200 BC) is the set of vessels designed for different purposes—the basin (with rim diameter of 22.5 cm and mid-body diameter of 30.5 cm) as a container for a beverage, the jug for pouring, and the beaker for drinking. All these are decorated, the cauldron and jug with similar motifs suggesting that they are closely associated. The three undecorated bowls may have been used to serve food or drink. This set of vessels is an early feasting service, with ornate vessels designed to serve specific purposes in the course of the feast.

The pottery sherds among the stones in the northern part of the outer frame, and the bronze objects just outside the stone setting on the west side and at the southeast corner, indicate that the performance of the funerary ritual included actions at the perimeter of the grave structure as well as the arranging of objects within the burial chamber.

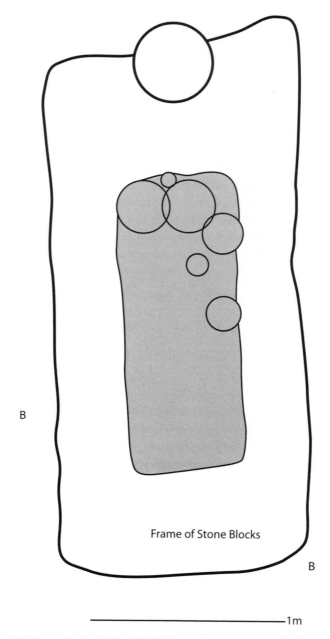

Frame of Stone Blocks

—————————————————————1m

FIGURE 34. Schematic plan of a late Middle Bronze Age grave at Mannsdorf, Lower Bavaria, Germany. This grave was framed by an outer structure of stone blocks and an inner rectangular pit in which the cremated remains of the individual were spread. Hatching: cremation remains. Circles: pottery vessels. B: bronze objects. (Drawing based on Engelhardt 2008.)

At Burgweinting, a cemetery of the Bronze Age D period included 120 graves. One consisted of a rectangular stone chamber set inside a grave pit measuring 3.2 by 1.7 m. On the floor of the grave was a paving of sandstone, measuring 2.3 × 0.8 m. The stone cist at the center of the chamber measured 1.8 by 0.9 m. Within the grave chamber but outside the cist, on the west side of the chamber, was a bowl and large sherds of a vessel of coarse ware, probably a storage jar. Some of the large sherds had been purposely stuck between the stones of the cist, a phenomenon known at other sites in the region. South of the chamber was a vessel with a cylindrical neck, decorated with rills. It had been set in place after the grave had been partly filled in, at a height of 30 cm above the floor level of the grave. In the same stratigraphic position but on the west side was a bowl. Inside the chamber were a decorated jug and a bowl, the latter with another bowl inside it. Two fragmentary rivets were found of a type used to fasten handles onto knives, but there was no trace of a knife.

Like the grave at Mannsdorf, this one at Burgweinting shows the importance of the stone frame as a defining visual characteristic. At the same time, features of the burial here illustrate other significant aspects of ritual in this period. The quantity of pottery placed outside of the central chamber raises questions about the meaning of different "layers" of framing. Why were some vessels placed inside the chamber and others in the space between the chamber and the outer stone structure?

The placing of sherds of the large vessel in openings between stones of the wall shows that objects that we might be tempted to consider simple trash played important roles in ritual performances. And the placing of two vessels in the fill of the grave, after some 30 cm of soil had already been replaced in the grave, provides insight into the time dimension, giving some sense of the duration of the burial process and the ceremony that accompanied it.

THE LATE BRONZE AGE (1200–800 BC)

The most common form of burial during the Late Bronze Age Urnfield Period was cremation, with the ashes then placed in a ceramic vessel, along with one or a few accompanying smaller pots and sometimes one or more bronze objects as well. A recently excavated grave at Fechenbach in Lower Franconia contained a large urn with a set of seven small vessels inside—four small bowls, one large bowl, a cauldron, and a beaker—that could be used in the consumption of an elaborate meal, or a feast. Ashes and burned bone from the cremation were at the bottom of the urn. Over these remains was a bronze pin that had been added after the fire.

This grave and other urn burials like it differ greatly from the chamber graves discussed above in having a very limited space in which objects could be arranged. The visual emphasis in the funerary ceremony was on the fire used in the cremation, rather than on space and the areal arrangement of objects in a roomy grave. But a small number of graves of this period, though also cremation burials, were set into chambers and in a few of these, such as that at Hart an der Alz in Upper Bavaria, an ornate four-wheeled wagon was buried, a practice that became more widespread in the Early Iron Age (see below).

On the North European Plain, cremation burials of this period were often accompanied by substantial structures that would have been plainly visible on the surface of the ground. At Telgte near Münster a large Urnfield Period cemetery contained graves that were enclosed by different kinds of ditches. In some cases, the ditches were "keyhole" shaped. In others, they formed long U-shaped enclosures. Still other graves were surrounded by circular ditches. Postholes indicate that some of the graves were covered by wooden structures. At Telgte and similar cemeteries, cremation burials were accompanied by burial monuments as visually striking and as complex as the chambers that housed inhumation graves.

THE EARLY IRON AGE, HALLSTATT C (800–600 BC)

At Grosseibstadt in Bavaria, a group of seven burial mounds was excavated in 1954 and 1955. The grave in Mound 1 is a good example of a well-outfitted burial of the early part of the Early Iron Age, Hallstatt Period C (Figure 35). The grave pit was 5.8 m long and between 2.1 and 2.8 m wide. A stone packing covered the pit. In the center of the northern part of the pit were the remains of a skeleton oriented north-south with the head toward the south and placed either on top of or underneath a four-wheeled wagon. Analysis of the skeletal remains indicate an individual about forty years old. On the right side of the skeleton was an iron sword and wooden scabbard. Near the middle of the east wall were bones of cattle, pig, and sheep or goat, with an iron knife alongside them. In the southern part of the grave pit were thirty-four ceramic vessels, arranged in what seem to have been two groups. One group was along the south wall of the chamber and included an exceptionally large vessel in the southwest corner and another in the southeast corner. Inside the large vessel in the southeast corner were remains of egg shells. The other group of vessels was situated in the northern part of the southern half of the chamber. Among the vessels of this group were a bronze amphora and two bronze plates. Between the two groups of vessels was a wooden yoke with numerous bronze attachments, as well as a number of bronze ornaments from a horse harness.

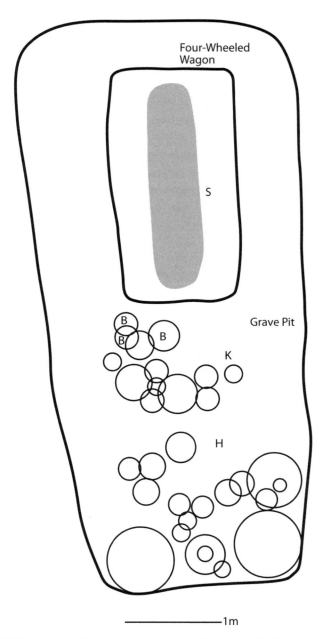

Four-Wheeled
Wagon

S

Grave Pit

B

B

B

K

H

1m

FIGURE 35. Schematic plan of an Early Iron Age grave at Grosseibstadt in Lower Franconia, northern Bavaria, Germany. Note the difference in size between this grave and those in Figures 33 and 34. Shading: body space. Circles: pottery vessels. B: bronze vessels. H: bronze attachments from harness. K: iron knife. S: sword. (Drawing based on Kossack 1970:46–61.)

Comparing the arrangements of this grave and others of Hallstatt Period
C in the central regions of temperate Europe with the arrangements of the
Bronze Age burials discussed above, two visual aspects are immediately striking. First, the burial spaces are much bigger here, with wooden chambers
much larger than those of preceding periods. The frame allowed expansive
open space on the floor of the burial chamber, and this space accommodated
larger displays of objects. Four-wheeled wagons and tens of ceramic vessels, unusual in the latter part of the Bronze Age, were now common in the
wealthiest graves. Second, a substantial amount of unoccupied space was left
within the chamber. The larger chambers and arrangements that left more
open space suggest that these graves were arranged for the participation of
larger numbers of people in the funerary ceremonies, and perhaps also that
more elaborate performances were conducted within the chamber involving
the display and manipulation of objects in the process of setting them into
their final positions.

Also new is the separation of the buried individual in one half of the grave,
together with the wagon and the sword, from the thirty-four pottery vessels
and three bronze vessels in the other half. This arrangement reflects the same
framing of space as does the separation of zones containing different kinds of
ornament on pottery of this period (see Chapter 5). In contrast to the earlier
graves, this one contained feasting vessels for multiple individuals.

THE EARLY IRON AGE, HALLSTATT D (600–500 BC)

Hochdorf is a key site for study of all questions relating to burial practice in
the latter half of the sixth century BC, because it was undisturbed when discovered, because the excavation and recording met the very highest standards
of archaeological research, and because the preservation of organic materials
was exceptionally good. In addition, the grave was among the most richly outfitted of its period. Since the grave has been much discussed and illustrated, I
shall refrain from describing the contents here and focus instead on the patterns of the arrangements.

The arrangement of objects in the grave is highly linear. The burial was
inside a wooden chamber measuring 4.7 by 4.7 m, a perfect square, and the
objects were set into the grave in a north-south orientation. The couch, placed
close to the west wall, is a strong linear element, and the cauldron was positioned in direct line with the couch, just north of it. The wagon and its pole
form a parallel linear element on the west side of the chamber. The result is a
strong linear band of objects on the west and on the east of the chamber, and
a large open space in the middle. Hanging on the south wall of the chamber

was the line of drinking horns with the largest horn, the only one of iron, significantly placed at the west end just above the man's head.

The geometric shapes of the major objects—those that would have garnered a great deal of visual attention from onlookers at the funerary ceremony—are consistent with those of the chamber itself and of the arrangement of objects within it. The couch is a rectangle, and the linear bars supporting it underneath are straight lines set at right angles. The wagon is also a rectangle. The wagon wheels, and the cauldron and its supporting ring, are all circles, as is the gold bowl. The horns, conical forms with curved ends, are less regularly geometrical. The man's ornaments are also essentially geometrical in shape—a rectangular belt plate and shoe ornaments, and a circular bracelet, neckring, and hat.

Visually striking is the way in which feasting equipment dominates the burial. The northwest and northeast corners are occupied by metal feasting containers—the cauldron and gold bowl in the northwest, nine bronze bowls as well as an axe (perhaps used to kill an animal for the banquet) in the northeast. Then, too, the entire south wall was devoted to the display of feasting equipment—nine drinking horns, one all metal, the others of natural horn adorned with gold.

GRAVES, MIDDLE IRON AGE: 500–200 BC

From the fifth century BC on, we see more uniform burial practices across much of temperate Europe than during earlier periods. Reinheim and Hochscheid 2 are good examples of relatively richly outfitted graves of the fifth century BC. The Reinheim woman was buried in a chamber roughly three meters square (though one side was destroyed before excavation), and the body was placed in the center of the chamber. Although, due to the acidity of the soil, the only surviving skeletal remains were fragments of teeth, the situation of the body could be reconstructed from the position of the jewelry. The woman was elaborately ornamented with gold-ring jewelry, brooches, and beads. Just to the left of her head was a container holding a quantity of jewelry. A bronze mirror had been placed next to her right shoulder. Vessels for feasting—an ornate gilded bronze jug, two imported bronze basins, and two gold attachments for drinking horns—were all to the left of the body toward the east wall.

Particularly noteworthy are the location of the body, with all of its decoration, in the center of the grave rather than on one side, and the distribution of mirror, jewelry container, and feasting set between her and the chamber walls. The only empty areas in the grave were small spaces between her head and the north wall and her feet and the south wall. The excavator believes that there had been a wooden coffin in the grave, no remains of which have survived.

Similarly, in the man's grave at Hochscheid Mound 2, the body was centrally placed in the burial chamber, and the accompanying objects were arranged on and around it. The grave pit was 3.8 by 2.4 m in size, and it was lined with an arrangement of stones, almost a dry-stone wall. Wood remains indicate the presence of a coffin or some other kind of wooden structure in the grave. At the very center of the grave was a sword, with a highly decorated scabbard (Figure 29), positioned with its decorated surface downward. Presumably this was originally at the right side of the buried individual, though the skeletal remains did not survive. Just as in the Reinheim grave, personal ornaments were positioned on the body, and other objects were arranged between the body and the walls of the chamber. In Hochscheid 2, the fibula and bracelet were in positions indicating that they were attached to the body, while pottery, spearheads, and a large knife were all situated around the body. As at Reinheim, there was very little empty space left in the chamber.

After 400 BC, graves containing gold and bronze imports, like the grave at Reinheim, and highly ornate scabbards, like Hochscheid 2, are rare. Most common are narrow rectangular graves with minimal space between the body and the coffin walls, lacking tumuli or stone-lined chambers, and containing modest sets of jewelry in the case of female burials and of iron weapons with some, but not all, males. Grave 14 at Radovesice in Bohemia is a good example. The grave pit was 2.22 by 0.75 m in size, and it contained probable remnants of a wooden coffin and the skeletal remains of a woman between thirty and forty years of age. The woman was outfitted with personal ornaments in the form of two fibulae, a bracelet, a belt with a large iron ring, two footrings, and fragments of another indistinguishable object. Remains of organic material were identified at both the head and foot ends of the grave. Aside from the objects on the body, there were no identifiable items added to the grave.

A different kind of grave was excavated at Marcelcave in the Somme region of northeast France. Slightly off center in the southern part of a square chamber, were the remains of a cremation. Close to the remains there was a mass of iron weapons. In the center of the chamber was a pair of andirons (firedogs). Near the east corner was a metal cauldron, and lined up along the northwest wall were ten ceramic vessels, along with a knife placed close to the northernmost vessel. The arrangement of objects left a considerable amount of open space (in contrast to Radovesice 14, above). Along with the open space, the visually most striking features of this grave arrangement are the pair of andirons set in the very center, with open space left around them, and the line of pots along the northwest wall.

GRAVES, LATE IRON AGE: 200–50 BC

During these final two centuries of the Iron Age, we see notable changes in the character of burials in temperate Europe. In the central regions of the continent, where we have rich evidence of burials from the Bronze Age, the Early Iron Age, and the earlier parts of the Late Iron Age, the practice of subsurface burial declined precipitously over the course of the second century BC. For major settlements such as the *oppida* at Altenburg, Heidengraben, Kelheim, and Manching, we have only a small handful of graves, where we would expect thousands.

On the other hand, among the graves that have been excavated elsewhere in temperate Europe, we note strong similarities of practice in locations separated by considerable distances. I will cite three examples, all dating from around the middle of the first century BC.

At Badenheim in the middle Rhineland a grave 1.65 by 0.95 meters in size was in an enclosure surrounded by a ditch. It contained seven ceramic vessels, all but one of them lined up along the west wall. They included three bowls, three jars, and one large bottle and may have comprised a set associated with feasting. In northern and eastern areas of the grave were the cremation remains and an animal skull, probably that of a pig. In the space between the remains and the pottery was an iron sword in its scabbard (Figure 32), both bent into a U-shape. The southern part of the grave pit was empty, though the author of the report speculates that wooden furniture may originally have been present.

At Welwyn Garden City, north of London in the United Kingdom, a burial chamber measured about 2.5 by 1.5 meters (Figure 36). Cremated bones of what is believed to have been an adult male were situated in the northern part of the grave, and space was left around them. Grave goods were placed along the wall of the grave, not close to the bones. A wooden object of some kind lay across the floor of the grave, separating the part with the cremated remains from the southern part of the grave where most of the grave goods had been arranged. Five Roman amphorae were positioned in a row against the east wall. A large number of ceramic vessels were placed within the southern area of the grave, thirty-six in total, thirty-three local and three imported.

As with the grave at Boiroux (Figure 11), the open space here is much reduced from that of Early Iron Age Grosseibstadt (Figure 35). Unlike the Mannsdorf grave, here the cremated remains were deposited in a concentrated circle, not scattered across the floor of the burial. In common with Grosseibstadt, the remains of the individual were spatially separated from the majority of vessels arranged in the grave, in this case by a physical barrier

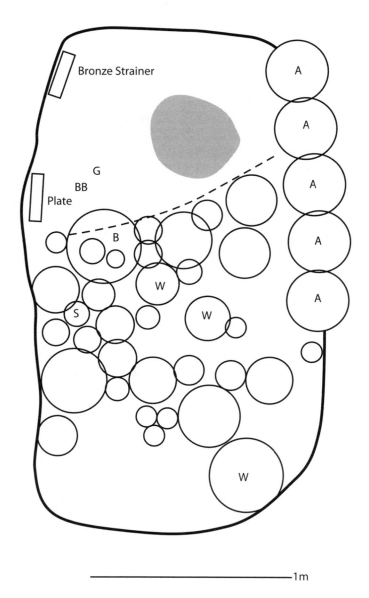

Bronze Strainer

G

BB

Plate

B

A

A

A

A

A

W

W

S

W

1m

Figure 36. Schematic plan of a Late Iron Age grave at Welwyn Garden City, north of London, England. Hatching: cremated remains. Circles: pottery vessels. A: Roman amphorae. BB: bead and bracelet fragments. B: bronze dish. G: gaming tokens. S: silver cup. W: wooden vessels with metal attachments. (Drawing based on Stead 1967.)

set across the floor of the grave, marked by the position of studs with bronze heads, apparently originally attached to a wooden board. As in the cases of both Grosseibstadt and Boiroux, the grave contained multiple ceramic vessels associated with feasting—thirty-six in this case, along with two of bronze, one of silver, and three wooden vessels. The most striking visual aspect of the Welwyn grave, and a feature that makes it representative of the major trend of its time, is the framing of the part of the grave containing the cremated remains of the individual with highly visible imported objects that arrived in Britain in the context of the great expansion in commercial activity during the late second and first centuries BC. On the east (right) side, five Roman amphorae formed the frame; on the west side were an imported bronze strainer and ceramic plate, both arranged vertically (rather than in the horizontal position in which they were intended to be used) to form the frame on that side. Finally, in the north end of the grave with the cremated remains were the rest of the grave goods: a set of gaming pieces, representative of both interregional interaction and the sociality of game-playing between the buried individual and other members of his group, as well as glass bead and bracelet fragments, also imported.

At Boiroux in the Corrèze region of central France, excavators uncovered a four-meter-long burial chamber (Figure 11) that provides strong evidence for the deliberate arrangement of objects in a visually meaningful fashion. The grave was oriented east-west, with the head at the west. A wooden coffin contained the burial and most of the grave objects, and the coffin was surrounded and covered by stones. Prominent at the foot end of the burial, but outside of the wooden coffin, were three Dressel 1B amphorae, all with their tops purposefully broken off and all arranged standing upright. The grave also contained twenty-four ceramic vessels, including plates, bowls, and jars, eighteen of them handmade and six wheelmade. The excavators note the highly systematic arrangement of the vessels on the floor of the coffin. According to their report, the finest vessels were placed at the head end, just above (west of) where the deceased individual's head would have been (no bone material has survived). These four vessels include a high-necked and footed vessel with bands of incised ornament that is the most elegant and delicate vessel in the grave, as well as two other wheelmade vessels. Storage vessels were situated along the sides of the coffin and at the foot end. Wide-open vessels, plates and bowls, were situated mainly from near the center of the grave extending eastwards, in the region of where the stomach and the legs of the deceased would have been. The location of these latter vessels led the excavators to ask whether a table might have been present originally, set over the deceased's midsection.

A lancehead was found on the right side of where the deceased would have lain. The location of a shield handle indicates that a shield lay across the individual's left side, probably from about the level of his ears to that of his knees.

The visual layout of the grave emphasizes the importance of the finest vessels, placed at the person's head; the individual's military significance, indicated by the lance placed prominently at his right side, the knife suspended from his belt, and the shield protecting his left side; and his social role in hosting a meal or a feast for a number of other persons. The four vessels at the head deserve special attention, since they are clearly separated by a considerable distance inside the coffin from the twenty other vessels. Besides the fact of their being among the finest of the vessels in the grave, and including, as we have mentioned, the only much-decorated vessel, they comprise a complete set of feasting vessels: an exquisite serving vessel for wine, presumably; a beaker for drinking; a bowl for food; and large jar for the storage of food. Thus, at a glance, the participants in the funerary ceremony saw represented here the individual's military status, his social role as a host, and the special quality and character of the personal feasting set with which he entertained other members of his community.

ARRANGEMENTS IN GRAVES: PATTERNS OVER TIME

The detailed descriptions of the graves above can be summarized as follows:

In the Bronze and Early Iron Age, we see a trend over time from minimal display in minimal space during the Early Bronze Age, to larger spaces during the Middle and Late Bronze Age, to the big open burial chambers of the Early Iron Age, in which objects were typically arranged around the outside edge of the chamber and considerable open space—affordance—left in the center. Associated with this increasing space devoted to the funerary display, and the expansion of the open space in the center, is an ever-increasing quantity of feasting vessels, culminating in graves such as Hochdorf and Vix, where the displays included enormous containers for beverages, sufficient to serve a sizeable party of retainers. Significantly, while Hochdorf includes individual feasting vessels for a team of supporters—both beverage containers (nine drinking horns) and food dishes (nine bronze bowls)—there were only two vessels for individual consumption in the grave at Vix; namely, two Attic *kylikes* (and two Etruscan bronze basins). At Vix, it seems that group consumption took place in the enclosure in the vicinity of the rich grave, and the vessels used in that event were deposited there. If this is correct, then the Vix enclosure can be regarded as representing a beginning phase of the practice of creating rectangular enclosures defined by bordering ditches for the conduct of ceremonial activities. We shall soon see this practice developed further at Gournay and other open air "sanctuaries."

During the fifth century BC, the nature of the displays associated with burials was changing. The big chamber spaces of the preceding century began to go out of fashion, replaced by the late fifth and early fourth centuries BC by much smaller spaces for even the most richly outfitted burials, such as Glauberg 1, Reinheim, and Weiskirchen. The big feasting sets so common in the seventh and sixth centuries BC, at Grosseibstadt and in many graves at Hallstatt in Austria, were replaced by much more modest sets intended for one or two participants. During most of the fourth, third, and the early second centuries BC, even such modest sets of feasting equipment became rare, and burial display was limited to at most the individual's personal accouterments (jewelry for women, weapons for men). Sometimes a single ceramic vessel was present, but more are rare.

These practices are abundantly evident in the great flat-grave cemeteries of the Middle La Tène Period, such as those in the Champagne region of France, at Saint-Sulpice and Münsingen in Switzerland, Nebringen in Germany, and Jenišův Újezd and Radovesice in the Czech Republic. Public display involving large quantities of objects shifted away from the burial ceremony to open spaces in the landscape. These open spaces featured enclosures created by digging ditches surrounding rectangular spaces (at Gournay, Ribemont, and Braine) and platforms built for the ceremonial deposition of objects into water (at La Tène, Fiskerton, and Kessel). At the same time, smaller-scale sites were also established at which objects were ceremoniously deposited (at Douix, Egesheim, and Duchcov). This shift from the display of objects placed in graves to the display of objects deposited so as to become part of the landscape, either in the ground or in water, was a profound change in the way that people thought about seeing their significant pieces of material culture.

Another series of important changes took place during the second century BC. It was at this time that the first of the *oppida* were established. These were the largest settlements of prehistoric Europe, and their often enormous walls of timber, stone, and earth were in themselves objects of display. Even Julius Caesar marveled at their appearance. Throughout much of temperate Europe, the custom of subsurface burial was replaced by some other means of disposing of the dead, the character of which is still unclear. Compared to the preceding centuries, we have only a very small number of graves for the period between the middle of the second century BC and the end of the prehistoric Iron Age. In the lands between the middle Rhineland and the English Channel, the practice of burial continued, and we know a significant number of burials from Britain in this period. Among the graves that are available for study, substantial chambers were often constructed, and sometimes large numbers of vessels associated with feasting were laid out on the chamber floor, as at Acy-Romance in France, Clemency and Goeblingen-Nospelt in Luxembourg, Wederath 1216 in Germany, and Welwyn Garden City in southern Britain. The inclusion of andirons in a number of burials underscores the importance of feasting display in these graves. In contrast to the situation in the earlier period (the seventh, sixth, and early fifth centuries BC) when chambers were common, now there was not the same emphasis on open space—affordance—in the center of the chamber. Objects were more likely to be piled together, one on top of the other, as in the graves at Mailleraye in France and Baldock in Britain, and in the deposit at Tintignac, rather than laid out in a broad spatial arrangement with a prominent open space in the center. Even in the large chambers at Clemency and Welwyn, most of the floor was covered with objects, in marked contrast to graves such as those at Grosseibstadt, Hochdorf, and Vix.

This new way of visualizing space and putting it to use was consistent with the Late Iron Age emphasis on production and commerce. In the earlier period of the wider, more open chambers, space was organized and used with social purposes in mind, the layout of objects in the grave being arranged so as to be accessible to the members of the community carrying out the funerary ceremony. Whether or not many people actually entered the burial chamber in the course of the ceremony, the visual openness of the central part of the chamber was a socially significant aspect of the performance of the ritual. The elimination of that open space in the final two centuries BC was one expression of the great social and political changes that accompanied the economic shifts brought about by increasing participation in far-flung commercial systems. We shall look more closely at this phenomenon in Chapter 12.

CHAPTER 9

∞∞∞∞∞∞∞∞∞∞∞∞∞∞∞∞∞∞∞∞

PERFORMANCES

Objects and Bodies in Motion

They threw swords into the lake at La Tène. They arranged bent and broken scabbards in the ditch at Gournay-sur-Aronde, and placed iron tools in the fire at Forggensee. At Snettisham, they buried gold neckrings. Prehistoric people *performed* all of these actions, for they were indeed *performances*, held in open spaces where they could be seen by others, in some cases by large numbers of them. And all of these performances involved objects, the seeing of which was crucial to the meaning of the ceremonies.

ARCHAEOLOGY AND PERFORMANCE

Archaeological evidence is static. In the arrangement of objects in graves, the accumulations of pottery and animal bones at settlements, the walls around hilltop fortifications, we seethe physical results of past actions, but we do not see the actions directly. The actions that led to the crafting of the objects that we recover archaeologically and to the patterns created in the archaeological evidence by arranging objects in particular ways were, however, critically important to how people saw those objects and patterns.

I use the word "performance" here to refer specifically to actions that people carried out in social contexts—"with an audience" and with their material culture. To be a performance, an action must be aimed at communicating with others. A performance involves some kind of movement by a person or persons, and our concern here is with those movements that involved the manipulations of objects.

MOVEMENT AND SEEING

Humans see things better when they are in motion, whether it is the object being viewed that is moving, or the observer. Richard Gregory notes that when a person is looking at an object in motion, that person does not move his or her eyes in the saccadic "jerks" with which the eyes view stationary objects (Chapter 2). Thus the eyes (and brain) can focus more fully on the object than if it were still. (This point is easy to test. Stare at a stationary object for more than a few seconds, and soon you will have difficulty "seeing" it clearly; the only way to bring it back into full focus is to look away from the object, and then back to it. But follow a running dog or a bird in flight, and you will find it easy to keep your visual and mental attention on the object in motion.) This enhanced ability to see moving things may well stem from our evolutionary past, when it was important for our ancestors to be able to focus clearly on potential predators coming toward them (or on prey running, flying, or swimming away from them).

When we witness someone moving an object, whether a priest lifting a chalice from an altar, a baseball player swinging a bat, or a master of ceremonies handing a trophy to a winner, another powerful aspect—that of bodily involvement—is added to the visual aspect of the object's motion. Experiments have shown that in such situations, observers unconsciously experience, through viewing the person moving the objects, the feel of the objects that are being manipulated in what is known as "embodied cognition." This experience is very different from simply viewing a stationary object, and it results in both feelings of participation in the moving of the objects, and more powerful memories of the objects, and the occasions, than would result from viewing static objects. Moreover, when an individual has experienced the motion of an object in the performance, subsequent sightings of the object can generate the same reaction as the person experienced when actually witnessing the performance.

We need also to consider the role of light in the experience of seeing objects in motion. Stationary objects tend to be in consistent light, at least during short intervals of time. But when a person moves an object—when the priest lifts the chalice, or the batter swings the bat—patterns of light, reflection, and shadow change rapidly, adding to the visual attraction and fascination of the object in motion. The effects of changing patterns of light are especially pronounced on three-dimensional objects, such as pottery, and on metal objects with ornament in high relief, such as some of the decorated scabbards and the ornate shields of Late Iron Age Britain.

ACTING IN FRAMED SPACES

Performances take place in specific places within defined spaces. The frames around the spaces are essential components of the visual experience of the viewer. The performance of arranging objects in a grave takes place within the confines of the edges of the burial pit or chamber. The deposition of objects at the enclosed sites of Gournay, Ribemont, and Braine was also carried out within clearly defined boundaries. The creation of these frames and spaces was in itself an important performance, one that was enacted and witnessed by members of the community and that had profound impact, both in direct participation and in memory, on the individuals who took part.

BODILY PARTICIPATION IN PERFORMANCE

The arranging of objects in burials, the setting into the ditches at Gournay of objects to mark that boundary, the erecting of lifesize statues on top of or next to burial mounds—all of these actions result in patterns in the material evidence that we recognize, but the results are for us static. We see the objects, we can identify the patterns, but we cannot see, directly, the motions, the performances. All of the evidence, however, suggests that these actions were performed with and for an audience—a community (for the purposes of the event) of people who witnessed the actions, and by witnessing them became active participants, whether or not they actually handled the objects or shoveled the dirt themselves.

In some instances, we have direct evidence for the active participation of viewers, witnesses to the proceedings. Rosalind Niblett notes evidence at several sites, including Clemency in Luxembourg and at Folly Lane in St. Albans in the United Kingdom, of intensive packing of the ground near a burial chamber, likely the result of a procession that took place as part of the funerary rituals. At Dun Ailinne in Ireland, Bernard Wailes has argued that the enormous postholes on the hilltop supported a grandstand of some kind that allowed participants to view ritual proceedings on this hilltop site.

PERFORMANCES WITH OBJECTS

Feasts

Meals in most societies are and have always been social occasions, whether they involve a family sitting down at a table together for a meal, a business lunch in a high-powered Midtown Manhattan setting, or a banquet such as Trimalchio's in Petronius's *Satyricon*. As social occasions, they involve performances, because, as Martin Jones observes, at meals people sustain themselves nutritionally and "constitute (themselves) as social persons." At meals "we . . . consciously put our worlds in order at a whole variety of levels." These themes are apparent in early literary accounts of feasts and banquets, such as Plato's and Xenophon's descriptions of *symposia* in Classical Athens and the scenes in the great halls of the early medieval epic *Beowulf*. All such occasions involve specific established practices and rules, whether it is "no elbows on the table," the "man of the house" carving the roast, or "pass the port to the left."

What we are interested in here, of course, are the Bronze and Iron Age performances that we can reconstruct from the evidence of material culture. Countless studies of pottery from Bronze and Iron Age settlements have shown that there were set patterns governing the use of particular vessel forms for particular purposes. Large, thick-walled, coarse-textured vessels with broad bodies and constricted necks—jars—were commonly used for storing foodstuffs. Bowls were used mainly for serving and consuming food, cups for drinking beverages.

The inclusion in burials of complete sets of vessels, with different individual vessels intended for different purposes in consuming food and drink, together with evidence from Situla Art, can give us an idea of how the performances of meals were carried out. In the Late Bronze Age grave at Hart an der Alz in southern Bavaria we encounter an early example of a complete set of feasting vessels, but one that was only sufficient for one or two persons. The eight ceramic vessels in the Hart grave include two storage jars, two bowls for food, two jugs, and two cups for drink. Most important are the three bronze vessels in the grave, because they mark it as different from others of the time and presage the bronze drinking sets of the Iron Age. The set included everything an elite man needed to serve himself wine (or to be served by someone else): a pail, a sieve to filter out the added spices, and a cup.

Seven hundred years later, the "performance" of a feast is more clearly represented at the grave at Hochdorf. Now, around 525 BC, there is not just a bronze pail, but a cauldron, made in the Greek world, with a capacity of 400 liters. A gold bowl found next to the cauldron served as a dipper for scooping out mead. On the wall of the chamber hung nine drinking horns, and nine bronze dishes were arranged on a wagon. The Hochdorf man was no solitary diner, nor did he serve just one or two others. The matching numbers of horns and dishes make apparent that those arranging the Hochdorf grave were marking the performance of feasting in which this man took part, feasting that involved at least his retinue of eight. Even though the objects in the grave are stationary, it does not require great feats of imagination to picture the performance that this equipment entailed. We can see the man sitting on his ornate bronze couch, holding his enormous iron-and-gold drinking horn and leading his followers, each holding his aurochs-and-gold horn aloft, performing the social and political rituals that are so strongly implied by the contents and arrangement of this tomb.

Never again is the theme of a group performance as clearly presented visually as in the tomb at Hochdorf. In the Vix grave (480 BC) there was a larger vessel—the largest bronze vessel known from the ancient world—along with a bronze jug and basins from Italy and wine-drinking cups from Athens, but no vessels for a retinue. Later at Clemency and at Welwyn Garden City, feasting is again represented by sets of vessels, but not in the multiple numbers found at Hochdorf. In one or possibly two of the four well-outfitted burials at Goeblingen-Nospelt in Luxembourg, however, we see something of the "performance for a retinue" theme, with a large and comprehensive set of vessels in Grave B, and a more modest set of feasting equipment in Grave A.

Scenes in Situla Art provide us with another source of evidence for the performance of feasts in Iron Age Europe. The majority of decorated situlae have been recovered in northern Italy and Slovenia, but one of the vessels with the most useful scenes of feasting is from Kuffarn in Austria. It is thought to date to around 400 BC, and it was recovered from a grave that contained a bronze ladle and an iron sword, among other objects (Figure 37).

The situla from Kuffarn has on it one of the more important scenes representing a feast, and it is a scene that is consistent with feast scenes on other situlae, notably those from Magdalenska gora and Vače in Slovenia. Unlike evidence from graves, this scene actually shows us a performance—an action scene. Three figures are depicted performing actions. The seated figure is holding aloft a bowl of a form that is familiar from Early Iron Age contexts in temperate Europe. The middle figure holds a situla in his left hand and with his right, which holds a ladle, he reaches toward the seated person and the cup that that person is holding. It is not clear from the scene whether the middle figure is offering to fill the cup or has just filled it. The figure on the left is carrying two empty cauldrons away from the scene to refill them. As Stefan Winghart observes, in the situla feast scenes each vessel form has its own specific purpose, so that the performance represented on the situla links

FIGURE 37. Feasting scene on the situla from Kuffarn, Austria. From Karner 1891, pl. 9.

function to form. If, after viewing the scene on the Kuffarn situla, one were to see a bowl, a situla, or a large jar in a different context, such as a funerary display, the observer would be reminded of the whole set, since the object-type had been linked to the performance in that important scene.

At the hilltop site of Dun Ailinne in Ireland, Bernard Wailes reports the remains of feasting activity associated with unusually large circular timber structures that are believed to have had important political and ritual significance (see above). The evidence of animal bones in different stratigraphic layers has been interpreted to indicate a series of chronologically distinct feasting events at the site.

FUNERARY RITUALS

Chapter 8 examined arrangements of objects in graves; here I will consider the performances of the rituals that led to those arrangements.

Archaeologists typically work with burial structures (mounds, chambers) and with objects placed in burials with the dead, and indeed these can be very important sources of information about many different aspects of early communities. As we know from ethnographic evidence, the disposal of the body of the deceased is only one part of what is often an elaborate performance of a series of interrelated ceremonies in connection with funeral rites. Rosalind Niblett, in her analysis of the grave at Folly Lane in St. Albans, provides unusual insight into just how complex these performances that take place both before and after the burial can be, and how important they are for our understanding of what went on, why, and what effect they are likely to have had on participants.

The floor surface of a grave, whether it consists of the natural earth, a stone pavement, or the timber base of a wooden chamber, is an affordance in Gibson's terms, a "whiteness" for Bender and Marrinan. It is a space with potential, where objects could be placed and displayed in emotionally and historically charged performances. At the outset, participants regarded the space as ready for action, ready to receive objects that conveyed meaning both about the individual celebrated in the funeral ritual and about the nature of the world in which the community lived. They knew that the open space would be transformed into an arrangement of significant objects.

Ethnohistoric, historical, and ethnographic studies show that funerary rituals are usually communal social events with a substantial part of a community taking part. Even the spectators observing funerary rituals are not really passive—their very presence and participation through a communication of feeling, and perhaps through gestures and sounds, made them active partakers in the overall performance.

In the Early Bronze Age, deceased persons were commonly buried with some elements of personal jewelry—bracelets or beads, and sometimes with a ceramic vessel (Chapter 8). In the Middle Bronze Age and especially the Late Bronze Age, more objects were being placed in some graves, including axes, swords, and in a few cases drinking vessels of bronze. The laying out of complex arrangements of grave goods—largely pottery in some cases, as at Hradenín and Grosseibstadt; wagons, equestrian equipment, and weapons in others, reached a high point during the Early Iron Age. In this period, expansive grave chambers were decked out with complex arrangements of objects in what must have been elaborate performances involving both verbal actions—speaking and perhaps singing—which are lost to us, and physical performances involving the arranging of objects in the graves, the results of which are available to us. Among the best-documented and most elaborate examples are the burials at Hochdorf in southwest Germany (525 BC) and Vix in eastern France (480 BC).

As noted in Chapter 8, in the second half of the fifth century BC, the quantities of grave goods and the elaborateness of ceremonies declined, so that even the wealthiest graves of the late fifth and early fourth centuries BC, such as Reinheim, Glauberg 1 and 2, and Weiskirchen, show much more modest arrangements in the grave spaces. The relatively few exceptionally well-equipped graves, such as those at Waldalgesheim on the middle Rhine and Ciumeşti in Romania, do not alter the general picture for temperate Europe as a whole.

In some parts of Europe, the latter half of the second and the first century BC saw a return to the practice of performing rituals that involved laying out quantities of objects in burials. In great chamber burials, such as Clemency in Luxembourg, Welwyn Garden City north of London, and Goeblingen-Nospelt in Luxembourg, we find once again the material result of performances that involved large numbers of objects that were no doubt displayed as they were set into place before an observant audience of participants.

Two exceptionally well excavated and reported graves, both from the late period, will illustrate these points.

A grave at Mailleraye-sur-Seine, dated sometime between 200 and 150 BC, contained a variety of visually potent objects, and its arrangement permits precise reconstruction of the process whereby the objects were put in place during the funerary ceremony. The bones are identified as those of an adult, the gender is uncertain. Since most graves that contain both weapons and well-preserved skeletal remains were those of men, it is highly likely that the individual was male.

In the center of the grave pit was placed a glass vessel that contained the cremated remains and two ceramic vessels, a bowl and another, taller vessel. A glass bowl, a bronze vessel, and a bucket with figural attachment were also set into the grave at this first stage. Near the vessels a bronze ring, a horse bit, and various fasteners were placed. Six iron tires that had been damaged by exposure to fire were arranged surrounding the centrally placed objects in the bottom of the grave pit. Then other bronze and iron objects, including axes, lance points, fibulae, and a chain from a cauldron, were set in place outside of the circle formed by the tires. Next a pair of andirons was arranged on top of the tires. Then a cauldron was placed upside down on top of the assemblage. Next two tires smaller than the first six were set in place enclosing the cauldron. As a final action, weapons were added to the deposit. Three swords in their scabbards were arranged parallel to one another on top of the cauldron, and a packet of three lance heads and three shield bosses were set at the southeast edge of the grave.

Because of the vertical arrangement of the objects in this grave, the order of placement is clear, which is not generally the case when objects are laid out separately on the horizontal surface of the grave base.

The grave goods buried in this deposit include objects related to military activity (the three swords, five lanceheads, and three shield bosses); horsemanship and chariotry (bits, harness gear, tires, and chariot parts); feasting (two andirons, a cauldron, a cauldron chain, and three spits); and personal ornamentation (three fibulae).

The visual aspects of the positioning of objects in the grave are clear and striking. It is highly probably that a social group witnessed and thus participated visually in the arranging of the grave. This group would have consisted of individuals with social connections to the buried person—immediate family members, members of the wider family, members of the residential community, and other members of the "warrior elite" to which the deceased belonged, some of them coming perhaps from considerable distances away. We do not know what transpired in other parts of the funerary ceremony, before and after the placing of these objects in the grave pit. But from these objects and their placement, we can say a great deal about the visuality of this arrangement and of the performance of this part of the ceremony.

The first part of the construction of this visible monument to the memory of the role in the community occupied by the buried individual was the placement of the urn with his physical remains. The cremation fire in which the individual's corpse had been reduced to these bone fragments was no doubt fresh in the memories of the participants, whether it took place just hours or days before the setting of the urn into the ground. (Niblett's 1999 study of the St. Albans grave alerts us to the fact that considerable time can elapse between one part of the funerary ceremony and another.) The physical act of placing the urn at the bottom of the grave pit, at its center, must have been, therefore a visually dramatic moment in the performance.

The second stage in the arrangement was the placing of the encircling iron tires on top of the urn and the accompanying vessels. (The six tires were fire-damaged, hence the wood on them would have burned away.) The practice of dismantling vehicles before arranging their parts in graves was common (in the Vix and Arras burials, for example). The placement of the circular tires as enclosing devices is, however, of particular visual significance. Like all enclosing devices, they formed frames around the central, vital, part of the burial. And like all frames, they served to highlight the importance of what was inside. This part of the ceremony and the arrangement of objects must have been very carefully thought out and planned by those conducting the ceremony, and then just as carefully performed as a powerful, vision-directing action.

The next layer placed on the assemblage consisted of objects that were used in feasting and that referred directly to both the feast itself and to the social aspects of the feast—to conviviality and high spirits, but also to the expression of social status and competition in social contestation within the community. These included the andirons that represented the hearth and fire at which meat was cooked for the feast, and the cauldron in which the meat was cooked or the beer or mead was brewed. We might speculate that the placement of the cauldron upside down referred to the fact that this individual would not be using it anymore.

On top of the cauldron and on top of the entire assemblage were placed three swords in their scabbards, arranged in precise parallel to one another across the central part of the base of the cauldron. One sword was set outer face down, the other two with their outer faces up. These clearly served the purpose of closing, and thereby completing, the assemblage. Of all the possible ways of displaying swords in the grave—set on the floor of the grave, laid around the edges, stuck into the ground—this arrangement was chosen so as to ensure that they would stand as the most striking aspect of the burial visually. After the process of laying out the cremated remains and accompanying vessels, then surrounding those with the tires, then adding the layer of objects pertaining to feasting and hosting, finally the whole assemblage was capped with the three swords. They would thus remain with the participants as the most powerful of all their visual memories of the performance.

The experience of witnessing the arrangement of these objects in the burial was a kind of visual tour through the principal physical attributes of the individual's roles in his society—as warrior most importantly, then as a host of feasts, and finally as horseman and charioteer.

It is worth noting that at this same time in the Greek and Roman worlds, individuals of status were commemorated at their burial sites by portrait sculpture and inscriptions. Portrait sculpture attempted to show them at their best and healthiest. Inscriptions told who they were and what they did, and why they should be remembered. In the nonliterate society of Iron Age Europe, similar kinds of information were being conveyed, not through realistic likenesses or written descriptions, but through physical objects whose visual qualities conveyed unmistakable and powerful messages to the viewers.

Finally, we must consider the relationship between this burial and the society of which it was part. As I explained above, it is much more productive to understand burials as reflections and expressions of societies than as statements about the individual in the grave. While it can be argued that a grave represents the relationship between the buried individual and his or her society, I would argue that by far the most important thing about a grave is what it says about the society, not the individual. It is, after all, the society that carried out and witnessed the funerary ceremony. In the case of this particular grave, we can cite the warrior accouterments and the feasting equipment as particularly obvious points of connection between the individual and the society. The warrior did not fight for himself but for his community. And he did not feast by himself, but with members of his community—for otherwise feasting loses its entire social value and purpose.

Around the time of the Roman conquest of Britain in the middle of the first century AD, a cremation burial ritual was performed at the site of Folly Lane at St. Albans, a site excavated and reported by Rosalind Niblett. A shaft had been dug into the ground within a rectangular enclosure defined by a ditch, and earth from the hole was used to create a mound in the center of the enclosure. In the bottom of the shaft, a wooden structure was erected, apparently for the purpose of housing the body before the cremation.

The cremation of the body was carried out on the mound—a highly visible location. Niblett suggests that if participants had stood on the bank constructed from soil dug out of the ditch, as many as several thousand people could have witnessed the event.

Before all of the material in the fire had fully cooled, some of it, including burned bone, pottery, and metal objects, was placed in the shaft, while other parts were placed in a pit dug for the purpose just northeast of the mound. The structure in the shaft had been purposely destroyed, and then, after the depositing of the cremated material, the shaft was filled in. This filling was itself carried out in a particular manner, since sherds of the same vessels were found at the base of the shaft and in the top layers of the backfilled soil. The deposition of sherds rather than whole pots appears to have been deliberate, a part of the ceremony conducted at this burial site.

Niblett notes that the soil around the shaft was especially hard packed and suggests that participants in the funerary ceremony left this direct evidence of their presence.

Quantities of pottery, including Roman amphorae, recovered from the bottom of the shaft were interpreted as the material remains of a feast that was held at the time of the ritual.

From the scattered, partial, and fragmentary nature of the burned bone, the pottery, and the metal remains that were recovered in the shaft and in the burial pit, Niblett draws the conclusion that the most important part of the ceremony was the cremation itself, carried out high on the mound for maximum visibility, rather than the burial of the remains afterwards.

Open-Air Depositing

Visually striking natural features were often sites where objects were purposefully deposited, including pottery and bronze implements. For example, at the base of the imposing limestone cliff known as the Schellnecker Wänd west of Kelheim in Bavaria, Germany, a massive quantity of Late Bronze Age pottery was deposited (Figure 38). In the current state of analysis, it is not clear whether the pottery was dropped off the top of the cliff to shatter below, or broken against the cliff face at the bottom. There are no signs of settlement activity on the spot, hence it is apparent that people deposited the pottery at this location purposefully.

From the end of the Early Iron Age on, we have evidence for the creation of ditched enclosures for purposes other than settlement. A well-documented example is the enclosure at Vix, situated just 200 meters from the famous burial. Here a ditch surrounded a rectangular parcel of land about 22 meters square. There was an entrance into the enclosure at a break in the ditch about 1.8 meters wide. A special purpose for this enclosure is suggested by the

FIGURE 38. Photograph of the cliff outcrop (just right of center) at Schnellnecker Wänd, Bavaria, Germany.

presence near the entryway of two near-lifesize stone statues, one apparently of a woman wearing a neckring and a tunic (assumed to represent the woman buried in the rich grave), the other of a man wearing a sword and holding a shield. The abundance of sherds of ceramic bowls and of particular animal bones in the ditch have been interpreted as the remains of feasting activity inside the enclosure. Ditched enclosures of roughly the same size and general character and of about the same date as the Vix enclosure have been identified elsewhere in Europe, for example at Weichering in Bavaria and at Závist in Bohemia.

During the Middle Iron Age, large open-air sites were created at which substantial numbers of objects, especially weapons, were deposited in ways that left them visible for some time. At Gournay-sur-Aronde construction of a ditch that enclosed a rectangular area about 45 by 40 meters in size began at the end of the fourth century BC, and the site was used for the next few centuries for the deposition of some 2,500 metal objects, as well as the remains of many animals. Among the objects deposited in the ditches were about 200 swords, 180 scabbards (found in over 700 pieces), 220 shield bosses, and 60 lance points.

The arrangement of weapons at Gournay shows a dense distribution of swords and scabbards all along the inner ditch, concentrated especially at either side of the entrance. Jean-Louis Brunaux, the excavator, and his colleagues argue that the weapons were originally hung on trophy stands, on the wall, and on the gateway to the enclosed space; but nothing remains of any such supports, and it is difficult to establish direct evidence for any such disposition. What we can say with some confidence is that the weapons lay in the ditch for a time. They may have been hung above it and fallen in, but they may also have been purposely and directly deposited in the ditches, as suggested by some of the reconstruction drawings and models. The purposeful bending and breaking of many of the weapons would accord well with this latter theory.

The regularity with which weapons and other objects occur in the ditches of later Iron Age enclosures, as well as the regular occurrence of other special objects in similar contexts (see amphorae, below), strongly suggests that they were purposely placed in these locations for specific visual reasons. They were meant to be seen in the ditches that defined the enclosure area, and they were particularly arranged on either site of the entrance, a key place in sanctuary enclosures. The sight of hundreds of iron and bronze weapons piled up along a stretch of tens of meters in the ditch, most of them showing clear signs of damage by breaking, bending, and hacking, must have been impressive. Besides being striking in their own right as weapons that had undergone severe damage, these objects added to the visual power of the ditches, the edges and boundaries that defined the enclosure.

Along with the military equipment for over two hundred individual warriors, Gournay yielded around a hundred fibulae and various metal objects associated with horses and wagons. Evidence at the site indicates deposition over a long period of time, and not in a single event. Gournay also yields abundant evidence for the sacrifice of cattle on the site. Apparently, over many decades, cattle were brought into the enclosure and dispatched there, and weapons were ceremonially broken or bent, and tossed or laid into the pits and ditches.

Ribemont-sur-Ancre, a site 50 km from Gournay, shows evidence of somewhat different but related practices. At Ribemont, the focal point of the display was not weapons, but rather human long bones. Sometime in the latter half of the third century, a rectangular construction was fashioned out of human long bones. Other bones were deposited in other arrangements nearby. Some skeletons were laid out, without skulls, along with iron weapons.

Considerable thought has gone into reconstructing what happened at Ribemont. Brunaux and his colleagues have hypothesized that the performance consisted in the erection of a huge trophy display, made up of mounted beheaded corpses outfitted with their complete weaponry—sword, shield and lance. This performance, together with the several bone houses that have been uncovered, would have presented viewers with a visually shocking display of defeated enemies and their military equipment, set forth in a highly ritualized context within and just outside the enclosure. According to the excavators' analysis of the material, the performance of the arranging of the trophy took place in a relatively brief period of time around the middle of the third century BC, perhaps following a specific battle. In this regard, Brunaux points to similarities with the site of La Tène, where the weapons are also typologically quite homogeneous, and of roughly the same date. If the dating is correct, both sites would represent vivid displays of trophies and the sacrifice of weapons to celebrate military victories during the third century BC. Greek and Roman texts tell of Celts sacrificing their war booty to their gods. Archaeology and the texts may correspond unusually well in this case.

We can only imagine the impact of the performances at these two sites on the participants. Since in both cases (as at many other similar sites in France and neighboring regions) the performance area was open and exposed, there is every reason to think that the ceremonies were public and indeed that all members of the communities were encouraged to witness the events. The Ribemont display, with beheaded bodies fully outfitted with their weapons, may have made a much more powerful impression on viewers—it would surely have been remembered and described for generations afterward. The Gournay performances, on the other hand, were ongoing over an extended period, so that witnessing them may well have become a regular practice for the community.

Enclosure B at Braine "La Grange aux Moines," constructed around 125 BC, is quite different from Gournay and Ribemont. It measures about 110 by 70 meters, the enclosing ditch varying in width between 1.5 and 2.5 m. There is an entrance across the ditch on both the east and west sides, and near each entrance are concentrations of deposited objects.

The principal material deposited in the ditch was imported Roman amphorae, but a few other items were included as well, most notably animal bones. What is particularly striking at Braine is not the huge quantity of special material as at Gournay, but rather the clearly patterned arrangement of the materials deposited in the ditch. As the plan indicates, amphora sherds are scattered all along the ditch, with strong concentrations around the middle of the east and west sides, near the two entrances to the enclosure. The excavators noted a particular pattern in the distribution of materials in the ditch, with some areas of highly fragmented remains (amphora sherds, fragments of metal tools, and animal bones), and other areas where objects are less highly fragmented. Near one corner were several horse skulls placed at the midsection of a horse skeleton. Two deer skulls, with antlers, were positioned close to the entrance. Cattle skulls, and occasionally dog skulls and fragments of human skulls, were placed close to large stones. Several complete ceramic vessels were found near the entrance. Among the relatively small number of tools found in the ditch were those commonly placed in wealthy burials during the final century and a half BC—a cauldron, a pail, a grill, a large fork, and a knife.

At Hayling Island on the coast of southern Britain, some human bones were recovered, but no evidence was found of the kind of trophy proposed for Ribemont. Nor were Roman amphorae present. But a substantial quantity of material was deposited at the site, including coins, personal ornaments, weapons, horse and vehicle gear, belt-hooks, two "currency bars," and animal bones. The coins, bronze objects, and iron objects were all found concentrated inside the outer entrance, just south of the opening, though there was also a general, but much lighter, scatter of material across the site. The concentrations of different materials suggest the existence of some special platform on which objects were originally arranged for display.

EARTH, WATER, AND FIRE DEPOSITS

Significant numbers of objects were deposited in pits in the ground, in bodies of water, and in fires. These three media of deposition share with graves the removal of objects from the view of the living, unlike the open-air deposits, which seem to have been intended to create displays that might remain visible for extended periods of time.

Throughout the Bronze Age, objects were purposely buried in pits. Pottery vessels were often so deposited, sometimes complete sets of vessels (see Chapter 5). Bronze objects were also often buried, especially in the Early Bronze Age and the Urnfield Period, when the hoards could be large, containing tens of kilograms of metal.

Pit deposits are less common during the Early and Middle Iron Ages, but they become common once again during the Late Iron Age. Some pits contain quantities of iron tools, as at Kolín in the Czech Republic, Wauwiler Moos in Switzerland, and Kappel in Germany. Others contain weapons, as at Tintignac in France. Many pit deposits of gold have been found, some containing gold rings, as at Snettisham in southern Britain, and some contain both gold rings and gold coins, such as St. Louis in Switzerland and Niederzier in the Rhineland of Germany.

Objects were deposited in bodies of water as well, throughout the period of our concern. Metal objects are the most likely to survive immersion, as they did in large quantities at La Tène, but special conditions of preservation show that wood and other organic materials were deposited as well, as at Flag Fen in eastern England and Hjortspring in southern Denmark. Deposits of jewelry items became abundant during the Middle Iron Age, as for example at the source of the Douix in Châtillon-sur-Seine in eastern France and at Duchcov in the Czech Republic, both sites mentioned in Chapter 6. During the Late Iron Age, weapons and tools were often deposited in rivers, as at Kessel in the Netherlands and in the rivers Thames and Witham in Britain.

Fire deposits are a special feature of the Alpine regions, including the foothills of the mountains. They typically involve the burning and subsequent deposition of animal remains, jewelry, tools, and weapons. Among the best documented of fire deposits are those at Forggensee and the Auerberg, both in the Alpine foothills in Upper Bavaria, and at Wartau-Ochsenberg in Switzerland.

MARTIAL ACTIVITY

Before the Early Iron Age, our main source of information about martial activity is weapons in burials and deposits. In the Early Iron Age, representations begin to show weapons as objects in the hands or worn on the persons of individuals. Men on horseback on the Strettweg vehicle hold spears and shields in their hands and wear helmets, but they are depicted as if displaying their weapons and not actually engaged in combat with them. The scenes on the back of the Hochdorf couch show eight individuals holding swords and shields. Both of the figures on the two ends of the panel hold a sword extended outward, with a shield in the other hand. In the central part of the panel are three pairs of sword-bearers. Each of these six individuals holds a sword behind his head as if about to deliver a slashing blow forward. The Hirschlanden statue is shown with a dagger in his belt, and the one figure from the Vix enclosure has a short sword hanging from his belt as well. The Glauberg statue also has a short sword worn on the man's right side.

During the Middle Iron Age we find the first representations of actual martial activity, and now of groups of warriors in formation as well. They occur on vessels decorated in the Situla Art style and on the scabbard from Grave 994 at Hallstatt, an object that deserves our attention here.

Grave 994 at Hallstatt was excavated in 1875, and a sketch shows the layout of the burial. The skeletal remains of a man 1.71 meters tall were found, oriented east-west with his head to the west. Next to his right arm was an iron sword in a bronze scabbard. Other objects in the grave were an iron knife, two iron spear- or lanceheads, a bronze cup, and a bronze sieve. The objects in the grave suggest a date for the burial around 400 BC.

The scabbard bears highly complex visual themes (Figure 39). The figural scenes have attracted the most attention and comment, but they are far from being the entire visual program of the object. Particularly striking in my

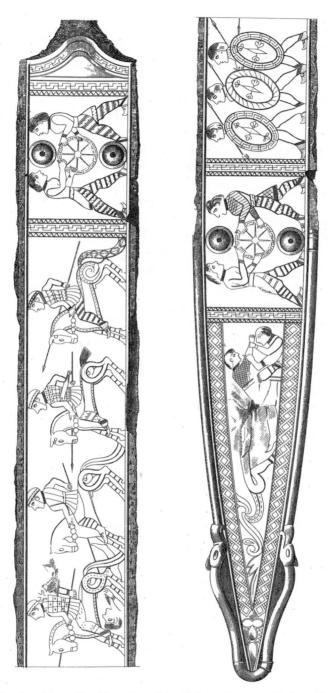

FigURE 39. Drawing of the scabbard from Grave 994 at Hallstatt, Upper Austria. From Lindenschmit 1891, pl. 9; the entire scabbard is shown in one piece in fig. 28, 7 (see page 118).

analysis are the many boundaries that catch the viewer's eye. The reason these are so important and striking is that they separate the figural scenes off from one another, in effect instructing the viewer to look at them as four distinct scenes and not a single one (such as the single scenes on such contemporary objects as the Stična belt-plates and the situla scenes). Moving downward from the top of the scabbard, we see a scene of two men holding a wheel. Next is the largest scene, with four horseback warriors and three marching infantry soldiers, all seven of them armed. Then comes a second scene of two men with a wheel. And finally two figures who seem to be wrestling.

The scenes are separated by complex borders that include in each case three separate vertical elements. These borders are important visual devices that force the viewer to look at the entire object in a particular way, as a series of separate, disconnected segments. At the top of the scabbard is a curving border of zigzag lines, a modified running dog pattern, and another tier of zigzag lines. Just under this is a straight border across the top of the scabbard, also composed of zigzag line, modified running dog, and zigzag line. This pattern combination recurs between the first two panels, between the second and third, and between the third and fourth. The basic function of separating the four panels could have been achieved with simple lines across the scabbard, but what the designer used was much more complicated. These broad, differentiated, internally patterned borders are objects of vision in their own rights, not just separators. They tell the viewer how to see this particular object, and also tell something about the nature of the world that the viewer inhabits—about how it is organized.

At the bottom of the scabbard, enclosing the two figures who seem to be wrestling, is a broad boundary band, as broad as the three-part bands separating the scenic panels, with a squared wave pattern in the center and dense hatching around it. This exceptionally broad and highly ornate border serves to highlight this scene, with its exceptional triangular shape. Also special about this scene is the substantial floral ornament at the tip of the triangle, different from anything else on the scabbard.

The visual aspects of the figures on the scabbard are significant. There are fourteen human figures, four horses, and part of some kind of creature—it is not clear what it is meant to be—in the middle of the triangular scene at the bottom end. None of the figures is represented by a simple outline. All show some degree of complexity in their detailing, with techniques that forcefully draw in the viewer and invite careful examination of what he or she is seeing. For example, on the legs of both figures in the right-most space, linear borders separate zones of smooth metal from those with stippling. In the largest space, three of the four riders wear what appears to be body armor, with stippling in boxed squares. All four horses have complex spiral ornament on their haunches, and three of them have stippled outlines around their bodies. All of the shoes shown are heavily stippled.

Finally, the end of the scabbard—the chape—is formed by what looks like a two-headed snake, its three-dimensional heads projecting beyond the edges of the scabbard.

The very orientation of the scenic representation on this object is important. The scene can only be viewed and comprehended if the scabbard is placed horizontally, not vertically as it would have been worn. This fact serves to emphasize the display aspect of swords and their scabbards. And this one is clearly an object of display, to be looked at, examined, and understood.

A striking feature of the Hallstatt scabbard and of the Situla Art of Kuffarn is the extent to which movement is represented in the narrative. On the Hallstatt scabbard, all fourteen distinctly represented figures are shown moving in some way.

Immediately eye-catching because they are the widest figures and occupy the widest space, and because there are four of them, are the horsemen. Although the horses' legs are not positioned in a way to indicate motion, their bodies look as though they are moving. And certainly the humans on the horses' backs look as though they are riding, not just sitting on standing animals. The way in which they grasp their spears in their right hands and the horses' halters in their left suggests that they are moving forward. Even the distinct spiral on the rear haunches of the back horse gives a feeling of motion. And the second rider is actively thrusting his spear downward and forward at the hapless victim lying on the ground beneath the first horse.

The three soldiers in the center are clearly marching along toward the left. Their legs make apparent that they are walking, but, as with the horses' legs and feet, the men's feet are not in natural walking positions—their shoes are flat against the ground, not bent with heel or toe touching the ground as we would see in a photograph of someone walking. This aspect of the object shows us that the creator of this narrative scene saw the world very differently from the way we see it. We would show horses in motion by showing their legs in different positions, and soldiers marching by indicating the bends in their feet.

In the Late Iron Age, weapons were often placed in burials, as well as deposited in open-air contexts, in pits, and in water, as noted above. On the Gundestrup Cauldron, made probably around 100 BC, we find a scene representing martial performance that is comparable to the scene on the Hallstatt scabbard (Figure 40). As on the Hallstatt scabbard, we find here both warriors on horseback and foot soldiers. The four on horseback all wear helmets, the front two with animal figurines on them, and two of the four carry lances. Six of the foot soldiers carry shields in their left hands and spears or lances in

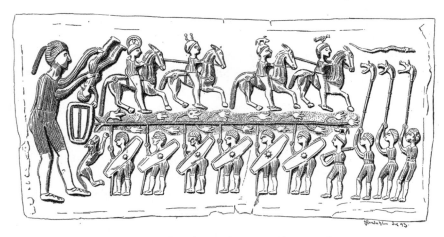

FIGURE 40. Drawing of inner plate E from the Gundestrup Cauldron, Gundestrup, Denmark. From
Steenstrup 1895, pl. 6.

their right, and with the spears they support a tree placed horizontally across
the middle of the plate forming a boundary between the two rows of troops,
cavalry above going toward the right, infantry below facing left. Behind the six
with shields and spears or lances is another figure with a helmet surmounted
by an animal, and behind him are three figures carrying and playing horns,
called "carnyxes," that are also represented in deposits such as that at Tintignac and on both Late Iron Age and Roman coins.

The position of the horses' legs is very different from that on the Hallstatt
scabbard. Here motion is indicated by bent forelegs. With the foot soldiers
it is not as clear, but the positions of some of the legs suggests that they are
marching along.

Also different visually from the Hallstatt scabbard is the lack of distinct
edges to this scene. There is no frame, aside from the limits of the silver plate.
The tree does function as a divider through the middle of the scene, and tall
verticals at either end—the giant figure on the left and the smaller figures with
their long carnyxes on the right—act as bordering devices on the two sides.

The two scenes can be contrasted from a number of viewpoints, both in
terms of their content—the differences between representations of martial activity around 400 BC and around 100 BC—and in terms of their techniques
of visual representation. My focus here will be on the representations alone,
leaving aside the matter of the different contexts—the scabbard on the one
hand and the large silver vessel on the other.

Overall, the content of the two scenes is similar, remarkably so given
that they represent military performances some three hundred years apart.
The most significant difference is the inclusion of the carnyx-blowers in the

Gundestrup scene, a category of participants that is not represented in the earlier context and indicates a more complex military organization at this later date. Both show foot soldiers armed with lances or spears and carrying shields, and troops mounted on horseback carrying lances and wearing helmets. In the Gundestrup scene, the foot soldiers wear some kind of head covering too, but it is not clear whether they are helmets, while those on the Hallstatt scabbard do not wear anything on their heads. Two of the cavalry helmets on the Gundestrup cauldron have animals as crests, and one of the marching soldiers does as well, while none of the Hallstatt helmets has a crest. The Hallstatt scene has no clearly represented additional group of military persons comparable to the three carynx-blowers on Gundestrup. Both scenes include other figures—the two pairs holding wheels and the "wrestlers" at the bottom of the Hallstatt scabbard, as well as the giant figure dipping the smaller one into a container on Gundestrup; in neither case is it apparent to us how these additional figures relate to the military scenes.

When it comes to the visual aspects of the two representations, the Gundestrup scene is considerably livelier. The horses are shown in motion. The pattern of cavalry riders going one way and marching troops going in the opposite direction gives the scene a visual tension that does not exist with the Hallstatt scene. Moreover, the giant figure on one side and the three figures-plus-tall-carnyxes on the other serve to create a much more complex composition than that on the Hallstatt scabbard, where every figure is tightly bound within the confining edges of the scabbard. Finally, the relief character of the Gundestrup figures gives them a three-dimensionality that is lacking in the incised figures on the Hallstatt scabbard and thus makes the scene livelier and more visually attractive.

CHAPTER 10

✧✧✧✧✧✧✧✧✧✧✧✧✧✧✧✧✧✧✧✧✧✧

NEW MEDIA IN THE LATE IRON AGE

Coins and Writing

NEW WIDESPREAD IMAGES

The development of coinage in temperate Europe and the first regular signs of writing are innovations that share some important features. Both were introduced from outside the region, specifically from the Mediterranean world, toward the end of the Middle Iron Age. Although both had existed in the Mediterranean world for centuries before their introduction and adoption in temperate Europe, both appear in temperate Europe at about the same time, during the third century BC and more abundantly during the second and first centuries. They were both adopted at a particular time in Europe's developmental trajectory, and under specific economic and political circumstances.

The coins produced in temperate Europe were initially modeled after Mediterranean prototypes. It has often been argued that coins were first introduced into temperate Europe by "Celtic" mercenaries, who are mentioned in a number of Mediterranean textual sources. They would have returned home carrying their pay in the form of the gold staters of Philip II of Macedon. This may well have been the case, but we need to think about the matter in much broader terms. The important issue is why communities in temperate Europe adopted this new medium when they did. There was plenty of opportunity to learn about coins during the fourth and third centuries BC. Along with returning mercenaries, merchants and other kinds of travelers are likely to have brought Greek coins into the heart of the continent, and coins may also have circulated from place to place as so much precious metal.

FIGURE 41. Gold coin from Crémieu, Isére, France. From Blanchet and Dieudonné 1912:25, fig. 21.

The early models for coinage in continental Europe seem on present evidence to have arrived in the east via the Danube valley from the Black Sea region, and in the west from Greek southern Gaul and up the Rhône valley and into Iberia. Some early European coinages, from early in the third century BC, followed the Mediterranean prototypes closely (Figure 41), but in the course of the third and second centuries BC, a wide variety of local designs and images developed. During the second and first centuries BC, Roman coinages served as models for silver and bronze coinages in Europe.

COINS

CONTEXTS

A great many Iron Age coins are recovered in deposits, which sometimes contain hundreds and even thousands of coins. Examples of recent discoveries are a deposit of 336 gold coins at Hohenfels in the Upper Palatinate of Bavaria, Germany, and another of 840 gold coins found near Wickham Market in Suffolk in southern Britain. The contents of coin deposits vary widely. Some contain all new coins of just a few issues, some combinations of new and used coins, and others consist entirely of used coins. Some hoards are all of one metal, some are mixed. A recent compilation of coinage data from Britain lists about 45,000 known Iron Age coins, a figure that gives some idea of the scale of finds. The number from the continent is much larger.

Coins are also found in settlement contexts, but in much smaller numbers than in hoards. In settlements of the Late La Tène Period, silver and bronze coins are often found scattered on the surface, suggesting that by the end of the second century BC, low-value coins were being regularly used, at least in the larger communities. But even smaller settlements, such as Berching-Pollanten in northern Bavaria, yield substantial numbers, indicating that coins were in use well beyond the major centers.

Coins also occur in graves, but only rarely, and then it is ordinarily only a single coin that is found, most often in a woman's grave. The earliest documented find comes from a well-outfitted woman's burial at Giengen in southwest Germany, dating to about 220 BC.

COINS AS VISUAL OBJECTS

European Iron Age coins are similar in basic appearance to our modern coins. They are round metal disks ranging in size from smaller than a modern dime to about the size of a quarter (some small fractional denominations were produced late in the sequence). Many, but by no means all, had an image of a head, usually in profile, on one side.

From a visual point of view, coins are disks that bear affordances. Coin blanks were cast in ceramic molds, then stamped with cut dies to give them their visual patterns. Some bronze coins were cast rather than struck. The unstruck disk, known as a flan, offered two flat, initially blank, circles with a surface area tightly circumscribed by the edge—the rim of the coin. The viewer's attention is riveted to what is inside that rim. From the perspective of the visual devices discussed in Chapter 2, a coin is a perfect attention-getting device.

COINS AS CHARMS

Metal disks of any kind were not common objects before the third century BC, so coins, which in their look and feel were so different from everything else that Iron Age Europeans saw and touched, must have presented a novel visual experience. Freshly minted coins, whether gold, silver, or bronze, were shiny and sparkled in the sun and in firelight. Gold coins remained forever untarnished. Even today, most of us feel a brief thrill when we receive a shiny new coin. When dumped together or carried in a purse or bag, coins jingled. They thus possessed many of the characteristics of charms—objects that by their appearance, feel, and acoustic properties delight the senses. Thanks to the aura that these properties conveyed, coins have played a special role in many contexts that have little to do with their role as currency. They were placed in the mouth of the dead in Roman burial practice, baked into cakes to bring luck to the person who got the piece with the coin in it, and for the past two thousand years we have been tossing them into wishing wells and fountains.

In addition to the special visual and tactile properties of coined disks of gold, silver, and bronze, Iron Age coins bore images.

IMAGES ON COINS

Images added to the charming and magical properties of coins. But more importantly, they made coins the first medium for the mass dissemination of images in temperate Europe. Before the expansion of coinage in the second century BC, images of any kind were relatively rare in most of the region, and, as we have seen in the preceding chapters, largely restricted to objects used by small groups of elites. On coins, images became abundant and widespread for the first time. The importance of this large-scale dissemination of images—"pictures"—should not be underestimated.

The majority of Iron Age coins bore images, in the sense of recognizable representations of things (Figure 42); but not all did. The styles and subject matter of this imagery varied with geography and over time. The most common image was that of a human head in profile on one side of the coin. Sometimes it was a naturalistic representation of a head, sometimes a highly abstract interpretation of the salient features, particularly the hair. The reverse side of the coin bore a variety of different kinds of images. Particularly common was that of a horse in profile, sometimes with a rider, sometimes not. As with the head, the style varied widely. Often other objects or shapes were represented underneath or around the horse. Some coins bore patterned designs on the reverse rather than a picture of anything identifiable. Some had on them the head of a bird.

CROSS-REFERENCING

The variety of objects of different kinds that are represented on coins makes them important vehicles of cross-referencing. Not surprisingly, these are objects of kinds that, as we know from other contexts (burials, deposits, and other representations), played special roles in the visual world of Late Iron Age Europe. Rings, especially neckrings, are often represented on coins, sometimes, but not always, around the necks of human figures (Figure 43). Fibulae are represented on some coins, and—as in other media—they are always represented open (see Chapter 6). They are shown at a size out of all proportion relative to horses and other objects that may appear on the same coin surface, suggesting that their visual importance in society was vastly out of proportion to their size. Swords are sometimes shown on coins, as are carnyxes (see Chapter 9). Roman amphorae are represented as well.

Coins were important media of inter-referencing as well, presenting visually a number of different kinds of objects that formed important components of the visual world of the Late Iron Age, and thus illustrating relationships

FIGURE 42. Bronze coin from the *oppidum* at Kelheim, Bavaria, Germany. Diameter 1.8 cm.

FIGURE 43. Silver-coated bronze coin from the *oppidum* at Kelheim, Bavaria, Germany. Diameter 1.4 cm.

between objects in the minds of the people who minted the coins. This particular kind of inter-referencing was new in the second century BC. I have argued above that in effect everything in material culture refers to other things that are part of the same cultural or visual system; that the color, texture, and decoration of Early Bronze Age storage jars reference the landscape, for example. But in the earlier periods, direct pictorial referencing is not common. The example of the head of the Late Bronze Age pin referencing a specific form of cup was mentioned above in Chapter 5.

In the Early Iron Age, visual referencing became more common. The Strettweg vehicle refers to warriors and their weapons, the Hochdorf couch-back to sword fighting and combat on wagons, Situla Art friezes and the Hallstatt 994 scabbard also refer to warriors and their weapons, and scenes in Situla Art not infrequently refer to feasting as well, and to the accouterments that accompany it—the vessels, furniture, and musical instruments, as well as supplies of food and drink brought for the occasion.

In contrast to these representations in which objects are shown being used by persons, coins in the final two centuries BC often refer to objects "out of context." Neckrings are sometimes sited on the neck of a person (Figure 43), but when fibulae are shown, they are not attached to a person or to anything else. What we see is simply the shape of the fibula, floating in the space of the coin surface. Swords on coins also typically occupy open space on the surface and are not associated with a human figure. Roman-style amphorae are similarly represented, not as part of a feasting scene (or a scene of trading or burial), but as separate, individual objects on the coin surface. These disembodied representations are indications of the importance of these objects. They convey meanings without the need for any obvious context to make their significance clear.

FIGURE 44. Gold coin of the CRICIRV type (see Allen 1972). From Blanchet and Dieudonné 1912:13, fig. 5.

Many coins bear writing. The early imitations of Greek coins have on them copies of the names on the prototypes, but later, on local coins, new names appear (Figure 44). In their wide-ranging study, Derek Allen and Daphne Nash note that some five to six hundred different names can be identified on Iron Age coins, and they argue that the majority of these are personal names (or fragments thereof). They suggest that the names are those of the individuals who certified the coins' value. The writing consists of either Greek or Latin letters, or, often, mixtures of the two. Allen and Nash interpret the prevalence of mixed inscriptions as evidence that even those with the power to commission and certify coinage had only a shaky command of of Greek and Roman writing.

The point that writing on coins was visually significant even when the issuers could not actually read is nicely illustrated by a series of Iron Age gold coins that derive from the gold stater of Philip II of Macedon. The initial copies reproduce the Greek letters of the name "Philip" accurately, but in later derivations what had been Greek letters become linear patterns with no recognizable textual meaning.

WRITING

The societies of Bronze and Iron Age Europe never developed a system of writing. They were exposed to the writing systems of the Mediterranean world, but before the start of the Roman Period, the only examples of writing known from temperate Europe are very short inscriptions, most often single names, occasionally a few words in Greek or Latin letters. Here our concern is primarily with the visual aspects of inscribed objects, not with the literary content of the writing.

INSCRIPTIONS

Although we have no real texts from Bronze Age or Iron Age Europe, a substantial number of inscriptions, generally no longer than a single name, exist. The largest context of such inscriptions is coin legends of the last two centuries BC, of which several thousand have been noted. But other inscriptions have also been identified, all in the writing systems of Mediterranean societies. (Some have suggested that the incised linear marks on the bases of some Late La Tène ceramic vessels, particularly the so-called "cooking pots" [*Kochtöpfe*] represent a form of writing, but attempts to derive any meaning from these marks have not yet been successful.)

A few examples will provide a sense of the character of the inscriptions from prehistoric Europe. A small carved amber object from Bernstorf near Freising in Bavaria, bearing incised letters in the Mycenaean alphabet known as Linear B, has received much attention. If the object is genuinely what it appears to be, it may date to the fourteenth century BC, the late Middle or early Late Bronze Age in the Central European chronology. However, the object was not recovered in a primary stratified context, and its authenticity has been challenged.

At the Early Iron Age settlement of Montmorot in eastern France, a pottery sherd has lines incised on it that have been interpreted as being related to Etruscan script. There are Greek letters incised on the neck of the Vix krater (about 530 BC) and on the bronze figurines that are attached to it, presumably as a guide for the assembling of the object. A coin from the Greek city of Massalia in southern Gaul dating to about 400 BC with the letters MA on it has been reported from Aubstadt in northern Bavaria. A glass bead from a grave at Münsingen in Switzerland dating to around 300 BC has Greek letters inscribed on it. A sword recovered at Port in Switzerland is stamped with the word KORISIOS on the top part of the blade. The letters are Greek, but the name is believed to be a local "Celtic" personal name. Two sherds of pottery from Manching have inscriptions incised into them, both in Greek letters. One is fragmentary, the other spells the name BOIOS. A neckring made of sheet gold from Mailly-le-Camp in Aube, France, has a series of inscriptions incised or hammered into the metal on the inside of the rings. Two of the bronze helmets from a deposit at Ženjak in Slovenia (commonly known by its German name Negau) dated to around 100 BC bear inscriptions in what is described as a "north Italian alphabet." The great majority of the coin legends also date to the end of the second and the first half of the first century BC. Finally, the presence of bronze frame pieces from Roman wooden wax writing tablets and bronze and iron *stili* of the kind used for writing on such tablets provide indirect evidence of writing at several *oppidum* sites, notably Stradonice and Manching.

As noted above, the inscriptions are generally very short, most often single words. Their purpose seems to have been to mark ownership in some sense, or to specify some kind of identity. (Since we do not know much about concepts of ownership in prehistoric Europe, nor about feelings of identity, we need to be cautious in making any assumptions about their purpose.) The words KORISIOS and BOIOS were probably, the linguists tell us, local individuals' names, but just what was being indicated by inscribing objects with these names is uncertain.

Significance

Even though we cannot be very specific about what these names meant at this stage in our understanding, we can appreciate the importance of this new medium, or new technology, for the visual world of late prehistoric Europe. Though writing was mainly restricted to single-word inscriptions, as it became more common from the second to the mid-first century BC, it began to supplant other visual media of communication, notably objects and the complex decoration with which they were sometimes adorned. In so doing, the use of writing gradually began to change people's social interactions with objects. As David Olson suggests, writing constitutes a fixed means of communication, whereas other, nontextual media, such as speech and the use of objects to communicate, are more fluid, flexible, and changeable. Once something is written, it is stated permanently, for anyone to consult and to read—at least until something causes the physical destruction of the text. Whether KORISIOS was the name of the blacksmith who made the sword or of the individual for whom it was crafted, the sword was for all time connected with that person's identity. Similarly the name BOIOS is permanent on the sherd from Manching, whatever it may have meant to the person who carved the letters.

But words spoken are ephemeral. It is impossible to go back and check what was said unless there is a written record, or in modern times a voice recording. And as with speech, objects can be rearranged and the meaning of an arrangement thus changed. (Though in a burial, once the grave is filled in, the arrangement of objects is for all practical purposes permanent.)

No doubt understanding of the Greek and Roman writing systems that are represented by the inscriptions in Iron Age Europe was limited to a small minority of people north of the Alps, possibly a handful of elite individuals who were in contact with members of Greek and Roman society, and perhaps merchants who interacted regularly with their Mediterranean-area counterparts. But as many ethnographic studies have shown, even if people are not themselves literate, they can appreciate the importance of writing as a powerful technology for conveying information between those who can read and write. Even nonliterate persons are directly and often strongly affected by the use of writing. When writing appears in highly visible places and in contexts associated with elites and power, its effects are especially significant. The addition of lettered legends to coins, linking them to individuals who controlled the coinage system and thus identified themselves with the new technology of communication, was thus a significant factor in the ongoing changes in the visual world of the final two centuries BC.

Greg Woolf has written of the "documentary mentality" that held sway in the Roman world by the time of the late Republic. From the middle of the second century BC on, Rome made increasing use of texts, especially for keeping records of various kinds. It is in this same period that we have increasing evidence for interaction between Rome and temperate Europe, in the form of a rapidly growing volume of Mediterranean products that were finding their way northward—wine amphorae, coins, medical instruments, and other materials. It is in this context of widespread economic change, and of the cultural changes that accompanied it, that we need to understand the increasing use of inscriptions in temperate Europe during the second and final centuries BC.

Burial practice offers an instructive example of the impact of writing on the conveyance of meanings. In the Roman world during the final two centuries BC, the preferred practice for elites was burial with few or no grave goods, but with funerary inscriptions—texts—engraved on stones set above the grave (Figure 45). These texts conveyed the information deemed important about the deceased. In prehistoric Europe, such information was carried instead by the objects placed in the grave and by the arrangement of those objects.

NEW PATTERNS OF COMMUNICATION AND PERCEPTION

The coins and writing that became important during the second and early first centuries BC were not only new technologies of communication, but also represented a change in something like the texture of communication. In terms of the degree of intimacy between these media and the people who used them, they were a far cry from the storage jars of the Early Bronze Age,

FIGURE 45. Inscribed Roman tombstone from Mainz, Germany. From Körber 1905:1.

marked with the potter's own fingertips, and from the jewelry of the Early La Tène Period, characterized by unique combinations of hybrid creatures and decorative S-curves. Coins and writing were part of the visual world of mass production: of wheelmade pottery, iron tools, fibulae, and other goods.

Coins by their very nature were mass-produced—a single pair of dies, or a coin mold, could produce thousands of nearly identical coins. The result was the bringing of images, and legends to Iron Age Europeans on a scale vastly greater than ever before.

The case of writing was similar. The Greek and Roman alphabet systems contained limited numbers of letters, and those letters appeared again and again on coins and on the other kinds of objects mentioned above. When letters were combined to form text, they created identifiers of a fixed nature.

The written name could not vary—if it was written according to the rules of spelling in the Greek or Roman writing system, it was inflexible.

Material culture as a system of conveying identity is different, and in some ways it is more like speech used for this purpose than it is like writing. The same immediacy that characterizes messages transmitted through speech can also be conveyed through arrangements of objects on a feast table, at a deposit, or in a funerary arrangement. Whereas texts are limited to the letters of the alphabet and the words that those letters can form, speech is open to an infinite range of variations through the impact of intonation and gesture on the understanding of words. Arrangements are similarly open to unlimited variation in the choice of objects, the physical character of those objects (size, color, texture, decoration), and the placement of those objects in relation to one another and in relation to the edges of the active space.

It might be argued that fashioning a pottery vessel of a particular size, shape, texture, and decoration is comparable to writing a text, because both are potentially fixed and permanent. But alphabetic writing is limited to the letters available in the alphabet, to the spelling rules for combining those letters into words, and to grammatical guidelines for connecting words into phrases and sentences. Fashioning pottery (or any other kind of object) is subject to no such restrictions (in theory at least—there may be cultural rules governing what is and is not permitted).

Another significant difference between writing and material culture lies in what is known as the "biography of objects." Once a text is written, whether it is a single word on an Iron Age coin or a decree written on parchment, that text is permanent, unless it is physically altered or destroyed. And if it is physically destroyed, it is obliterated—it cannot be turned into something else. But objects can be turned into something else, and when they are, that is part of their biography—the story of their continued use in different form. The frequency with which we encounter pottery that has been intentionally broken, swords and scabbards that were purposely bent or snapped in two, and objects of many types deliberately buried in the ground or deposited in water, makes clear that objects can go on "living" as other things. The sherds of the smashed vessel become part of the structure of a Middle Bronze Age grave chamber. The sword snapped in two becomes part of the display of objects arranged around a space in which ceremonies are carried out. Objects thrown into water play roles in meaningful performances.

Whereas writing specifies and fixes, material culture reminds and alludes. The name written on the KORISIOS sword or the names inscribed on coins say it all—the single word links, specifically and directly, the object with a person. But the decoration on the object is more subtle and nuanced. It is a reminder, a suggestion. The object can lead the person who views it to other memories and connections, in addition to the principal one intended by the maker.

A single word or name states a fact; the object or even the image of the object opens up a whole range of associations, as explored in this book. The fibula connects with the themes of garments, of the body, with status, identity, ritual, and surely with other meanings that remain as yet unknown to us.

CHAPTER 11

∞∞∞∞∞∞∞∞∞∞∞∞∞∞∞∞

CHANGING PATTERNS IN OBJECTS
AND IN PERCEPTION

In the preceding chapters, I have examined three categories of objects—pottery, fibulae, and swords with their scabbards—and two ways of manipulating objects—arrangements in graves and performances involving human bodily action with objects—over the two-thousand-year period from the Early Bronze Age to the end of the prehistoric Iron Age. My focus has been on visual aspects of objects, and my main subject the changes in their visual character over time.

My argument is that by examining these categories of objects and their use by early Europeans, we can discern something of how prehistoric Europeans "saw" in both the literal and metaphorical senses of that verb, how they perceived things visually, and how they understood their places in the world. My approach is different from that of most studies of Bronze and Iron Age Europe, in which investigators try to understand changes in terms of categories of organization and practice that correspond to those familiar to us from studies of the historical past and of the modern world (social structure, political organization, trade systems, and so forth). Instead I attempt to understand the world of the past in terms of how the people who lived in it viewed and understood it. The systematic analysis of visual structures and details points up how makers and arrangers in early Europe fashioned the material world and how the people who inhabited that world perceived objects visually.

The concepts outlined in Chapter 2—the visual world, ecological psychology, and extended mind theory—help to situate the objects of study in a theoretical framework. The visual world concept helps us to appreciate the coherence of the visual experience of any individual in the environment in which he or she lives. Ecological psychology teaches that everything in that environment contributes to the individual's perception and experience, that seeing needs to be considered as part of an experience that involves all of the senses, and that the individual does not just experience one thing in an environment—one object—but rather the totality of that environment. Extended mind theory emphasizes the importance of the object, or the arrangement of objects, as a device to think with as well as to see.

By focusing attention on a specific selection of visual features—including lines, edges, surfaces, and figures—it has been possible to compare and contrast visual aspects of objects and arrangements from different times during the two millennia under consideration. Gibson's idea of affordances, together with Bender and Marrinan's of white spaces, helps us to appreciate the importance of the parts of objects and arrangements that are not filled in but left open, on purpose. These can be as important to visual perception and response as the incised spirals, hybrid animals, and other visually more striking features.

The notion of the crafted object as a diagram is central to the entire discussion. Neidich argues that paintings are diagrams of the societies that produce them, and Bender and Marrinan show how the engravings in Diderot's *Encyclopédie* are diagrams of that cultural context, but the concept can be applied just as usefully to all crafted objects, designs, and images, as well as to arrangements of things. Every object shaped and decorated by human hands can be understood as representative of the society in which it was fashioned. Some, such as the paintings that Neidich has in mind, provide much more complex information than others, but the principle is valid for all objects, including handmade Bronze Age pottery and simple mass-produced Late Iron Age fibulae.

In this chapter, I synthesize the material laid out in Chapters 5 through 10. I draw attention to the consistency of the patterns in the visual character of material culture in each of the three main periods of time considered in this book, and to the character of the changes that took place in the fifth century BC and in the second century BC.

FROM THE EARLY BRONZE AGE TO THE EARLY IRON AGE

The first time period examined in this book is characterized by strongly geometric patterning in material culture, a characteristic that unites the developments of the millennium-and-a-half from the beginning of the Bronze Age to the Early Iron Age, 2000–500 BC. The use of straight lines and of geometric shapes, including squares, triangles, rhomboids, and circles, is the outstanding feature of the decorative patterns on the pottery, fibulae, and scabbards examined above, and also on other categories of material, most notably straight pins during the Bronze Age and belt plates during the Early Iron Age. This consistent use of geometric patterning applied to all categories of material culture indicates a particular way of seeing and of understanding the world.

Significant changes in visual aspects of material culture are also apparent during this fifteen-hundred-year period, and they reflect changes in ways of seeing and in attitudes toward the natural and social environments. Changes in the character of pottery are especially valuable as indicators of these changes. Throughout the Bronze Age, three categories of vessel dominate assemblages—jars, bowls, and cups. Jars are often large and bulbous in shape, with constricted necks, and they were commonly used to store grain and other foodstuffs, as finds at settlements demonstrate. They are ordinarily rough-textured, not polished, and often show sizeable pebbles in their fabric. Jar decoration includes a variety of motifs impressed into the clay by the potter's fingers or by other tools, and it commonly occurs both on the rim and on one or two raised bands around the top of the shoulder. I have argued that jars were fashioned in this way so as to refer to the fields on which the produce that was kept in the jars was grown. The tan to brown color and the deliberately rough texture of the exterior surface strongly evoke the appearance of the fields when ready for planting or freshly planted. These particular characteristics of jars change gradually during the Early Iron Age, indicating a decrease in the desire to reference the fields through the visual characteristics of this category of pottery.

In contrast to jars and cups, bowls are ordinarily undecorated during the Bronze Age. They are usually polished so that they have smooth surfaces both inside and outside, but are otherwise strikingly plain compared to the other two categories. In the Early Iron Age, however, some large bowls are highly decorated on the inside, the surface that is visible when the bowls are in use.

Cups show a distinctive pattern of change over the course of the Bronze Age. In the Early Bronze Age, they are larger than in the following periods, and they commonly have only one of two kinds of decoration—either a series of three or four sharply incised horizontal lines around the top of the shoulder or a single incised line at the top of the shoulder and incised and filled triangles dropping down from that line. In the Middle Bronze Age, cups are much more varied in character. Some have little or no ornament (sometimes a modest row of impressed dots around the vessel at the top of the shoulder), while others, much smaller than the cups of the Early Bronze Age, carry elaborate incised ornament. The decoration of each of these small cups is unique, in marked contrast to the two ornamental alternatives of the Early Bronze Age. In the Late Bronze Age, this trend toward individualizing decoration reaches its apogee in small, thin-walled, often highly ornate cups, each unique in its pattern of incised decoration.

In the Early Iron Age, a significant change takes place with the addition of patterns of zonal decoration. Jars of this period tend not to have the rough textures and relatively simple linear ornament of Bronze Age jars, but have instead incised geometric shapes on their bodies and shoulders. The same kinds of shapes now decorate both bowls and cups as well.

These changes in the ways that these features of pottery were fashioned can tell us important things about the visual world of the people of the time and about how they conceived their relationships with the world in which they lived and with the society of which they were part. The texturing of jars in the Bronze Age points to a special concern with the productive capabilities of the landscape. This characteristic of the jars is evident during the entirety of the Bronze Age, well over a millennium of time. In contrast, this aspect of jars gradually diminishes during the Early Iron Age, suggesting a shift in concern from relationships with the natural world and its productivity to relationships within the social sphere.

The patterning of cups during the Bronze Age and the decoration of all categories of vessels during the Early Iron Age reflect these social concerns. The change in the character of cups during the twelve hundred years of the Bronze Age is particularly significant. The limited decorative repertoire of the larger Early Bronze Age cups suggests that they were used communally (by members of a family perhaps) and that it was therefore not necessary to mark each in such a way as to designate association with a particular individual. Many families used cups with similar ornament. In the Middle Bronze Age we encounter the new individuality of the much smaller cups. Each is decorated differently from every other; this, and their size suggests individual rather than group, use. Then, in the Late Bronze Age, we again find highly decorated cups, each small and with its own individual patterning, representing specific individuals.

In the Early Iron Age, the growth in the use of zonal patterns of decoration indicates increasing concern with differentiation. The structure of the ornament on pottery of this period, similar to that on belt plates and other objects of the time, emphasizes separation and difference, themes that are not apparent in the material culture of the earlier stages of the Bronze Age.

The patterns of change in pottery, then, indicate a gradual shift of focus over some fifteen hundred years from concern with the natural environment, to concern with the social environment, reflecting a shift from a society in which members of communities were regarded first and foremost as members of groups, to one in which individual group members express their differences from others.

Changes in the visual patterns of fibulae and scabbards can be understood in a similar way. The earliest fibulae of the Bronze Age are geometric in form, with a parallel pin and thin bow, sometimes with flat circular forms extending from the head and foot ends. Late Bronze Age fibulae tend to be much thicker and to employ new shapes, such as semicircular bows and wire spirals. In the Early Iron Age two significant changes occur. One is the introduction of the S-curve, in the bow of serpentine fibulae and finally in the overall shape of the *Fusszier* and *Pauken* fibulae. The second change is the inlaying of materials, most often on the foot, a practice indicative of the same visual differentiation that we notice in the pottery. These changes in the fibulae can be understood as reflections of an increased emphasis on the differentiation of individuals. The use of a compelling visual device, the S-curve, enhanced the effectiveness of the fibulae in capturing the eye of the viewer.

The visual aspects of swords and scabbards, as well as of the Early Iron Age daggers and sheaths, show similar patterns. Scabbard and sheath decoration is consistently geometric throughout the period, with an emphasis on straight lines running the length of the surface. In the Late Bronze Age, the often highly ornate patterns of incised decoration on the hilts parallel the ornament on the fine cups of the same period and, like the cups, the decoration on each sword is different from that on any other sword. In the Early Iron Age, some swords are distinguished from the majority by special decoration on the handle or the pommel, sometimes of sheet-gold and ivory. In the latter part of the Early Iron Age, details of the handles and pommels often show a similar individualizing, sometimes with inlay as we have seen on some fibulae.

With respect to the arrangement of objects in graves and the manipulation of objects in performances, the evidence shows a gradual and steady increase in scale and complexity. In the early phases of the Bronze Age, graves tend to be simple, irregularly shaped pits in the ground, with few grave goods other than personal ornaments attached to the body and clothing of the deceased. In the Middle Bronze Age some chambers appear, with a small number of objects arranged in the open space between the body and the grave wall. In the later phases of the Bronze Age, chambers become more common, and the displays of objects more extensive. This process reaches it culmination in the Early Iron Age, with tens of objects, mostly ceramic vessels but also weapons and equipment associated with horses and wagons, arranged in the chambers, as at Hradenín, Grosseibstadt, Hochdorf, and Vix. In concert with the expansion of the burial space and the quantity of objects arranged on the floor is the increasing importance of feasting equipment in the graves. Sets of vessels, both ceramic and bronze, associated with feasting are first clearly identifiable in the Late Bronze Age, and by the time of the Grosseibstadt and Hochdorf burials, the feast is fully established as a performance to be represented in the grave by vessels appropriate to it.

Concurrent with pottery and fibulae that evoke differentiation; swords, scabbards, and daggers that, through the use of inlay and exotic materials signal the special status of the owners; and the use of extra space and greater numbers of objects—especially those associated with feasting performance, the graves also present us now with pictorial representations of performances of martial activity. Figures represented on the Strettweg vehicle and on the Hochdorf couch hold weapons, reflecting a new concern not just with displaying weapons as objects set in burials, but with showing them in action, in the hands of performers.

In summary, the gradual changes in visual patterns and representations during the Bronze Age and Early Iron Age show a shift from a primary concern with relationships with the land to a concern with relationships within social communities; an increase in complexity reflected in more differentiation in the decoration of pottery, fibulae, and swords and scabbards; and in greater burial spaces and more extensive arrangements of objects. By the end of this phase, more attention was being given to the social roles played by specific individuals, represented in the most richly outfitted burials, such as those at Hochdorf and Vix. Finally, the increased display of materials and products from distant sources, such as the amber, coral, and ivory used to decorate fibulae and sword handles, as well as the sets of imported vessels in the richer burials, point to the importance of growing contact with communities in other regions beyond temperate Europe.

THE MIDDLE IRON AGE

The key to understanding the changes in visual aspects of material culture during the fifth century BC is the increasing connectedness prehistoric Europeans were feeling with the larger world beyond the communities and regional groupings that had in previous times framed their lives. The new visual expressions of the fifth, fourth, and third centuries BC can be interpreted as expressions of these changing feelings about and perceptions of their relationships not just with the natural world or with the communities in which they lived and interacted daily, but with this larger world that was opening to them as a result both of travel experiences (by mercenaries, merchants, and diplomats) and the much more common experiences of new goods coming into their communities and into their consciousness. Chapter 12 develops this theme.

This new attitude constituted a repositioning of worldview and of the sense of self. Relations with the local elites were no longer so important, replaced by a sense of relationship to the larger world. One widespread sign of this new attitude was the prevalence of the attention-getting S-curve in both the shape of objects and the decoration on objects. Its use marks a departure from the geometric patterned ornament of the preceding period and an entrance into the new visual world of the next three centuries. Especially at the beginning of this process, the S-curve is important in drawing our attention to the fact that new kinds of relationships were taking precedence over old ones.

If we adopt this approach, there will be no need to posit the "revolution" or "overthrow" of the Hallstatt D elites that has been a research problem for so long. What happened in the fifth century BC was not a revolution but a change in perspective, in outlook, in worldview, and with it came changes in visual expression.

Nor does the old idea that the "Early La Tène Style," or "Early Celtic Art," developed because local craftworkers copied designs on Greek and Etruscan imports hold up to scrutiny of the accumulating evidence (for discussion of this issue, see Chapter 12).

Pottery of the fifth and following centuries BC was no longer decorated in the zonal fashion of the previous period. Most now had no decoration on the surface, but when there was decoration, it was with patterns in the new style, with incised S-curves and sometimes with representations of plants and animals. The shape of pottery vessels often incorporated the S-curve into their profiles, as is especially apparent in a new vessel type: a bottle with a lens-shaped lower portion and a long neck with a flaring rim. It is also notable on bowls and jars with sharply angled sides.

In this period, potters borrowed ideas about vessel shapes directly from imports. Particularly noteworthy are ceramic versions of the Etruscan bronze beak-spouted jugs (*Schnabelkannen*) that have been recovered at a number of different places in temperate Europe, including Mont Lassois in France and the Dürrnberg in Austria. Also significant are efforts to transform imported vessels by adding to them or reshaping them. Examples are the gold attachments added to the *kylikes* at Kleinaspergle and the reshaping of the Etruscan bronze jug from the grave at Schwarzenbach. All of these actions indicate that Europeans had adopted a different attitude toward the visual character-istics of Mediterranean imports from that of their predecessors. The Greek and Etruscan imports found in Early Iron Age contexts were unaltered—the Europeans who received, possessed, and used them were content to keep them as they were. But with all of the changes that marked the fifth century, in particular changes in Europeans' ways of conceptualizing their place in the world, a desire developed to alter imported items so as to transform them into objects visually consistent with Europeans' new ways of visualizing.

Fibulae are particularly noteworthy expressions of this new way of seeing. The S-curve is fundamental to the shape of fibulae from the fifth, fourth, and third centuries BC, and it is this shape, combined with the three-dimensional formlines, that makes the fibulae of these centuries so attractive. The hybrid creatures that appear now on fibulae, as well as spiral patterns and areas of hatching, are yet other visual devices to attract and hold attention.

Scabbards are decorated with the same kinds of motifs as fibulae: incised patterns based on S-curves, hybrid creatures, sometimes integrated into the S-curve pattern, and patterns of hatching and open spaces (affordances).

Grave arrangements are now much less spacious than those of the Early Iron Age, though a few of the richer burials of the fifth century BC still have chambers comparable to those of the preceding period (such as the burial at Vix in France around 480 BC and at Reinheim in Germany around 400 BC). By the fourth century BC, graves are ordinarily just big enough to accommodate a body and a small number of grave goods, if any. Women's graves are characterized by personal ornaments and sometimes contain a ceramic vessel as well. Some (but not the majority) of men's burials contain sets of iron weapons, and sometimes a vessel.

Whereas in the Early Iron Age, performances were organized around the funerary ceremonies associated with individuals, in the Middle Iron Age performances were situated in open spaces and not linked to particular persons. This change represents a shift away from performances highlighting individuals and their roles in communities and toward an emphasis on public participation in community rituals and a new awareness of landscape. The latter may be related to the growing self-awareness of European communities of their place in the larger world, an awareness that lends new importance to one's *own* space and landscape. Performances involving the display and deposition of objects customarily took place in settings of unusual natural character, such as the stone arch at Egesheim, the springs at the source of the Douix in France and Duchcov in the Czech Republic, and in spaces created specifically for the purpose, such as the enclosures at Gournay and Ribemont in France.

Performances of martial activity are represented as larger-scale and show a higher level of organization than was suggested by earlier examples. The scene on the scabbard from grave 994 at Hallstatt and those on several of the situlae show well-armed troops portrayed as members of organized military units. As their awareness of other parts of the world and of their place in it grew, Europeans became more involved and aware of systematic military activity, especially when some began serving as mercenaries in lands around the eastern Mediterranean.

In summary, the visual patterns of the Middle Iron Age suggest progressively less concern with the relationships of elite individuals to the communities in which they lived, and more concern with relationships to the larger world. The prevalence of S-curve motifs can be understood as a means to express this new sense of identity in relation to a larger social universe than that of the immediate community or even of the society. The appearance and proliferation of hybrid creatures in the ornament of the fifth century BC on fibulae and scabbards (as well as on other categories of personal ornamentation not discussed here) can be viewed both as means of attracting attention through their visual qualities, and also of fashioning new signs of community identity in the changing world. The shift of major performances from the graves of individuals, such as those at Hradenín, Hochdorf, and Vix, to open public spaces as at Gournay and Ribemont similarly reflects this change in perceived relationships from those of individuals within communities to those of communities with other communities in the larger universe.

THE LATE IRON AGE

The changes in ways of seeing after 200 BC are also best understood with reference to the increasing experience of belonging to a bigger world, but with a different focus. The new ways of perceiving of the Middle Iron Age relate primarily to the experience of a bigger world, of new ideas and new themes; those of the Late Iron Age relate primarily to commercial participation in that larger world. Feelings about belonging to the larger world are of course part of this, but in the Late Iron Age, much of what was perceived, understood, and felt about relationships was tied specifically to commerce and to the increased production and movement of goods that commerce entailed.

The visual world of the Late Iron Age was much affected by the technological and social fact of mass production, which was a direct result of participation in the expanding "world system" of Mediterranean, Asian, and African commerce (see Chapter 12). The potter's wheel came into general use during this time, and the majority of pottery, especially at large settlements, was made on the fast wheel. The dominant fibula types were designed to be mass-produced rather than individually crafted. And scabbards, as well as many other kinds of objects, were decorated much less elaborately than they had been in previous times. Every aspect of seeing and of design was affected by the increased efficiency of manufacturing and the changed character of objects that resulted.

The pottery assemblages of this period have four special characteristics that differentiate them from those of earlier periods. One is the fact of wheel manufacture, which resulted in both more standardized sizes and shapes, and in sharper profiles for many vessels. A second is the use of vertical line decoration, sometimes created by a comb, at other times by a stylus drawn down the side of an almost-dry vessel. The third is the development of thin-walled, beige colored, painted wares, the finest and most delicate of the categories of pottery. The fourth is a new shape, a cylindrical jar with a narrow base, a swelling central part, and a very wide mouth; it was an elegant form new to the pottery repertoire of temperate Europe.

Fibulae are much less ornate than in either of the previous periods, and they have for the most part lost the S-curve in their morphology. One distinctive aspect of some fibulae late in the sequence is the openwork treatment of the foot, which includes a small ornamental join across the center of the opening.

Scabbards rarely bear incised ornament over their entire surface, as some had in the Middle Iron Age, but instead often have distinctive ornament at the top. A new form of openwork decoration appears on the top parts of some scabbards at the very end of the Iron Age, in a technique similar to that used on contemporary fibulae.

Fundamental changes took place in practices involved in the disposal of the dead. The practice of burial, common from the Neolithic Period through the Middle Iron Age, now declined precipitously. Other ways of treating the bodies of the dead are apparent at some sites, such as Ribemont in France and Leonding in Austria. At Manching and many other settlements, including Knovíze in Bohemia and Basel-Gasfabrik in Switzerland, substantial human remains have been recovered from settlement surfaces and in pits, suggesting new kinds of rituals. A very small proportion of people were buried in chambers reminiscent of those of the Early Iron Age, and with substantial feasting materials, including now sometimes Roman wine amphorae, andirons, and grills.

Performances involving the manipulation of objects were again practiced in the outfitting of rich burials, as had been done at the end of the Early Iron Age. Some enclosures of the types constructed in the Middle Iron Age continued to be used for the display of objects through performances, but they tended to be smaller than those at Gournay and Ribemont. Well-documented sites of this period include Braine in France, Hayling Island in southern Britain, and Empel in the Netherlands. Performances that are not directly linked to graves take place in smaller, and perhaps much less public settings than had been the case in the Middle Iron Age, as for example the burial of gold and silver objects at Snettisham and St. Louis and related sites, and iron deposits at Kolín and Wauwiler Moos. Gabriele Kurz has noted, and mapped, a significant differential distribution of deposited materials from this period, with coin deposits more numerous west of the Rhine and iron deposits more numerous to the east. Martial performance is now well represented iconographically, as on the Gundestrup cauldron, and in special deposits, such as that at Tintignac.

Two new elements entered the visual world of late prehistoric Europe in the late fourth, third, and second centuries BC—coins and writing. Both were introduced from outside, from the Mediterranean world. While coins with writing on them had reached temperate Europe from Greece by the end of the fourth century BC, neither coinage nor writing became major factors in the northern visual world until the latter half of the second and the first centuries BC.

Coins became part of the visual world of mass-produced objects during the final two centuries BC, together with wheelmade pottery, serially manufactured fibulae, and all of the other kinds of objects that were made in series now, rather than individually crafted as they had been earlier. Coins are the archetypal mass-produced object—hundreds or thousands of nearly identical objects were stamped and cast. They fit smoothly into the trend toward mass production that was already under way, and they contributed to the rapidly expanding volume of mass-produced goods.

Writing was different. On the one hand, it was a new technology in temperate Europe—nothing like it had been practiced previously (though, as we have seen above, some earlier imported objects bore inscriptions). Minters of coins adopted writing insofar as they used Greek and Latin letters to inscribe their names on coin dies. It is thus apparent that they understood this new technology to some extent and appreciated its value for communicating the information that they wanted on their coins. Even the very limited dissemination of writing in this medium during the latter part of the second and the first centuries BC brought the new technology to the attention of a large proportion of Late Iron Age Europeans. No doubt this early familiarity with writing played an important part in the reception of Roman inscriptions after the conquests, even though the vast majority of Europeans could not read or write.

On the other hand, the letters that were struck onto coins and inscribed on other objects were new elements in the visual world *as* visual elements, quite aside from their meanings as texts. The importance of this aspect of writing is clear when we look at derivative versions of original Greek coins that turn what had been Greek letters into linear patterns that no longer form recognizable letters. Alphabetic writing as linear patterning played an important role in the developing visual world of the Late Iron Age.

CHANGING PERCEPTIONS AND INTERACTING WITH
THE LARGER WORLD

Changes in ways of visualizing things and corresponding changes in the design and arrangement of objects enable us to discern three fundamentally different worldviews and approaches to marking connections between people and the world in which they live. In my argument here, the two big shifts happened as a result of people experiencing new ways of understanding the larger world and participating in it. The first, beginning in the fifth century BC, was expressed in new shapes, motifs, and forms associated with the perception of the larger world and expressive of a connectedness to that larger world on the one hand and of feelings of one's own identity on the other. In the second shift, which took place in the second century BC, the change was primarily a response to joining into a much larger world-system of commerce that engulfed much of the eastern hemisphere during the final two centuries BC.

In both instances, new ways of looking at the world were expressed materially through new styles of material culture, which affected every aspect of people's lives, from the pottery vessels from which they ate and drank to the ways in which they used objects in the performance of ceremonies.

The changes that took place during the second and first centuries BC in a very real sense prepared the peoples of temperate Europe for the conquest by Rome of about half of the European continent. Without these changes the conquest would have been a much more disruptive series of events. As it was, much of temperate Europe was well along the way to acquiring a new, world-commercially based mode of visualization more than a century before Caesar led his legions into Gaul in 58 BC. And as a result, although the Romans introduced a sizeable number of changes—including a new political system, taxation, stone architecture, paved roads, and Mediterranean-type cities—a great deal of this change remained superficial. As I have shown elsewhere, much of the local cultural tradition persisted throughout the Roman presence. Even modes of visualization did not change completely with the Roman conquest, as the material culture of the so-called "Celtic Renaissance" makes plain (Chapter 13).

CHAPTER 12

∞∞∞∞∞∞∞∞∞∞∞∞∞∞∞∞∞∞∞∞

CONTACTS, COMMERCE, AND THE DYNAMICS OF NEW VISUAL PATTERNS

ATHENA IN BAVARIA

In 1994, archaeologists found a bronze statue of the goddess Athena in a pit at Dornach, a Late Iron Age settlement dating to around 70 BC, 10 km east of Munich. The figure, on a small cylindrical base of sheet bronze, stands 16.4 cm high. She is clothed in a wrap-around garment called a *chiton* and wears a Corinthian-style helmet with a plume on the top and with a horn on either side. In her right hand she holds a bowl, in her left a cylindrical box called a *pyxis*. Figures of gods and goddesses from the Mediterranean world are unusual in temperate Europe before the time of the Roman conquest (in 15 BC in this region). This little Athena was found in the second layer down from the top of the pit, about a meter below the modern ground surface. It had been deposited intentionally, in a layer of soil that also contained a number of other objects that mark the deposit as very different from typical settlement debris. A leg bone of a newborn calf had been placed in the pit, as had part of the pelvis of a bear. Sherds of pottery vessels were also present, but no entire vessels. All of the evidence suggests that the figure of Athena as well the other items had been deposited as specially selected objects in a ritual offering.

The most important thing about the Athena statue is that this Mediterranean object had been integrated into local practices. The character of the associated objects in the pit indicate that the inhabitants of the settlement were in a sense welcoming Athena into their own ways of doing things, depositing her along with objects that they had been offering for centuries. This is just one particularly instructive piece of evidence that illustrates the extent to which communities in temperate Europe were becoming increasingly integrated into the larger world of the Mediterranean basin and beyond, and an example as well of how the process of integration worked. The fruits of that process would significantly impact the modes of visualization of temperate Europeans.

EXPANDING HORIZONS AND CHANGES IN VISUALIZATION

The two major changes in the visual structure and patterning of objects that I have highlighted in the preceding chapters, one in the fifth century BC and the other in the second century BC, took place in the context of major changes in the relationship between societies in temperate Europe and societies elsewhere, specifically in the Mediterranean basin, in Asia, and in Africa. The changes emerged internally, from within the societies of temperate Europe. They were in no sense "caused by" outside societies, nor by trade relations with outside societies. Instead, they came about as responses on the part of individuals and communities in temperate Europe to ideas and opportunities that became available to them through the widespread expansion of interaction throughout the eastern hemisphere from the sixth century BC on.

The responses of Europeans in the two periods of change were different, and they happened under different historical circumstances. The changes in the visual character of fifth-century-BC objects resulted principally from the expanded dissemination of ideas, embodied in new objects, styles, motifs, and designs. The changes in the second century BC resulted mainly from the expansion of commerce—of trade in goods.

EXPANDING CONTACTS, NEW IDEAS, AND THE CREATION OF NEW VISUALITIES: FIFTH CENTURY BC

INTENSIFIED INTERACTIONS AND THEIR EFFECTS

The issue here recalls the perennial question that has dogged European archaeology since the early part of the twentieth century: How did the Early La Tène Style, or "Celtic Art," originate? Paul Jacobsthal laid the groundwork for possible answers to this question in his great work of 1944, *Early Celtic Art,* and many distinguished researchers have pursued the matter since. They include Otto-Herman Frey, J.V.S. Megaw, Frank Schwappach, Martin Guggisberg, Felix Müller, Dirk Krausse, and Rudolf Echt. The problem with their approaches, I am going to argue, is that they have conceived the question much too narrowly. In Jacobsthal's study, he mentions the possible importance of "influences" from other regions, but his focus, and that of his successors, is firmly on the Mediterranean world, in particular on Greece and Etruria. Most of the discussion about origins of the new style has focused on identifying motifs and elements in Greek and Etruscan art and connecting them with motifs in the Early La Tène style. Now that we possess a great deal more information about the archaeology of other regions of the world than was available to Jacobsthal, we can view the matter differently. But as my argument will show, what is critical is not only that we can see a wider diversity of possible "models" for the new style, but that we can also adopt a new approach to the question that will allow us to propose explanations for the emergence not only of a new style, but of a whole new way of seeing.

My argument is that the great change in the European mode of visualization came about as the result of the people in temperate Europe experiencing a range of new things, styles and motifs that derived not from Mediterranean societies alone, but from a much wider range of sources, and in the context of very specific historical circumstances. The exposure to new visual ideas alone would not be enough; only a specific set of cultural circumstances within which that exposure took place can account for the widespread adopting of new visual themes and motifs and the emergence of a whole new mode of visualization. I shall consider both of these matters in turn—first the direct evidence for exposure to new visual themes, and then the evidence for the particular circumstances in which these contacts took place.

It is now clear that changes in the style of ornament began well before the generally accepted starting date of "Early La Tène Art." For example, S-curves on the dagger sheath from Salem show that the motif was known well before the full development of the new style. And recently reported gold ornaments from the Heuneburg are decorated with curvilinear lines and dots in a pattern not unlike Early La Tène examples. Curvilinear lines occur in other contexts, too, in Late Hallstatt associations. Curving lines in the form of garlands are a regular feature of Early Iron Age decoration on pottery, and it can be argued that the garlands on the ornate cups of the Late Bronze Age are precursors to this practice of applying curvilinear ornament to objects. Furthermore, a whole series of settlements that show occupation associated with materials attributed to both Late Hallstatt and Early La Tène have been reported from France and Germany, at Charmay "Le Haut des Marquettes," Allaines Mervilliers, Remseck-Neckargröningen, and Erdwerk I at Niedererlbach, to name just four examples.

In an elegant passage, Andrew Sherratt argues that the impact of long-distance contacts was critical for human societies, suggesting that everyone involved was affected. Most directly relevant to our discussion here is his sentence: "The experience of contacts with a wider world was an integral part of the developmental history of all societies and civilizations, as communities defined their identity by reference to a widening circle of neighbors." While there is evidence that manufactured goods from other regions of the world reached temperate Europe earlier, the quantity of crafted objects fashioned in other regions became much larger from the middle of the sixth century BC on. Examples from around that time include the Grächwil hydria and the Kappel jug, both bronze vessels from the Greek world made before the mid-sixth century BC. Made later in that century and also from the Greek world were the Hochdorf cauldron, the bronze tripod and the ivory and amber decorated couch from Grafenbühl, and the Vix krater. Attic pottery and western Greek transport amphorae dating to between 520 and 480 BC are well represented at a number of sites throughout the central and western regions of temperate Europe. During the fifth century BC, Etruscan bronze vessels arrived in substantial numbers, including bronze basins and, especially, beaked jugs (*Schnabelkannen*), and a number of Etruscan bronze figurines have been reported from different places as well. These imports have been familiar in the archaeological literature since the middle of the twentieth century, but the quantities of such finds and the number of sites at which they are represented have grown substantially in the past two decades.

Equally important are objects from other regions of the world. A whole series of sword hilts, including several from Hallstatt in Austria and specimens from Deisslingen and Kinding in southern Germany, dating from the seventh and sixth centuries BC, are crafted of elephant ivory, indicating a source connection with the Near East or Africa. A small bronze situla made in Syria was found in a fifth-century-BC grave at Straubing. Silk textiles, perhaps from the Mediterranean region, perhaps from further east, have been reported in graves of the late sixth and fifth centuries BC.

From the evidence currently available, it is apparent that surviving imports from the Mediterranean region are much more numerous than those from other, more distant, regions. But the fact that the majority of foreign objects in sixth- and fifth-century-BC contexts were Mediterranean in origin does not mean that those objects and the societies that produced them were necessarily the only or even the primary sources of the new visual themes and ideas. In fact, I argue here that in the past, researchers have been misled by the quantities of Greek and Etruscan imports and the similarities of style and motif exhibited by some European and Mediterranean products into drawing a causal connection. Large number of imports + some similarity in motif and style = source of influence, motifs, inspiration. This approach takes a much too narrow view. If we look at the larger world of the sixth and fifth centuries BC throughout Eurasia and Africa, we can understand the motifs and styles apparent in the products of both Mediterranean and European crafts-workers as resulting from a common pool of shared ideas and themes that were circulating throughout Eurasia. Taking this broader view also helps us to understand why and how the new types of design and ways of seeing developed in temperate Europe at just this time.

At the time when the new style developed in Europe, during the fifth century BC, curvilinear patterns—S-curves, spirals, formlines, and stylized, sometimes hybrid animals—can be found across much of temperate Eurasia. They are by no means limited to the Mediterranean basin and Europe. A few examples selected from a wide range of available objects will serve to make the point. A bronze belt buckle from Aul Tseia in the Causasus, dated between the seventh and fifth centuries BC, is decorated with an animal composed of S-curves, spirals, and formlines. A gold pectoral from Arzan in Tuva, southern Siberia, dated to the seventh century BC, is decorated with spirals and formlines. At Vani in the Republic of Georgia, mid-fifth-century-BC gold ornaments bear floral motifs, especially palmettes and blossoms, very like those that are found in Early La Tène art of the Rhineland. Other gold ornaments from the site bear striking resemblances in form and technique to gold jewelry from Grave 1 at the Glauberg. As far away as China, bronze figurines strikingly similar to those in temperate Europe occur on bronze vessels, as for example on a vessel from Nanshangen, Ningcheng that dates to the eighth or seventh century BC. A gold tiger fitting from Weijiaya, Chencang District, Baoji City, dating to the Warring States Period (475–221 BC), has decorative spirals on its haunches very much like many of the animals found in Early La Tène contexts—the dogs on the rim of the Basse-Yutz flagons and the hybrid creature on the lid of the jug in Grave 2 at the Glauberg, for example. In the region of Xinjiang in western China, ornamental objects from a number of sites bear spirals and S-curves very like those on Early La Tène figurines in Europe. A wooden box from a grave at Zagunluk dating to the eighth century BC has on its side a relief carving of a wolf with spirals on its haunches remarkably like those on figurines from Basse-Yutz and the Glauberg. Several sheet-gold objects from grave 30 at Alagou dating to the fifth or fourth century BC show similar spirals on the bodies of animals, in this case animals identified as tigers. From the same grave is a sheet-gold representation of a lion, the entire figure in the shape of an S-curve.

Gold bracelets from Pasargadae in Iran show S-curves and spirals, while gold bracelets in the Oxus Treasure show both high relief and hybrid animal forms reminiscent of those on Early La Tène gold rings.

Animal figurines that bear similarities to sixth- and early fifth-century examples from temperate Europe include a bronze horse from Gordion in Turkey, a bronze horse-and-rider figure from the northern Caucasus dating between the ninth and seventh centuries BC, and stags dating to the sixth or fifth centuries BC from Inner Mongolia (China) and from Mongolia. These are just a small number of examples to illustrate the point that bronze figurines of animals very similar in basic character to those of temperate Europe were made and used at the same time in many different regions of Eurasia, always with local variations in specific visual features.

Humans and animals represented in horizontal rows in friezes, as in the Situla Art of the eastern and southeastern Alpine region of Europe and on the scabbard from Grave 994 at Hallstatt, occur in remarkably similar form in Georgia in the Caucasus. Correspondences in detail are striking, with horseback riders, stags, birds, and hunters represented in both sets.

Another strong indicator of contact and interactions across Eurasia during the Early Iron Age is the distribution of bronze mirrors. They become common in burial contexts, as at Reinheim and Hochheim, at about the same date—the fifth century BC—as temperate European modes of visualization underwent the many changes that we have outlined. And it was at approximately this same time that mirrors came into fashion in the Scythian regions of Eastern Europe and Western Asia, and further east in China and all the way to Japan.

I am not suggesting a direct connection between any of these individual objects from Asia and those of Early La Tène Europe. But the similarities in style, motif, and execution are striking, as is the fact that the practice of making and using mirrors began in so many far-flung areas within the same period. Since these developments are all roughly contemporaneous, it is fair to say that a whole package of interrelated decorative elements was shared across Eurasia during the fifth century BC, from Iberia in the west to China in the east.

Rather than seeing Greek and Etruscan arts as the sources for the new elements and combinations in temperate Europe, we should consider Greece and Italy as regions that shared in a much larger, pan-Eurasian development of motifs, styles, and decorative elements during this time, with communities in some regions emphasizing certain features of the package, while other communities emphasized others.

The model that derives "Early Celtic Art" from Greek and Etruscan sources (with possible influences from Scythian and Persian regions) belongs to an earlier era in research history, before investigators appreciated the extent of contacts, interactions, and influences over great distances that already existed by the Bronze Age. Now that archaeologists have investigated regions of Western and Central Asia much more extensively than before, and now that results of excavations in China and neighboring regions are becoming more available in the West, is it becoming ever clearer that there were long-distance contacts across Eurasia from at least the beginning of the Bronze Age, and also that these contacts had very real effects in introducing peoples all along the routes to new visual styles, motifs, and ideas. Sometimes people responded to the new ideas, sometimes they did not. The outcome of experiences with new themes and ideas depended upon specific circumstances at any given time.

In past discussions, the question of the origins of the Early La Tène style has been seen as related to the material culture of the elites within European society. Many of the most striking objects in the new style were of gold and were recovered in richly equipped burials, as at Reinheim, the Glauberg, and Weiskirchen. Thus, much of the discussion has revolved around the notion that the elites were commissioning items in the new style in the context of social competition and other elite concerns.

This viewpoint also requires rethinking. As more of the imported items are being recovered archaeologically, an ever-larger proportion of them are seen to derive from non-elite contexts—from what appear to be typical settlements and not-particularly-rich burials. It seems that early objects in the new style were much more widely distributed across society than was at first believed. As there is a trend today to see burials as community representations rather than as statements about the deceased, objects such as the ornate gold-ring jewelry and fibulae from these burials are increasingly being understood as belonging to community groups rather than to individuals. With this shift in our orientation, it becomes much easier to understand the new style as one part of a large-scale change in ways of seeing than as the prerogative of a narrow elite.

THE LARGER CONTEXT OF INTERACTION

Results of recent research show that interaction between peoples across sometimes great distances was much more extensive in the past than most interpretations have suggested. During the Bronze Age, there is evidence of contacts between the central regions of Europe and the eastern Mediterranean, as well as between communities of western and eastern Asia. Throughout the Early Iron Age, from the eighth century to the fifth century BC, raw materials such as elephant ivory and coral, as well as finished goods including silk, textile dyes, Greek bronze vessels, and Etruscan figurines attest to goods reaching temperate Europe from distant lands.

For the latter part of the Early Iron Age and from the Middle Iron Age, a variety of different mechanisms are likely to have been involved in these interactions, which brought with them not only goods but also ideas from other regions. Trade, in the sense of an exchange of goods, was surely involved. From Greek texts, we learn of the need in Greek cities for a wide range of things that were available in or via temperate Europe, including furs, pitch and tar, honey, timber, amber from the Baltic Sea shores, and perhaps grain, preserved meat, metals, and other substances as well. Diplomatic relations between elites in temperate Europe and societies of the Mediterranean basin also played a part. The Vix krater most likely arrived as a diplomatic gift of some kind, as the nature of the object and a passage in Herodotus suggest. Other unusual imports, such as the cauldron in the Hochdorf grave and the furniture in the Grafenbühl burial, are also likely to have changed hands in the context of political relationships.

Especially during the latter part of the fifth and start of the fourth century BC, movements of peoples brought Europeans into contact with others. The evidence, both textual and archaeological, for the migration of peoples from temperate Europe into Italy, Greece, and Asia Minor during the fourth century BC is the subject of much debate, but whether we understand the evidence as indicating large-scale migrations of populations or movements of small bands of people, these movements in any case involved interaction between peoples who had inhabited different parts of Europe and Western Asia. David Anthony has shown that migratory movements are ordinarily accompanied by return migrations, as people very often move back to the place from which they originally came. The archaeological evidence in Italy during the fourth and third centuries BC indicates that groups in northern Italy maintained regular relations with regions north of the Alps in eastern France and Germany.

The service of mercenaries from temperate Europe in armies in Greece and other lands of the eastern Mediterranean is well documented in Greek textual sources during the fourth and third centuries BC. Archaeological evidence seems to support the textual sources to some extent, but it is more complex and ambiguous.

Thus from the sixth through the third century BC, a series of mechanisms were in operation that brought together people from temperate Europe and the Mediterranean basin. Whether Europeans went farther east and south is not clear from the available evidence. Elephant ivory and silk may well have come into Europe via trade centers in the Mediterranean, but there is no reason why Europeans could not have reached Africa and Central, Southern, and Eastern Asia. In any case, it is clear from the evidence in Europe during the fifth and succeeding centuries that Europeans were open to new materials, objects, and visual designs coming from distant lands.

Creating a New Mode of Visualization

Given that Europeans, as well as peoples in many parts of Asia, experienced a great widening of interactions with other regions during the sixth and fifth centuries BC that exposed many of them to new sights and ideas, we might ask what it was that made them internalize those experiences in such a way that a whole new style of ornament, and way of looking at the world, emerged. I want to suggest three main ways of approaching this question.

First, the adoption and intensive application of S-curves, spirals, and animal ornament was a way of expressing, through material culture, new feelings of cosmopolitanism, of belonging to a larger world of which Europeans were becoming increasingly aware through the mechanisms discussed above. By adopting and integrating into their own pottery, fibulae, scabbards, and other objects motifs that were common in parts of the Mediterranean basin, Western Asia, and elsewhere in the wider world, they could feel that they belonged to this vast commonality. This feeling may explain why we find floral ornamental motifs over such great expanses of space—from central France to the Caucasus, for example.

Second, while borrowing design elements and ideas from beyond their own regions, they at the same time transformed them and made them distinctively European. Though S-curves and spirals were shared by peoples from Iran to western France, the peoples of each region used them somewhat differently. This part of my argument does not contradict the first, though it may seem to. On the one hand, Europeans wanted to share in the larger style; but at the same time, they wanted also to mark themselves as distinct. To this end, they applied the style in a manner uniquely characteristic of their part in the world. The addition of the gold foil palmettes to the Kleinaspergle cups is a striking example of this process. We should also note that none of the other design traditions that shared the S-curve, the spiral, the floral ornament, or the animal style created hybrid animals in the way that the peoples of temperate Europe did. That was a distinctive visual feature of the region.

Third, the phatic character of much of Early La Tène ornament is one of its most distinctive features. As I have argued above, much of the design of fifth-century-BC fibulae, rings, scabbards, and other objects was executed in such a way as to attract notice, much more so than objects made earlier or later. Craftsworkers motivated by this goal incorporated in their work many of the attention-catching devices described in Chapter 2. We need to explain why it should have been so important at this particular time to create objects whose first purpose was to demand attention.

The answer lies in the particular historical situation of the time. The broadening horizons of Europeans, elite and otherwise, during the late sixth and fifth centuries BC created a frame of mind different from those of earlier times. With the possibilities opened up by migrations and other kinds of travel, both regional and long-distance, social and political structures in temperate Europe became less rigid, more open to change. In this dynamic context, new elites could emerge through competition for influence and power. The new styles of decoration that were applied to fibulae, scabbards, and other objects worn by individuals were designed in large part to serve in this competition, by exploiting the attention-getting devices discussed above in Chapter 2.

The extensive new use of animal subjects, both in three dimensions on fibulae and rings and in two dimensions on pottery and, especially, on scabbards, can be also understood in this context of rivalry. Lotte Hedeager has argued that the animal representations on early medieval fibulae were symbols or totems of specific groups competing for prominence in the power vacuum left by the collapse of the Roman Empire. I would suggest that in our earlier context of Middle Iron Age temperate Europe, the animals, including hybrids, served a similar symbolic function in the contention for authority in a newly expanding world. They may well have represented creatures from myth and thus have religious significance as well, as Mircea Eliade might argue. But it is no accident that the hybrid animals had a short span of use, usually no more than two or three generations. Their limited currency supports the idea that they were created for a specific historical purpose.

EUROPE IN THE COMMERCIAL AND CONSUMPTION REVOLUTION OF THE SECOND CENTURY BC

THE INCREASING CONSUMPTION OF IMPORTED COMMODITIES

The situation of the Dornach Athena, placed in the pit with other apparent offerings, gives it a special resonance—it is not just an interesting foreign object, but an accepted and fully integrated element in the performance of local ritual, not a foreign intruder to be looked upon as exotic and (possibly) melted down. The style of the figurine certainly must have had visual impact on the people who handled and deposited it. But more important than this one striking object are the thousands of others that were transported from the shores of the Mediterranean Sea and beyond into temperate Europe during these two centuries.

Most abundant are ceramic amphorae that the societies of the Mediterranean world used as containers in which to transport wine, olive oil, and *garum*. The sixth- and fifth-century-BC trade in wine from the Mediterranean to the regions north of the Alps has already been mentioned (Chapter 5). The evidence of the ceramic amphorae indicates that this trade grew vastly larger in scale during the second and first centuries BC. Now it was not only the wine that was valued, but amphorae themselves, as visual objects, played special roles.

Matthieu Poux's distribution map of Roman amphorae in Gaul provides a striking view into the huge quantities of these vessels that were transported into the interior of Gaul and ended up in different kinds of deposits during the second and first centuries BC. As we have seen in Chapter 5, Roman amphorae were visually very different from any objects that had circulated previously in temperate Europe. They are taller than most ceramic vessels of the region, and, as Poux has argued, they can be viewed as approximating the shape of a person, with narrow base, a broad "waist," shoulders, handles as "arms," and the rim as the "head."

The ways that communities used these imported vessels tells us that they were much more important to them than simple containers. Poux shows that amphorae were carefully set into the enclosing ditches of many "sanctuary" sites of this period, in quantities and arrangements that seem very much to have been intentional, meant to be seen by people participating in activities in the enclosed spaces. Among the sites at which people arranged amphorae in ways to be visible to those within the enclosures are the French sites of Ribemont-sur-Ancre, Braine, Balloy, Fontenay-le-Comte, Corent, and Cleppé. While this practice is especially well documented in France, similar depositions of amphorae are known elsewhere as well, for example at the *Viereckschanze* at Nordheim in southwest Germany.

Some performances involving these imported objects were more complex than the simple business of arranging them in the frame of enclosures. Poux documents also the practice of "killing" amphorae—chopping off their "heads" with swords and depositing the parts.

Finally, Roman amphorae were frequently placed in wealthy burials of the final two centuries BC. If we think about this from the perspective of our lives in the twenty-first century, it seems strange. In the Roman world, ceramic amphorae were utilitarian transport containers—cheap vessels for shipping wine, olive oil, fish sauce, and other commodities. It would seem peculiar to us to place a cardboard box or an olive oil tin in a burial. The fact that amphorae were set into burials indicates that they had other, less pedestrian meanings for the people of temperate Europe. We find amphorae prominently arranged, often set against the wall of the burial chamber, as at Boiroux (Figure 11) and Fléré la-Rivière in France, at Clemency in Luxembourg, and at Welwyn Garden City north of London in Britain (Figure 36), for example.

All of these uses and practices indicate that imported ceramic amphorae had a significant visual presence in the second and first centuries BC. Not only was their size and shape different from all forms of local pottery, but their finish—their color and texture—also distinguished them. The shapes, colors, and textures of some local Late La Tène pottery is likely to have been influenced by the character of the Roman wine amphorae. Elegant tulip-shaped vessels with wide open mouths and gently curving sides are very similar in form to amphorae with their necks broken off (which were often put to use in that very state), and the formal similarity suggests that local potters borrowed the idea of the form from such altered amphorae. Some of the pottery in graves dating to the final century BC is of the same color as the Roman amphorae and has a similar surface finish. A connection seems likely, but more research will be required to confirm that the high value accorded imported amphorae stimulated local potters to borrow some of the features of those amphorae and incorporate them into their own wares.

Other objects from the Mediterranean world, and especially from Roman Italy, are also regularly recovered from settlement sites and from graves and other deposits. While not as abundant as the amphorae, they attest to the broadly based interactions that brought goods, and ideas, from the shores of the Mediterranean to communities in Late Iron Age Europe. Among the major categories are bronze jugs and pans, Campanian pottery, glass vessels, coins, fibulae, writing equipment, and medical tools. As noted above in regard to the Dornach Athena and Roman amphorae, imported objects were used, or consumed, in ways that integrated them into local beliefs and practices.

THE COMMERCIAL REVOLUTION OF THE SECOND CENTURY BC

In the preceding chapters, I have drawn attention to second-century-BC changes in the visual characteristics of pottery, fibulae, scabbards, and other objects. These changes were contemporaneous with other major transformations that affected the visual world of Europeans, including the establishment of the *oppida* with their enormous walls and relatively dense concentrations of population, the decline in the practice of subsurface burial, and the adoption of the new mass technologies for the production of pottery, ornaments, and iron tools. All of these changes north of the Alps happened in concert with the commercial expansion of Rome and other centers during the second century BC (Figure 46).

Trade both within and beyond the Roman world expanded rapidly during the second century BC, with its direct effects being felt north of the Alps and elsewhere. The large-scale production in Italy of wine for export was a phenomenon of this century, made visible to us in the form of the ceramic amphorae found throughout temperate Europe and elsewhere. Rome's political and military presence in southern Gaul expanded as well, resulting in a much strengthened Roman presence in this region, with major impact northward in the form of trade and the dissemination of the practices of writing and coinage.

Figure 46. Map showing some of the commercial centers of the second and first centuries BC in Eurasia and Africa, and sites near the Black Sea mentioned in the text.

As Steven Sidebotham points out, it has long been customary in studies of economies of this period to view the Mediterranean region as the dominant center. One consequence has been the tendency for European archaeologists to examine Late La Tène developments in terms of interactions with the Roman world, without looking further afield at the larger picture. As the results of recent archaeological studies in Africa and in Central, South, and East Asia are published, it is becoming increasingly clear that Rome and the Mediterranean basin were only parts of much larger systems of commerce that were expanding at this time.

At the end of the second century BC, Polybius (*Histories* I.3) wrote: "Previously, the doing of the world had been, so to say, dispersed, as they were held together by no unity of initiative, results, or locality; but ever since this date history has been an organic whole, and the affairs of Italy and Libya have been interlinked with those of Greece and Asia, all leading up to one end." The archaeological evidence, as well as the historical records of the great empires from the Roman Empire in the west to Han China in the east, attest to this interconnectedness.

Excavations carried out in 1978 at Tillya-Tepe in Bactria (now northern Afghanistan), uncovered six richly outfitted burials. Among the thousands of objects in the graves were a gold coin of the Roman Emperor Tiberius, minted at Lyon, a gold coin of the Parthian king Mithradates the Second, a coin and an ivory comb from India, two bronze mirrors from China, gold clasps that show Greek and Central Asian features, gold plaques of a style deriving from Scythian and Sarmatian traditions, and two glass vessels from the Mediterranean world. The graves date to the years just before and after the birth of Christ. A similarly rich assemblage of objects from diverse places of origin was recovered in two sealed rooms at the site of Begram, also in Afghanistan. This find has been interpreted as either a stored treasure or a warehouse full of luxury trade goods, including objects from China, India, and the Roman world, as well as items from the surrounding region, most dating to around the middle of the first century AD. The extraordinary diversity of origins represented at these two sites attests to widespread and very active contacts across Eurasia.

Christopher Ehret speaks of a "Commercial Revolution" during the first millennium BC that affected much of Africa and Eurasia. He argues that during this millennium, a major change took place in the organization of long-distance trade in the Mediterranean region, the Near East, and Africa. The dynamic moved from systems that revolved around the desires of kings and other potentates for luxury goods to a merchant-based system in which individual merchants were concerned with maximizing their profits rather than serving a king. W. V. Harris supports this idea by noting that names identified on objects in ships' cargoes of the time are those of individual merchants, not of government officials. This change, Ehret argues, led to expansion of commercial systems, greater competition between merchants, and the development of urban centers, the primary purpose of which was to foster trade.

In his study of the trade port of Berenike on the Red Sea, Sidebotham identifies five different commercial networks along which goods circulated in the latter part of the first millennium BC. One was from China overland across Central Asia to the Mediterranean. Lothar von Falkenhausen refers to this system as the "Silk Routes," emphasizing the complexity and variability of the specific tracks that different caravans followed at different times. A second linked ports in both the Persian Gulf region and on the coast of the eastern Mediterranean Sea with the southern part of Arabia. A third was a sea route from South and East Asia to Arabia and Africa. A fourth route ran between sub-Saharan Africa in the south to the Mediterranean Sea in the north. And a fifth was the "Amber Route" across temperate Europe to the shores of the Baltic Sea. When we think about these different systems and look at the publications coming out with new data from the many different regions along these routes, we get a very different perspective on Roman trade in the Mediterranean.

Direct archaeological evidence for these far-flung commercial connections consists in Roman imports found in graves at Meroë in Sudan (ancient Nubia), at many locations throughout India, and further eastward in China.

The regularity and intensity of these commercial transactions across Eurasia and Africa is indicated by the existence of the *Periplus Maris Erythraei*, a guide for merchants traversing the seas between India and Africa. Lionel Casson places the date of this text, which has been a matter of some dispute, in middle of the first century AD. The archaeological evidence clearly indicates that the commercial conditions to which it attests had developed centuries earlier.

THE VISUALITY OF COMMERCE AND THE GROWTH OF CONSUMPTION

Beginning in the latter part of the third century BC, the visual mode in Europe underwent another gradual change. As we have seen in the preceding chapters, pottery was increasingly shaped on the fast-turning wheel, fibulae were produced serially rather than individually crafted, and scabbards tended to have less ornament. Iron smelting and forging proliferated, and a wide range of tools were being manufactured, the great majority of them serially produced with minimal ornament or elaboration. Coins were minted, and their numbers increased greatly in the latter half of the second and first centuries BC. The overall pattern was one of increased levels of manufacture of many different kinds of goods, and a sharp reduction in handcrafting and in decoration. Objects became much simpler in their visual aspects than they had been. The elements calculated to excite visual attraction that we have discussed above—the S-curve, the spiral, and texturing effects—were much less often applied to objects.

These fundamental changes in design and decoration can be understood in terms of basic changes in attitudes and desires on the part of Europeans during the final three centuries BC. Communities in temperate Europe were increasingly engaged in a "world system" of expanding commercial activity and the increasing consumption associated with it. Susanne Sievers describes some of the evidence for participation in the now extensive commercial systems derived from excavations at Manching, the most thoroughly explored *oppidum* site in Europe. Fibulae from all over the continent are represented, as are coins from all directions. Roman amphorae attest to the wine trade. Among trade goods shipped from Manching and other centers in Europe southward to the Mediterranean basin, slaves, iron implements, woolen products, pitch, and honey are mentioned. Several chains for the securing of humans have been recovered at the site, perhaps direct physical evidence of the slave trade. Similar evidence has been recovered at other *oppida* across Europe.

All of the evidence thus suggests that in this final period of the prehistoric Iron Age, communities were concerned more with producing goods for commerce, in order to participate in the consumption of goods available through trade, than with fashioning objects and setting arrangements for visual display. From the start of the sixth century BC on, the placing of Greek bronze vessels in graves and the outfitting of sword handles with gold and ivory ornaments marked the beginning of a phase during which the display of connections with the outside world was important. From the start of the fifth century BC, visual aspects of material culture no longer focused solely on the display of connections with the larger world so much as on demonstrating participation in that larger world. From the late third century BC, the emphasis turned increasingly to the efficient production of goods as the cost for participation in the growing "international" commercial system. The crafting of complex, individually fashioned and elaborately decorated objects was deemphasized.

Although at this same time the practice of subsurface burial and hence the arrangements of objects in funerary displays declined, a small number of graves were constructed and outfitted to display wealth in objects and participation in feasting practice. These included the chamber graves at Clemency in Luxembourg and Welwyn Garden City in Britain. These were not altogether unlike earlier burials such as Hochdorf and Vix, although the placement of objects in the graves in the two periods was distinctly different (Chapter 8). But now, at the end of the Iron Age, the objects placed in graves were no longer the intricately decorated items that appear in those earlier graves. At the very end of the Iron Age, in a final effort to create visually distinctive objects, a new "baroque" fashion was created with openwork ornament that can be seen on a few special fibulae and scabbard attachments.

The visual world of the Late Iron Age was strikingly similar to that of Rome at this time, marked by quantities of mass-produced goods and a dearth of individually crafted objects. The increasing use of writing, however limited in temperate Europe, was already having a powerful effect as its use in communicating information decreased the need for communication via complexly shaped and decorated objects.

VISUAL PERCEPTION, CEREMONIAL PRACTICE, AND MASS CONSUMPTION

It remains to draw together the connections between the changing visual nature of material culture, ceremonial practice displayed in burial and arranged deposits, and the mass consumption of the final century and a half BC. (I use "mass consumption" in a relative sense here. Compared to the production and use of objects before 200 BC, the quantities of pottery and iron manufactured and consumed after the middle of the second century BC were vast. But compared to the mass consumption of our modern industrial societies, the levels were quite modest.)

In the course of the second century BC, *oppida*—walled settlements larger, in many cases much larger, than any that had existed before—were established across the whole of the central regions of temperate Europe (Figure 47). These were the first settlements in that region that can arguably be designated "cities," though there is much debate about whether or not they meet the criteria of urban centers. Population estimates are difficult to make because of the lack of substantial cemeteries associated with them, but an educated guess puts the population of the larger *oppida* at between three and five thousand. Excavations at many, such as Bibracte in France, Manching in Germany, Stradonice in Bohemia, and Staré Hradisko in Moravia, reveal densely built-up central areas with remains indicative of all of the functions of major central places in the landscape. These functions include the mass production of commodities such as pottery and iron tools and the on-site minting of coins. All of the substantially excavated *oppida* yield evidence for the interregional and intercontinental commerce noted above. Another indication of the urban and cosmopolitan character of these centers is the prevalence, for the first time in temperate Europe, of door locks and keys, suggesting that these communities were so large and complex that people no longer felt comfortable leaving their houses unsecured.

Visual Perception and Crafting Practice in the Context of Growing Mass Consumption

The visual character of objects changed as new and much larger communities formed, interregional and intercontinental interactions increased, and techniques of mass production replaced handcrafting. These changes took place in concert, and they reinforced one another.

Most pottery came to be produced on the potter's wheel for the first time in temperate Europe. Forms became simpler than they had been, with a decline

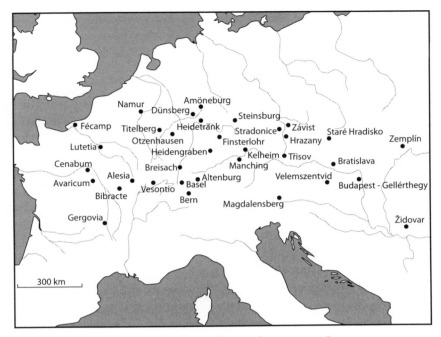

FIGURE 47. Map showing the locations of some of the *oppida* in temperate Europe.

in the distinctive S-shaped profiles of the Middle Iron Age. In contrast to the storage jars of earlier periods, such as the Bronze Age and Early Iron Age, storage jars now bore no added ornament, and nothing distinguished one from another. As I argue above, some of the new shapes and colors of the pottery may have been borrowed from the visual characteristics of Roman amphorae. The most important change from earlier periods is the sharp decline in special visual features that distinguish one vessel from another, such as fingertip impressions on rims or on ridges at the shoulders of vessels. The visual aspects of pottery that had frequently distinguished the products of one village from those of another disappeared, as pottery became a commodity rather than a craft product. There is little difference between the character of individual pieces produced at the various *oppida* or at the smaller settlements.

With fibulae the situation is similar. The most significant change was the sharp decline in complex and unique objects with the advent of mass production. It was the need to produce fibulae in great quantities that dictated the kinds that were manufactured, and the result was a limited repertoire of types, with most of the fibulae in each category looking just like all the others.

With scabbards, too, the trend was toward much less decoration, and what decoration was applied came from a limited repertoire of themes. As with pottery and fibulae, visual distinctiveness was given up in favor of more efficient production.

Coins and imported amphorae were consonant with this trend. Within the limited range of coin types, every individual coin is like every other. Amphorae made to transport wine, oil, and other commodities, were of a single, undistinctive shape.

Thus, people who grew up in this world of mass-produced pottery, fibulae, and coins experienced a visual environment very different from that of their Bronze Age and earlier Iron Age predecessors. When they made and arranged objects themselves, they did so in the visual mode to which they became accustomed in these new circumstances.

This new and different visual world is also apparent in the bronze figurines of animals that are relatively common at *oppidum* sites of this period. The stylized figurines characteristic of Early La Tène were replaced for the most part by more realistic, and always more easily identifiable (for us) representations of animals, including especially bulls, horses, rams, and stags.

CEREMONIAL PRACTICE

Changing patterns of visual perception and behavior are apparent not only in the character of objects, but also in ceremonial practices.

In much of temperate Europe, the practice of burying the dead declined at the same time that the *oppida* developed and European communities became more involved in the intercontinental commercial systems discussed above, that is during the second century BC. Between the middle Rhine and the English Channel and in southern Britain, the old practices of subsurface burial continued, but west of the upper Rhine, throughout southern Germany, Bohemia, Moravia, Austria, and in other lands to the east, there are none of the large cemeteries that we would expect at settlements as large as the *oppida*. Instead, other practices of disposing of the dead developed. The quantities of human bones that have been recovered on settlement surfaces (see above, Chapter 8) have been interpreted as the remains of some kind of ritual involving the bodies of the dead that replaced the former practice of burial in graves. As I have emphasized (Chapter 8), burying an individual in a grave, often with quantities of objects placed in the burial space, was a visual event of community-wide importance. The scattered nature of the finds of human bones at Late Iron Age settlements suggests that whatever ritual was practiced, it was not one that called special attention to the individual in the way that a grave did.

In those parts of Europe where burial was retained, we can distinguish significant changes in the associated ceremonies. In wealthy burials such as those at Mailleraye, Clemency, Welwyn Garden City, and Goeblingen-Nospelt, the floor space of the grave pit or chamber was filled with objects, in contrast to the practice in the earlier graves, such as those at Hochdorf and Vix. In those earlier instances, buried objects, including the corpse, were arranged around an open space in the center—an affordance—which must have played an important part in the visual performance of the ceremony of arranging the grave. Now, in this later period, that visual space was not left open, but was filled with objects. Perhaps in a visual world in which most pottery and personal ornaments were mass-produced commodities rather than individually crafted objects, participants did not feel the need for an open space that would afford them a close view of each object, since few objects had any special visual features that would be meaningful to viewers. The general character of the objects could be perceived even when they were packed together covering the entire floor space.

Another departure from earlier practice was the arranging of the largest and visually most obvious imports as part of the frame of the grave. At Clemency, the amphorae were placed in two corners of the burial chamber, two in one, eight in the other. At Welwyn Garden City, the five amphorae were arranged along the east wall of the burial chamber, and the bronze sieve-bowl and an imported plate were set on their rims to form part of the western edge. At Boiroux, the three amphorae were arranged in a row to frame the grave chamber at its lower end. The importance of this practice is that it shows the very significant role that those objects that represented the new cosmopolitanism played in the visual aspects of the burial ritual. In earlier contexts, such as Hochdorf, Vix, and Reinheim, the imported pottery, amphorae, and bronze vessels were never used to form part of the frame of the grave.

The character of deposits of valued objects also changed in the world of mass consumption at the end of the Iron Age. Whereas in earlier times, bronze weapons and vessels, fibulae, and iron weapons were the dominant categories of objects that were purposely deposited in water or in pits in the ground, now deposits were dominated by coins and iron tools. Both of these were commodities. Individual coins and individual iron tools were indistinguishable from others of the same type.

Finally, we see similar changes at the enclosed "ritual" sites that are characteristic of the Middle and Late Iron Age in France. At Middle Iron Age sites such as Gournay and Ribemont, weapons were the dominant category of object deposited in the ditches, especially swords and scabbards. At Late Iron Age sites, imported Roman amphorae dominated. At sites such as Braine and Lyon Verbe Incarné, there are ditches lined with amphorae, most of them fragmentary, arranged in such a way as to be visible from inside the enclosed space. The situation seems similar to that of the graves in which imported amphorae formed the frame. At these enclosure sites, the imports formed the very visible frame around the space created for the performance.

MASS CONSUMPTION AND VISUAL PERCEPTION

The formation of the *oppida*, the beginning of mass production, and a growing entanglement in the expanding commercial world of Eurasia and Africa—factors that were themselves closely interrelated—resulted in the development of a new kind of society in temperate Europe, a changing visual world, and of course a new way of seeing things. People became accustomed to seeing objects that looked very much like other objects. Things became less distinctive; they spoke less of where they were made, by whom they were made, and for whom they were made. According to extended mind theory, these changes in the character of the objects that people saw and used every day meant profound changes in *how* they saw and *how* they thought, in their experience and perception of the world in which they lived. The character of the decoration on a Middle Bronze Age storage jar provided visual reminders of your connections to your family and community, and perhaps to past social experiences of meals; and the details of the stylized representation of a figure on an Early La Tène fibula encoded kinship connections with individuals in neighboring communities. But what kind of information could be conveyed by a Late Iron Age wheelmade jar that looks exactly like hundreds of others in use in the settlement? If the Nauheim fibula that you are wearing looks just like those that five hundred other people are wearing, how much information does that fibula convey? These changes in the basic character of material culture during the final two centuries BC point to profound changes in visual signaling and visual experience that resulted from the gradual shift to a political economy that emphasized ever larger-scale production to satisfy both local needs and desires and to generate goods for exchange in expanding commercial networks. The visual properties of objects were now those of mass-produced goods, not of unique handcrafted items. This shift was consistent with a deemphasis in society on kinship and social relationships, for which the earlier individually designed objects were more important, and a growing emphasis on urban life and the manufacturing and trade systems that fostered it.

All of these changes took place in an overall context of increasing prosperity as the result of mass production and expanding commerce. The best evidence for a general increase in wealth in society is the widespread distribution of even the finest pottery—thin-walled painted jars and graphite-clay cooking pots—not only at the large population centers but also at small settlements.

Coins are also recovered in substantial quantities at the smaller settlements, and the iron tools to which those communities had access were the same kinds of tools as those produced and used at the *oppida*.

The world of the final two centuries BC was a very different place economically, socially, and visually, from that of the Bronze and early Iron Ages.

CHAPTER 13

∞∞∞∞∞∞∞∞∞∞∞∞∞

THE VISUALITY OF OBJECTS,
PAST AND PRESENT

ROMAN AND POST-ROMAN EUROPE

As I have argued elsewhere, the Roman conquest was not as comprehensive in its consequences for temperate Europe as many popular accounts would have us believe. In the preceding three chapters we have seen that the visual world of Late Iron Age Europe was already similar in important ways to that of Republican Rome. During the final two centuries before the conquest, Rome and temperate Europe were both participating in a "commercial revolution" that involved much of Asia and Africa as well.

After the conquests—of Gaul by 51 BC, of lands south of the Danube in 15 BC, of Britain in the years AD 43–47, and of what is now Baden-Württemberg in the latter half of the first century AD—it was a couple of generations before Roman administration and infrastructure were fully established in the new provinces. The European provinces enjoyed only a couple of centuries of prosperity, from the middle of the first to the middle of the third, before things began to unravel for Rome. Even at the peak of Roman control, the populations of the provinces continued many of their pre-conquest practices. The Heimstetten group of graves of the middle of the first century AD in southern Germany shows that burial traditions of the Iron Age were still current in conquered territory two generations after the conquest. In fact, people continued to make pottery very much like that of the prehistoric Iron Age for centuries into the Roman Period, and La Tène-style metal ornaments still were produced in large numbers during the second and third centuries AD.

Widespread changes after the middle of the third century AD, associated with the "fall of the limes" under pressure of the Alamanni and other related happenings, brought about a return to many circumstances of earlier times. But even at the height of Roman political power, a great many objects were being made and used in ways that harkened back to earlier visual practices, before the changes of the third and second centuries BC. This looking back over centuries to find sources of visual themes underscores the close association of the changes in material culture during the Late Iron Age with the visual culture of the Roman world of the time, an association that in the second and third centuries AD was less attractive to large numbers of people in the Roman provinces, who preferred to identify once again with the visual characteristics of their earlier native Middle Iron Age traditions. This phenomenon of the resurgence of the La Tène style has been called the "Celtic Renaissance," but the maintenance, or re-creation, of the visual patterns of earlier centuries is much more fundamental than the term "renaissance" suggests. In the fourth, fifth, sixth, and seventh centuries AD, many indicators point to the creation of a way of seeing and crafting that bears striking similarities to those of the Middle Iron Age. We see once again the use of S-curves, formlines, hybrid creatures, and the other means of shaping visual perception discussed in Chapter 2 that were favored before temperate European communities became involved in the global economic expansion of the final two centuries BC.

The lesson for European history is that the "Roman conquest" of parts of temperate Europe was not as all-changing as most history books would suggest. It resulted in a temporary occupation by Roman forces of conquered European provinces, but it did not change all aspects of cultural tradition or ways of crafting and seeing, nor did it last more than a couple of centuries. With this perspective in mind, the new creations of late Roman and post-Roman times in the so-called "Germanic kingdoms" of the early Middle Ages, become understandable as direct descendants of Middle Iron Age European ways of seeing. The phenomena of the persistence of Middle Iron Age "ways of seeing" during the Late Iron Age and early Roman Period, and of their subsequent resurgence in early medieval decoration, have not been systematically explored. Such an investigation would shed fascinating new light on the hybrid character of the material cultures of the Roman provinces.

In most accounts, the end of the Roman Empire in Europe came about sometime around the middle of the fifth century AD, depending upon what criteria are taken as indicative of that "end." In Britain, the end date is usually given as AD 410, when Roman Britain's call for reinforcements from Rome went unanswered. But it can reasonably be argued that in effect the end came much earlier, perhaps around the middle of the third century AD, when Rome was forced to pull its defenses in the middle of Europe back from the *limes*, which had only been completed some 140 years earlier, to the upper Rhine. Rome had not gained effective control over the Rhineland until around 15 BC, when Augustus established military bases there as defense against raiding parties coming across the Rhine from the east; and in that year Tiberus and

Drusus conquered the lands south of the Danube. It could therefore be argued that Rome really only controlled the Rhine and Danube borderlands for some two hundred and fifty years altogether. Moreover, the persistence of native-style pottery, metalwork, and burial traditions into the third century raises questions about the extent and the character of that Roman "control."

But however partial Rome's sway over people's hearts and minds—and ways of seeing and understanding their place in the world—may have been, Rome's "legacy"—its mythology—loomed large. On what, exactly, was it based? When Charlemagne had himself proclaimed "Emperor of the Romans" in AD 800, what exactly did he have in mind? Did he think that Rome had successfully ruled the European provinces for half a millennium? How "Roman" did he think that the inhabitants of the Roman provinces of Gaul and Germany had become? I would venture to suggest that Charlemagne's conceptions of Rome, like those of his successors, from the Renaissance thinkers to the Founding Fathers of the United States and on into our own times, were based principally on Roman texts—on the writings of Roman authors about the ways in which they understood the world in which they lived. The still-standing remains of Roman architecture must surely have played a role as well. It would have been difficult to ignore massive stone and brick structures such as the temples in Rome, the Porta Nigra and Constantine's Basilica at Trier, the Roman wall in London, and fortresses such as that at Portchester. Ever visible as well were the remains of the great walls that connected the middle Rhine and upper Danube frontiers on the continent (the *limes*) and the remains of Hadrian's Wall that separated conquered lands from unconquered territories in Britain.

Thus, I would argue that the idea of a "Roman Europe," in the sense of European provinces practicing Roman culture—in particular, Roman ways of seeing—needs considerable revision. As noted above, much evidence suggests that Middle Iron Age modes of visual perception and ways of crafting objects continued throughout the period of Roman political domination to reemerge in the so-called "early Germanic" style of the early Middle Ages, as well as in "Celtic" objects such as the Book of Kells and the traditions known as "Anglo-Saxon" and "Viking" art.

THE SPREAD OF LITERACY AND THE ROLE OF OBJECTS

The final two centuries BC were a critical time in Europe, when Europe's joining into the expanding commercial systems of Eurasia brought about fundamental change in ways of understanding the individual's and the community's place in the order of things. Mass production of goods, the proliferation of coinage as a medium of exchange, and exposure to the alphabetic system of writing were especially significant elements of this transformation.

As far as the time span of this book is concerned, this was the final period in which objects and their visual characteristics played the exclusive roles that they had from the Bronze Age on as media through which people created and expressed their relationships—with one another, with their social and natural environments, and with the wider world in which they lived. When writing was adopted, first in the form of legends on coins, objects gradually lost their function as the exclusive visual signaling devices, yielding the ground to texts, which became the media of instruction and record-keeping. As Jack Goody and others have shown, whether a particular individual is literate or not, the presence of writing in his or her environment has powerful psychological and social effects. Greg Woolf has demonstrated that from the second century BC on, Rome was becoming a very textual society, producing huge numbers of texts as aids to administering its expanding domains. After the conquests of the different regions of Europe, writing and the production of texts in a variety of media (notably papyrus, stone, bronze, and wood) spread rapidly throughout the provinces (Figure 45).

Objects did not lose their potency as media for communicating, but with the Roman conquests, texts largely supplanted them for the purposes of transmitting and recording information, particularly on a governmental and administrative level. For the administration of a huge and highly complex imperial system, texts had desirable properties. They were precise, unambiguous, and permanent. As media for conveying meaning, objects are less precise; they allow for more flexibility of interpretation and understanding than words. The visual properties of objects had served the purposes of the societies of prehistoric Europe well, but they had shortcomings when it came to communicating the kind of detailed and unequivocal information that the administrators of the Roman Empire needed to convey across space and through time.

When the power of Rome in Europe began to decline from the middle of the third century AD on, writing became once again less important in the daily lives of the inhabitants of temperate Europe than it had been when Rome's power was at its height. Objects and the special visual features with which they were endowed again assumed the near-exclusive roles they had played during the Middle Iron Age. In this context, we can understand the factors behind the expressive decorative themes that once again characterize the brooches, belt buckles, and other ornaments of the Late Roman and early medieval periods. Not until the wider dissemination of writing and reading began during the seventh century would writing begin again to usurp from objects their centrality as a means of communication.

OBJECTS, VISUALITY, AND COMMUNICATION IN
HISTORICAL AND MODERN TIMES

As David Olson has argued, writing was fundamentally different from earlier oral communication in that its meaning was fixed and permanent; a text meant the same thing in whatever context it was read. Olson contrasts this characteristic with oral communication, which, he argues, is considerably less rigid as meanings can change depending upon who the speaker is, the tone and volume of voice used, and other such variables. The same principle applies to objects as media of communication. Their meanings can vary, depending upon how visual elements are positioned, where the object is situated, and with what other objects it is associated.

In a study of the spread of writing in medieval England, M. T. Clanchy shows how for centuries, objects were still used as devices for communication, even as writing was gradually adopted for ever more purposes. In some transactions, for example, a knife was passed from one party to another to signify an agreement. Clanchy cites as another example the ivory handle of a whip inscribed with a text indicating that it signified a gift of four horses. In another instance, a horn was given as a symbol of the change of ownership of a forest. Clanchy goes on to argue that seals attached to documents may have been understood originally as objects that accompanied the written contracts, representing the earlier way of concluding agreements, now joined together with the new medium of writing. The inclusion of such objects to accompany written documents illustrates nicely the persistence of the older, traditional medium alongside the newer one.

Beginning with the Renaissance in Europe, official documents were to an ever-increasing extent recorded as texts. Examples are legion: codes of laws, real estate transactions, probate inventories, military plans, medical studies, religious doctrines, ritual procedures, descriptions of historical events, standard versions of literary works, not to mention recipes, personal letters, and other such ephemera. A relationship between the visual qualities of objects and the meanings in texts is especially richly demonstrated in the media known as illuminated manuscripts, including such examples as the Book of Kells and the Lindesfarne Gospels of the late first millennium AD, the Bayeux Tapestry of the eleventh century, the Luttrell Psalter of the fourteenth century, and illuminated bibles printed in the fifteenth century. In all of these cases, visual elements similar to those of the Bronze and Iron Ages explored in this book played important roles in linking the viewer through his or her visual experience with the text.

But even as the societies of Europe, and later those of the Americas, have become steadily more textualized, objects and their visual qualities have continued to serve as powerful media for communicating meanings of different kinds. They sometimes represent unofficial means of communication and operate in a system independent of the texts. A good example is to be seen in paintings by the seventeenth-century Dutch artist Jan Steen. Many of his works depict a number of different objects that seem not to pertain to the central theme of the image but that convey significant messages from the painter to the viewer. Since these messages are not spelled out in text, the viewer needs to be conversant in the meanings of different kinds of objects and associations of objects in order to appreciate the ideas that the painter wants to convey via these representations.

Sometimes craftsworkers used the special visual devices that we have explored in this book to supplement or reinforce meanings conveyed in texts. Christian reliquaries provide instructive examples. They are commonly crafted of gold or silver and incorporate in their designs many of the visually enchanting features that were discussed above in relation to fibulae, scabbards, and vessels. Linear patterns, S-curves, and frames are employed to capture and hold viewers' attention, to engage them in interaction, and to stimulate responses. The role of these reliquaries was to complement the texts and to provide a different physical and visual medium through which people could contemplate the themes and stories of Christianity.

What about us? Do we respond to objects and to the visual patterns on them in ways that are similar to those of our predecessors in pre-literate and Renaissance Europe, or are today's conditions so utterly different that there is no basis for comparison? Our lives are certainly dominated by texts, all the more so now that we have email, Facebook, Twitter, and other electronic media, all of which are text-based. But objects and their visual qualities continue to play major roles in our modern world, even though many of us are not as aware of our responses to them as we are of our reactions to the texts that confront us at every turn in our daily lives.

Advertisements, a category of media designed to make us look, pay attention, remember, and respond, illustrate this point. Print ads in newspapers, magazines, and on billboards make use of the same visual devices—lines, S-curves, formlines, and frames—that I explore in Chapters 2 and 4. The kinds of analyses that I apply to arrangements of objects in graves (Chapter 8) can be used to deconstruct the patterns and the imagery of contemporary promotions. Advertisements that incorporate motion—on television, in the movies, and on the Internet—operate in ways similar to those I have discussed in the chapter on performance (Chapter 9). In such ads, objects move in front of our eyes—cars, phones, slices of pizza—so that we can see them better than we would stationary objects. The movement of these objects helps us to remember what they look like and with what other objects and themes they are associated. In each case, the promised benefits are social in nature. A car offers status and respect; the phone provides easy and happy connections with people about whom we care; the pizza associates us with friendly and fun-loving companions.

It is interesting to note that many of the visual devices and design principles that underlie the decoration of the prehistoric pottery, fibulae, and scabbards examined in this book, as well as the arrangements in graves and in open-air structured sites, are the very devices and principles that enable us to engage in the textual communication that so pervades our modern lives. I think of smart phones in particular, but laptops and electronic readers of all kinds are other examples.

Recent studies by Janet Hoskins, Sherry Turkle, Daniel Miller, and Bjørnar Olsen, to cite only four scholars, document peoples' relationships with objects that have special meanings for them. Their studies demonstrate that today, in our text-saturated world, people often have emotionally powerful relationships with particular objects, clear evidence that objects are still important media with which people relate to other people and to society at large. In many cases, these relationships between people and the objects that they value are not unlike those between early Europeans and the ornate fibulae and scabbards discussed in Chapters 6 and 7, especially if we understand them in terms of extended mind theory.

Professionals in fields such as advertising, marketing, product design, and architecture regularly employ principles similar to those examined in Chapters 2 and 4. Their work is based on discovering which visual forms and structures evoke the most positive responses. And, as it turns out, those forms and structures are usually the very same ones (or very similar to them) that worked in the period covered by this book. In a recent article on "Intelligent Artefacts at Home in the 21st Century," the authors note how much can be learned about a person from where in a house pictures are arranged on walls, part of what they call "the ecology of place." They go on to note the significance of the arrangements of refrigerator magnets on the framed spaces of refrigerator surfaces. One could argue that the principles at work here—the ideas about what kinds of information are transmitted to viewers by particular arrangements of objects on surfaces—were already well established by the Bronze Age and operative in the arrangement of significant objects in particular patterns in the context of burials.

UNDERSTANDING THE PAST TO UNDERSTAND THE PRESENT

The study of the visual patterns constructed in later prehistory, when objects and their design—rather than writing—were the principal mode of visual communication, thus provides us with rich insight into how our relationships with objects and with visual media have developed over the past four thousand years. Understanding the creation and evolution of these forms helps us to appreciate why we respond the way we do to different visual patterns. It helps us to appreciate that even while most of our conscious actions are guided by written texts—the news we read, the email messages we exchange, the laws we obey—we are still powerfully influenced by the appearance of the objects around us.

Our responses to designs and patterns have been shaped by at least four millennia of human creativity and experience. By understanding how and why our predecessors used particular shapes and decorative designs for their pottery, personal ornaments, and other objects, we gain a deeper understanding of the world we live in and of our responses to it.

BIBLIOGRAPHIC ESSAY

Preface

Standard translations of Caesar and Tacitus are those in the Loeb Classical Library published by Harvard University Press. Recent study of Caesar: Goldsworthy 2006. On the Gallic War: Riggsby 2006. Roman conquests on the continent and in Britain: Wamser 2000, Wells 2003, Mattingly 2006. Literacy rates: Moreland 2010:290. Recent surveys of the period covered by this book, from other perspectives: Moscati et al. 1991, Green 1995, Kristiansen 1998, Harding 2000, Kristiansen and Larson 2005, Cunliffe 2008, Müller 2009.

PART I: THEORY AND METHOD

Chapter 1: Of Monsters and Flowers

A New Style for Iron Age Europe

Early La Tène style, with illustrations: Jacobsthal 1944; Megaw 1970, Megaw and Megaw 1989; Moscati et al. 1991; Guggisberg 2000; Müller 2009. History of European archaeology: Kühn 1976. Site of La Tène in Switzerland: Dunning 1991, Alt et al. 2007. Hallstatt in Austria: Barth 1991.

Written History and the Archaeology of Objects

Early writing in Mesoamerica: Monte Alban: Blanton et al. 1999, Olmec: Mora-Marín 2009. Mediterranean Europe: Chadwick 1990. China: Demattè 2010. Indus Valley civilization: Wright 2010. William James on different perceptions by different individuals: Duffy and Kitayama 2010.

Understanding the Past

Things that look familiar may be very different: Darnton 1984. Samuel Pepys: Tomalin 2002. Pliny the Elder: 1944–1947. Images as sources of historical information: Burke 2001, Lenman 2005, Lange and Ohlsen 2010. Riis's photographs: 1890; Fenton's: Baldwin et al. 2004. Every object embodies culture of its society: Morphy 1994, Mukarovsky 1988, Miller 2010. In non-literate societies, objects more important transmitters of information than in societies with writing: Jones 1998, Budden and Sofaer 2009:205, Searle 2010.

Objects in Times before Writing

Overviews of the material culture of the Bronze Age: Harding 2000, Kristiansen and Larsson 2005; Iron Age: Collis 1984, Moscati et al. 1991, Green 1995, Kristiansen 1998. Effects of the adoption of writing: Goody and Watt 1968, Ong 1982, Neidich 2003.

Seeing and Experience

Brett quote: 2005:2. Seeing depends upon what we have been before: Gregory 1998, Stafford 2007. Brain sorts visual stimuli, making us conscious of only a small fraction: Wilson 2002. Perception involves bodily interaction with environment: Johnson 2007.

Ways of Visualizing Things in the World

Studies of different perceptions in different societies: Goldhill 1996, De Bolla 2003, Sewell 1986, Forge 1970.

Visual Structures and Diagrams

Isherwood quote: 1939:10-11. Miller quote: 2010:53. Geertz on the Balinese cockfight: 1973. Songs and stories as models of societies: Lord 1991. Schama on seventeenth century Holland: 1987. Morphy on modern Australian material culture: 2005, 2007.

Greek and Roman Texts

On interpreting Greek and Roman texts that pertain to the peoples of temperate Europe: Champion 1985, Christ 1995, De Caro 1996, Lund 1998, Wells 2001, Grane 2003, Künzl 2008.

On Social Structure and Political Systems

Literature on the Hochdorf debate: Eggert 1999, Krause 1999, Olivier 1999, Krausse, ed., 2008. Problems of determined social and political systems in prehistoric Europe: Hill 2006, 2007; Collis 2007; Sharples 2010.

CHAPTER 2: SEEING AND SHAPING OBJECTS

Eye-Catching Objects

A good color reproduction, with discussion, is in Rebel 2008:46-47; images can also be found on the Internet.

The Basic Mechanics of Vision

Valuable recent discussions are Gregory 1998 and 2009; Zeki 1999; Wilson 2002; Ramachandran 2004, 2011.

What We Actually See

On the involvement of the whole body in visual perception: Johnson 1987 and 2007, Barsalou 2008. Enlarged hippocampus in London taxi drivers: Maguire et al. 2000. How the experience of seeing things teaches us how to see: Zeki 1999:82, Neidich 2003, Wexler 2006, Stafford 2007, Smail 2008, Boyd 2009. Art objects as maps of neurobiological perception: Neidich 2003.

Approaches to Visual Perception

Concept of the visual world: Gibson 1979. Ecological psychology: Gibson 1966, 1979; Shaw and Bransford 1977; Lakoff and Johnson 1980; Heft 2001; Brett 2005:28–34, Morris 2009. Perception of landscape: Tilley 1994, 2008. Extended mind theory: Clark 2008. Material engagement theory: Malafouris and Renfrew 2010, Malafouris and Renfrew, eds., 2010.

What Objects Do in the Visual World

Objects as agents of communication: Kopytoff 1986, Gell 1998:74, Barrett 2001, Brett 2005, Harper et al. 2008, Sutton 2008, Robb 2010.

Shaping the Experience of Seeing

Dictionary definition of "line:" *American Heritage Dictionary,* third edition, 1992,
p. 1045. In his new study of mirrors, Jody Joy (2008, 2010) develops a valuable
method for analyzing shapes of incised patterns. Lines: Poffenberger and Barrows
1924, Brett 2005, Ingold 2007. Bridget Riley: Riley 1965, 2009. Pollock: Cernus-
chi and Herczynski 2008. S-curves: Hogarth 1734, Mitchell 1978, Hallett 2006.
Spirals: Mitchell 1983. Formlines: von Jenny 1935, Holm 1965. Structures: Edges:
Shapiro 1969, Brett 2005, Andersmit 2003. Surfaces and textures: Gibson 1979,
Brett 2005: 53–55. Arrangements: Bender and Marrinan 2010. Images: Faces:
Bruce and Young 1998, Zeki 1999: 167–179, van de Vall 2003, Goodale and
Milner 2004:59; Animals: Eliade 1959, Kalof 2007, Jennbert 2011. Phatic images:
Virilio 1994, Gell 1992, 1998.

Affordances

The concept was developed by Gibson 1977, 1979. See also Heft 2001, Natsoulas
2004, Clark 2008:65. Bender and Marrinan 2010, 21, 23, 29.

Patterns, Connections, and Diagrams

Brett 2005:6, Bender and Marrinan 2010.

CHAPTER 3: THE VISUAL WORLDS OF EARLY EUROPE

Visual Ecology before Electric Lights

Blühm and Lippincott 2000 emphasize the need for us to situate ourselves in other
times and circumstances with respect to light in order to understand visual
perception in those contexts. Teniers's painting is reproduced in color in Solkin
2009:157 pl. 50 and can also be found on the Internet.

The Visual World of Bronze and Iron Age Europe

Useful overviews of prehistoric landscapes are Küster 1995 for central regions
and Pryor 2010 for Britain. A great number of local studies exist, frequently
published as parts of field research reports. On general issues, see Brück 2001,
2005; Fleming 2006, Barrett 2009. On excavations at Hascherkeller: Wells 1983.
Useful representations of seasonality in premodern landscapes can be found
in Brueghel's "seasons" paintings, the Luttrell Psalter (Backhouse 2000), and in

the narrative accounts in Homans 1941, Hartley 1979. Bodily interaction in the landscape: Johnson 2007. Adams on ideas about landscapes: 2002. Constructed landscapes: Gosden and Lock 2007, Fontijn 2008. Importance of existing earlier structures: Bradley 2002, Gerritsen 2007.

Settlements in general: Haselgrove 2007. Settlement at Allaines Mervilliers: Casadei et al. 2005. Elp: Bourgeois and Fontijn 2008. Weelde: Annaert 2008.

Houses: Gerritsen 2008. Beck and Steuer 1997 for central Europe, Lambot 2002 for Late Iron Age France, Arnoldussen and Fokkens 2008 for northern Europe. House Interiors: Lorenz 1986: 40–56, Bankus 1995, Webley 2003, 2007, Gransar et al. 2007. Photographs of reconstructions of Iron Age house interiors: Kreuz 2002:75 (fig. 47); Méniel and Lambot 2002, back cover. Capelle 2002 on furniture, Werner 1987 on Bronze Age folding stools, Cordie-Hackenberg 1989 on a table in a Late Iron Age burial; imported furniture: Fischer 1990. In Situla Art: Kastelic 1965. Changes in the Visual World: Scania pollen diagram: Berglund et al. 1991, 110 (fig. 4.1:1). Sixth century BC centers: Krausse, ed. 2008. Lorenz 1986:28 on trees felled to build walls and smelt iron. *Oppida:* Collis 1995, Fichtl 2000.

Light

On sources of light: O'Dea 1958, Hinz 1976, Brox 2010. At Pompeii in Italy during the Roman Period: Allison 2004:99–103. Importance of lighting for perception: Gombrich 1976: 3–18, Bille and Sørensen 2007. Fire in folklore and superstition: Ward 1984, Edsman 1987.

CHAPTER 4: FRAME, FOCUS, VISUALIZATION

Directing Vision

Early Bronze Age cup: Wells 2010. La Tène scabbard: Keller 1866, pl. 74, 4. Boiroux grave: Dussot et al. 1992.

Frame and Focus

On frames as borders: van Os 1995; van Thiel 1995a and b; Gregory 1998, 6, 49, 87; Brett 2005:43ff. Shapiro's paper: 1969.

Diagrams

Bender and Marrinan 2010. Neidich on art as providing maps of neurobiology of visual perception: 2003.

Modes of Visualization

Bender and Marrinan 2010. Ways of seeing: Berger 1972, Baxandall 1988, Deregowski 1989, Rasmussen and Spivey 1991, Goldhill 1996, Gregory 1998, Frank
2000, Nelson 2000, Elsner 2007. Portraits of Elizabeth I and Elizabeth II: National
Portrait Gallery NPG 541 and NPG 5882 (3).

Ways of Visualizing in Early Europe

Consistent visual patterns: These topics will be elaborated in Chapter 5–10 and are
  presented in summary here. Structured deposits: Hill 1995.
Changing ways of visualizing: Bronze Age: Harding 2000, Kristiansen and Larson 2005;
  Early Iron Age: Moscati et al. 1991. Hirschlanden: Zürn 1970. Hochdorf: Biel 1985,
  1996. Kuffarn: Lucke and Frey 1962. Strettweg: Egg 1996. Sopron: Hoernes 1891.
Middle Iron Age: The literature on the "origins of the Early La Tène style" is vast.
  This question has absorbed researchers from the middle of the nineteenth century on, when investigators in the field first realized that this apparently radical
  change had taken place in the "style" of decoration during the fifth century BC.
  Fundamental is Jacobsthal's *Early Celtic Art* (1944), which incorporated all of the
  important earlier studies and effectively defined the field for future studies. Especially important later treatments include Megaw 1970 and Megaw and Megaw
  1989, Frey 2002a. Among recent literature, particularly important are Verger
  1987; Guggisberg 2000, 2004, 2006; Haffner 2003; Echt 2004; Krausse 2006; Jung
  2008. Moscati et al. 1991 provides a useful overview of thinking about these
  matters up to 1990, with short articles by experts on all of Europe and a great
  number of excellent illustrations of the material under discussion. Müller 2009
  is an updated version, with excellent maps and photographs. For changing views
  of the "Mediterranean imports" and their significance both in social and political
  terms and with regard to development of style and motif, see Jacobsthal 1944,
  Haffner 2003, Guggisberg 2004, Pape 2004, Dietler 2010.
Late Iron Age: Krämer 1985, Rieckhoff 1995, Wells 1999, Müller 2009. New vessel
  forms: Hill 2002a and b, Desbat et al. 2006. On Roman imports: Werner 1954,
  1978, Feugère and Rolley 1991, Stöckli 1979, Will 1987, Poux 2004. For Britain,
  Hill 2007 and Hunter 2008 are valuable syntheses of this period.

The Dynamics of Creating the Visual Environment

Making: Helms 1993, Shimada 2007. Acquiring: Helms 1988. Long distance contacts
  and interaction across Eurasia during the Early Bronze Age: Kohl 2007, Kristiansen 2007; during the Early Iron Age: Wells 2006. Current views on Mediterranean imports: Guggisberg, ed. 2004.

Pottery, Fibulae, and Swords: Ideal Materials for Analysis

On the role of textiles in visual worlds, see Eicher 2010. Textiles in prehistory: Barber 1991. On Danish textiles, the classic work is Hald 1980. See also recent detailed study of the clothing recovered at Huldremose, along with more general discussion and recent references, in Nørgaard 2008. Recent study of Bronze Age textiles: Grömer 2006. On the well preserved, rich, and thoroughly analyzed textiles from Hochdorf, Banck 1996 and Banck-Burgess 1999. On silk in Early Iron Age graves: Good 1995. Recent discussion of clothing from Iron Age burials in Ukraine and Russia: Gleba 2008. Textile fragments adhering to iron objects in burials in Champagne: Schönfelder 2004.

PART II: MATERIAL: OBJECTS AND ARRANGEMENTS

CHAPTER 5: POTTERY: THE VISUAL ECOLOGY OF THE EVERYDAY

The Visual Ecology of a Jar

On this object and materials recovered with it: Wells 2010. Hascherkeller excavations: Wells, ed. 1983.

Pottery in Early Europe

Uses: Dietler 1996, Deffressigne-Tikonoff and Auxiette 2002, Meunier 2002, Morris 2002, Saurel 2002, Tappert 2006, Wells 2009, 2010. Imported: Krausse 2004, Pitts 2008:497. Imported ceramic amphorae: Greek: Dietler 2010; Roman: Peacock and Williams 1986, Poux 2000, 2004. Pottery deposited in pits: Petrosino and Putz 2003, Maier 1976, Brunaux and Malagoli 2003:32 (fig. 17). Braine: Auxiette et al. 2000. Mirebeau: Joly and Barral 2007. Dropped into wells: von Müller 1964. Deposited at base of cliff: Müller 2000.

The Visual Characteristics of Pottery

Materiality of Pottery: Shepard 1956, Rice 2005.

Pottery in the Visual World

Visual ecology: on similarities between pottery and landscapes: Hill 2002a, Jones 2007. Pottery and the body: Hill 2002a, Woodward 2002, Poux 2004, Brück 2006. Early Bronze Age reconstructed interior: Hänsel and Medovic 1991:77 (fig. 11). Lejre interior: Kreuz 2002:75 (fig. 47).

Pottery in the Visual Ecology of Late Prehistoric Europe

Recent overview of archaeology of Bavaria: Sommer 2006. Three major journals of international importance publish annual reports on archaeological research in the region : *Das archäologische Jahr in Bayern, Bayerische Vorgeschichtsblätter,* and *Jahrbuch der bayerischen Bodendenkmalpflege.* In neighboring Baden-Württemberg, *Archäologische Ausgrabungen in Baden-Württemberg* publishes annual reports on finds, and *Fundberichte aus Baden-Württemberg* publishes longer papers. In Austria to the east, *Archaeologia Austriaca* publishes annual reports.

Definitions of the principal forms of pottery: Tappert 2006.

Early Bronze Age pottery: earlier studies are cited in Wells 2010, and that paper explores in detail some of the topics treated here. Brück 1999 on the Enlightenment distinction between "ritual" and "secular." Middle Bronze Age pottery: Torbrügge 1959, Hochstetter 1980. Ornate cups in the British Isles: Needham and Woodward 2008.

Late Bronze and Early Iron Age pottery: Reinecke's chronology, 1911. On the lack of any distinction between the pottery traditionally ascribed to the Late Bronze Age and that to the Early Iron Age, see recent discussions in Reichenberger 1994, Meiborg and Müller 1997, and, for Britain, Sharples 2007. Late Bronze and Early Iron Age pottery here: see recent bibliography in Wells 2009. On the zonal decoration that particularly characterized the eighth and seventh centuries BC: Engelhardt 1985, Bauer 1988, Stegmaier 2009 and 2010. Belt plates: Kilian-Dirlmeier 1972.

Recently investigated settlements with material that traditionally has been ascribed to both Late Hallstatt and Early La Tène: Joachim 1999, Hénon et al. 2002, Müller-Depreux 2005, Baray 2007, Kohlberger-Schaub and Schaub 2007.

Middle Iron Age: Birngruber et al. 1996, Rind 1989:61–63, Möslein and Prammer 2001: 33 (fig. 38), Ettel and Irlinger 2006:173, Uenze 1986:85, Tappert 2006. Ceramic versions of Etruscan bronze *Schnabelkannen*: Abels 1992. Attic pottery: Krausse 2004, Pape 2004. Kleinaspergle *kylikes:* Kimmig 1988.

Late Iron Age: Detailed and well illustrated catalogues of pottery from Manching provide basic documentation of the different varieties of pottery: Kappel 1969, Maier 1970, Pingel 1971, Stöckli 1979, Krämer 1985 on pottery in graves. Tappert 2006. Special forms: Jerem and Kardos 1985, Haffner 1989, Böhme-Schönberger 1998. Fine figurally painted pottery from central France: Guichard 1987, 2009. Diverse pottery of latest Iron Age: Rieckhoff 1995, Gebhard 2004. Greek coins and local imitations: Mannsperger 1981. Roman amphorae: Peacock and Williams 1986, Bonnamour 2000, Poux 2004.

Pottery and the Visual Worlds, 2000–50 BC

New pottery and new eating practices at the end of the Iron Age: Desbat et al. 2006, Tappert 2006, Hill 2007, Pitts 2008.

CHAPTER 6: ATTRACTION AND ENCHANTMENT: FIBULAE

The Charm of Fibulae

For an excellent overview of fibulae in prehistoric Europe, see the section "Fibel und Fibeltracht" in *Reallexikon der germanischen Altertumskunde,* vol. 8, 1994, 411–607. With fibulae being such common objects in archaeological contexts from the Late Bronze Age through into the Roman Period (and well beyond), it is surprising how little attention has been paid to them as visual objects. Investigators have approached them primarily as chronological indicators (for which they are very important) and as indicators of interactions between communities in different regions of Europe ("trade"). Great attention is generally paid to fibulae recovered from settlements, in graves, and in deposits, and they are among the most commonly illustrated of all archaeological finds. Fundamental studies of fibulae include Beltz 1911 and 1913, Almgren 1923, Mansfeld 1973, Gebhard 1991, Völling 1994, Haselgrove 1997. Jope quotes: 2000:150, 151.

Fibulae in Prehistoric Europe

Settlements: Heuneburg: Mansfeld 1973; Manching: Gebhard 1991.

Graves: Oberstimm: Weinig 1991; Hochdorf: Biel 1985; Saint-Sulpice: Müller 2009:95 (fig. 97); Burgweinting: Zuber 2006; Dubník: Müller 2009:86 (fig. 84); Giengen: Biel 1991; Deal: Parfitt 1995.

Deposits: Heidentor at Egesheim: Dehn 1992, Dehn and Klug 1993. Source of Douix: Buvot 1998. Duchcov: Heger 1882, Kruta 1991. La Tène: Lejars 2007:363 (fig. 5). Villeneuve: Bataille 2008. Cornaux: Müller 2007a:353 (fig. 6). Empel: Roymans and Derks 1994. Hayling Island: King and Soffe 2001.

Representations: Krämer 1996. Examples of coins with fibulae shown on them: Allen 1972. Hirschlanden: Zürn 1970. Vix statues: Chaume and Reinhard 2003. Glauberg statue: Frey 2002b.

Fibulae as Visual Objects

Mansfeld's study of the Heuneburg fibulae: 1973. Diagram is on p. 4, fig. 1.

Middle Iron Age: Megaw 1970, Megaw and Megaw 1989, and Müller 2009 provide excellent illustrations of fibulae from this period. Panenský Týnec fibula: Megaw 1970:71 and fig. 65. Baitinger 2002:290 (fig. 325).

Late Iron Age: Nauheim fibula designed to be mass produced: Drescher 1955. "Baroque" openwork treatment of fibula foot: Great Chesterford: Jope 2000 (pl. 267, j-m). Hörgertshausen: Gebhard 2004:109 (fig. 4).

CHAPTER 7: STATUS AND VIOLENCE: SWORDS AND SCABBARDS

The Visuality of Scabbards

Bugthorpe scabbard: Stead 2006:186–187, 258 (fig. 92).

Swords and Scabbards in Prehistoric Europe

Swords in late prehistoric Europe: *Prähistorische Bronzefunde,* Abteilung IV: *Schwer-ter* series for Middle and Late Bronze Age swords; Sievers 1982 on daggers and their sheaths; de Navarro 1972 on Middle La Tène scabbards; Pleiner 1993 and Schauer 2004 on swords in general.

Where Swords Are Found

Graves: in Bronze Age: Stary 1980. Mailleraye: Lequoy 1993.

Landscape Deposits: Deposits of swords at open-air sites: Gournay-sur-Aronde and Ribemont: Brunaux 1988, 1996, 2006. Analysis of scabbards from Gournay: Lejars 1994. Deposits at water sites: overview in Torbrügge 1971, Schönfelder 2007. Bronze Age swords in the Thielle River in Switzerland: Müller 2007a, in the Saône in France: Bonnamour 2000. Hjortspring in Denmark: Kaul 2003. La Tène: de Navarro 1972. Tiefenau: Müller 1990. Danube: Wehrberger and Wieland 1999. Kessel in the Netherlands: Roymans 2007.

Iconographic representations of swords and daggers: Hirschlanden statue: Zürn 1970. On the back of the Hochdorf couch: Biel 1985. Warrior statue at Vix: Chaume and Reinhart 2003. Hallstatt Grave 994 scabbard: Egg et al. 2006.

Swords and Scabbards as Visual Objects

Bronze Age scabbards of wood or leather: Thrane 2006:499. Wooden scabbards of first part of Early Iron Age: Gerdsen 1986. Sheet bronze sheaths for Late Hallstatt daggers: Sievers 1982.

Patterns in the Visuality of Swords and Scabbards

Middle Bronze Age: Stary 1980, Schauer 2004. Late Bronze Age: Hilt from the Main at Untereisenheim: von Quillfeldt 1995:56 and pl. 14, 42. Early Iron Age: Hallstatt sword from Gomadingen: Gerdsen 1986:119 and pl. 6, 1. Sword from cremation grave at Oss: Gerdsen 1986:167–168 and pl. 4, 1. Sword with ivory hilt and pommel inlaid with amber from Hallstatt Grave 573: Gerdsen 1986:170 and pl. 5, 1. General discussion of Hallstatt period swords and scabbards: Pare 2004. Ivory pommel from Kinding/Ilbling: Meixner et al. 1997. Iron dagger and sheath from Wolfegg: Sievers 1982: 32 and pl. 20, 106. Salem sheath: Sievers 1982 pl. 14, 80.

Middle Iron Age: Weiskirchen scabbard: Müller 2009: 188–189. Glauberg: Nortmann 2002:37. La Tène scabbards: Sievers 2004. Hochscheid: Haffner 1992:55 and Plate 1, Megaw and Megaw 1989:59. Inlay and other coloring materials on scabbards: Rigby 2006, Giles 2008. Dragon pair motif/griffons: Fitzpatrick 2007, Müller 2009:283; distribution map: Stöllner 1998, Beilage 2. Examples: Montigny-Lencoup near Paris: Müller 2009, 112 (fig. 141), 283 (no. 69); Dubník in Slovakia: Müller 86 (fig. 84); Taliándörögd and Kosd in Hungary: Müller 2009, 283 (nos. 70, 71); Münsingen in Switzerland: Müller 2009, 283 (no. 72); Hammersmith: Stead 2006, 205 (fig. 39, 2) and Müller 2009, 283 (no. 73); Battersea: Stead 2006, 208 (fig. 42) at London. "Hungarian Sword style" examples: Müller 2009, 216–217. Witham scabbard: Müller 2009, 113 (fig. 144), 282 (no. 68). La Tène scabbard with three relief horses: Müller 2009:113 (fig. 143), de Navarro 1972, pl. 31, 2a and pl. 95, 32. Kirkburn scabbard: Stead 2006, 184–185.

S-curves: Cernon-sur-Coole in France: Duval and Kruta 1986. Drňa in Slovakia: Müller 2009, 216 (nos. 285, 286). Bölcske, Tapolca, Szob in Hungary: Müller 2009, 282 (nos. 63, 64–5). Dobova in Slovenia: Müller 2009, 282 (no. 67). Batina in Croatia: Müller 2009, 282 ([no. 66]). Sheperton in England: Stead 2006, 214 (fig. 34). "Swiss style:" Müller 2009, 113 (fig. 143).

Late Iron Age: Amerden Lock: Stead 2006:172–173, 235. Bird head scabbard ornaments in north European bog finds: Jørgensen et al. 2003; Kelheim vulture: Wells 1989. Badenheim: Böhme-Schönberger 1998.

CHAPTER 8: ARRANGING SPACES: OBJECTS IN GRAVES

Everything in Its Place

Hochdorf: Biel 1985, 1996; Verger 2006.

Visual Information from Graves

Heidetränk: Schlott et al. 1985. Folly Lane: Niblett 1999.

Graves as Frames and Spaces

Vix: Moulhérat and Rolley 2003.

Graves as Diagrams

Graves represent the community more than the individual buried: Williams 2004, Brück 2006:307–310, Hayden 2009, Searle 2010. Model for grave arrangement: Villard 1993.

Graves, Bronze Age through Early Iron Age: 2000-500 BC

Early Bronze Age: Poing: von Quillfeldt 1990. Mötzing: Schröter 1998. Alteglofsheim: Pászthory and Mayer 1998:35, Sommer 2006:110.
Middle Bronze Age: Untermeitingen: Krahe 1990. Bastheim: Gerlach 2000. Mannsdorf: Engelhardt 2008. Burgweinting Bronze Age D: Petzl 2009.
Late Bronze Age: Fechenbach: Hoppe 2006. Hart: Müller-Karpe 1955. Telgte: Wilhelmi 1974.
Early Iron Age Hallstatt C: Grosseibstadt: Kossack 1970.
Early Iron Age Hallstatt D: Hochdorf: Biel 1985, 1996; on visual aspects of the arrangement at Hochdorf: Wells 2008:65–69.

Graves, Middle Iron Age: 500-200 BC

Reinheim: Keller 1965, Echt 1999. Hochscheid: Haffner 1992. Radovesice: Waldhauser 1987:118–119. Marcelcave: Buchez et al. 1998.

Graves, Late Iron Age: 200-50 BC

Badenheim: Böhme-Schönberger 1998. Welwyn: Stead 1967. Boiroux: Dussot et al. 1992.

Arrangements in Graves: Patterns over Time

"Flat grave" cemeteries of Champagne: Charpy 1991. Saint-Sulpice: Kaenel and Müller 1991. Münsingen: Hodson 1968. Nebringen: Krämer 1964. Jenišův Újezd: Waldhauser 1978. Radovesice: Waldhauser 1987. Fiskerton: Field and Pearson 2003. Kessel: Roymans 2007. Acy-Romance: Lambot 2002, 2006, 2007. Clemency: Metzler et al. 1991. Goeblingen-Nospelt: Metzler 1995. Wederath: Haffner, ed. 1989. Welwyn: Stead 1967. Baldock: James and Rigby 1997:79 (fig. 90).

CHAPTER 9: PERFORMANCES: OBJECTS AND BODIES IN MOTION

Forggensee: Zanier 1999. Snettisham: Stead 1991.

Archaeology and Performance

Mitchell 2007.

Movement and Seeing

Gibson 1979:223–237. Gregory 2009:74–75 on seeing objects in motion; "embodied cognition:" Oberman et al. 2010; effects of viewing people manipulating objects: Johnson 2007:19–32 and Oberman et al. 2010.

Bodily Participation in Performance

Niblett on packing around burial chambers: 1999:59. Dún Ailinne: Wailes 1991, Johnston and Wailes 2007.

Performances with Objects

Feasts: Petronius *Satyricon* 1965; Poux 2002; Hayden 2009:43; Jones 2009; LeCount and Blitz 2010. Bronze Age feasting: Needham and Bowman 2005. Iron Age feasting: Dietler 1990, 1996; Krausse 1996; Arnold 2004. Basic pattern of vessel use in later European prehistory: Deffressigne-Tikonoff and Auxiette 2002, Morris 2002. Grave at Hart an der Alz: Müller-Karpe 1955. Hochdorf: Biel 1985, 1996. Vix: Rolley, ed. 2003. Situla Art: Kastelic 1965, Kern et al. 2009. Kuffarn situla: Lucke and Frey 1962, Urban 2006. Uses of bowls and cups: Kossack 1964, 1970. Feasts in Situla Art: Winghart 1992. Feasting at Dún Ailinne: Johnson and Wailes 2007:22, Crabtree 2007:169.
Funerary Rituals: Folly Lane: Niblett 1999. Hradenín: Gerdsen 1986:174–176. Reinheim: Keller 1965, Reinhard 2004. Glauberg: Baitinger and Pinsker, eds. 2002. Waldalgesheim: Joachim 1995. Ciumești: Rusu 1969. Welwyn Garden City: Stead 1967. Direct evidence of performance of ceremony: Surface of walkway at Folly Lane shows trampling: Niblett 1999:59. At Clemency: Metzler et al. 1991:142. Evidence for "circumambulation rites": Brunaux 1988. Mailleraye-sur-Seine: Lequoy 1993. Arras burials: Stead 1979.
Open-Air Depositing: Schellnecker Wänd: Müller 2000. Vix enclosure: Chaume et al. 2000, Chaume and Reinhard 2002, 2009. Weichering: Becker 1992. Závist: Motyková et al. 1991. Gournay: Brunaux 1988, 1996, 2006; Lejars 1994; Müller 2007b:367–371. Ribemont: Brunaux 1999. Braine: Auxiette et al. 2000; Poux 2000, 2004, 2006. French "sanctuaries" generally: Brunaux 2006; Bataille 2007, 2008; special case of Acy-Romance, Lambot 2006, 2007. Hayling Island: King and Soffe 2001.
Earth, Water, and Fire Deposits: Iron deposits: Fischer 1959, Pieta and Moravcík 1980, Rybová and Motyková 1983, Hingley 1997, 2006. Weapons: Dubreucq and Piningre 2007, Maniquet 2008, 2009. Snettisham: Stead 1991. Deposits in Water:

Torbrügge 1971, Bradley 1990; Pryor and Bamforth 2010; Douix: Buvot 1998; Hjortspring: Kaul 2003; Duchcov: Kruta 1991; La Tène: Alt et al. 2007; Fiskerton: Field and Pearson 2003; Llyn Cerrig Bach: Fox 1946; Kessel: Roymans 2007. Fire Deposits: Forggensee: Zanier 1999; Auerberg: Krämer 1966; Wartau-Ochsenberg: Pernet and Schmid-Sikimić 2007.

Martial Activity: Strettweg: Egg 1996. Hochdorf couch back scenes: Biel 1985. Hirschlanden statue: Zürn 1970. Vix warrior statue: Chaume and Reinhard 2003. Glauberg: Frey 2002b. Hallstatt 994 scabbard: Egg et al. 2006, Barth 2009. Gundestrup: Klindt-Jensen 1961, Nielsen et al. 2005. Warrior representations on coins: Hunter 2005. Carnyx player representations: Hunter 2001, Veres 2009.

CHAPTER 10: NEW MEDIA IN THE LATE IRON AGE: COINS AND WRITING

New Widespread Images

Iron Age coinage: Allen and Nash 1980, Mannsperger 1981, Kellner 1990, Kos and Wigg 2002. "Celtic" mercenary activity: Szabó 1991, Tomaschitz 2002.

Coins

Coinage in late prehistoric Europe: Allen and Nash 1980, Kos and Wigg 2002. Contexts of coin finds: Haselgrove 2005a and b. Hohenfels coin hoard: Brandt and Fischer 1988. Wickham Market: "Iron Age Gold Hoard." In graves: Polenz 1982; Giengen: Biel 1991. Legends: Allen and Nash 1980:107–130. Philip II staters and local versions: Mannsperger 1981, Schmutz 2009. Process of striking coins: Kellner 1990.

Writing

Overview: Prosdocimi 1991. Marks on bottoms of pots: Zeidler 2003. Bernstorf: Gebhard and Rieder 2002; critical view: Harding 2006. Montmorot incised lines on sherds: Verger 2001. Vix krater: Rolley 2003, Ellmers 2010. Massaliote coin from Aubstadt: Overbeck 1988. Glass bead from Münsingen: Gambari and Kaenel 2001. KORISIOS sword: Wyss 1956. Writing on sherds at Manching: Krämer 1982, Mees 2006:206–207. Mailly-le-Camp ring: Adler 2003. Negau helmets: Nedoma 2002. Writing implements in Late Iron Age Europe: Jacobi 1974a.

New Patterns of Communication and Perception

Significance of the adoption of writing: Goody and Watt 1968, Olson 2009. Great expansion in use of writing in second century BC Rome: Woolf 2009. Biography of objects: Kopytoff 1986, Gosden and Marshall 1999.

PART III: INTERPRETING THE PATTERNS

CHAPTER 11: CHANGING PATTERNS IN OBJECTS AND IN PERCEPTION

From the Early Bronze Age to the Early Iron Age

Bronze belt plates: Kilian-Dirmeier 1972, Wells 2008:64–66. Changes in grave arrangements: Müller-Scheessel 2005.

The Middle Iron Age

Transforming imported forms into local media: Mötsch 2008.

The Late Iron Age

Leonding: Pertlwieser 2001. Human bones at settlement sites at the end of the Iron Age: Manching: Hahn 1992; Knovíce: Matiegka 1896; Basel-Gasfabrik: Furger-Gunti and Berger 1980. Kurz on coin and iron deposits: 1995.

CHAPTER 12: CONTACTS, COMMERCE, AND THE DYNAMICS OF NEW VISUAL PATTERNS

Athena in Bavaria

Athena find: Irlinger and Winghart 1999.

Expanding Contacts, New Ideas, and the Creation of New Visualities: Fifth Century BC

Evidence for increased openness, contact, effects: On origins of "Early Celtic Art," see references cited in Chapter 4. Gold ornaments from the Heuneburg with curvilinear patterns: Kurz 2008:183 (fig. 12). Charmay "Le Haut des Marquettes:" Baray 2007; Allaines: Casadei et al. 2005; Remseck-Neckargröningen: Joachim 1999; Erdwerk I at Niedererlbach: Müller-Depreux 2005. Sherratt quote: 2006:31–32. Grächwil hydria: Guggisberg, ed. 2004. Kappel jug: Kimmig and Rest 1954. Hochdorf cauldron: Biel 1985. Grafenbühl tripod: Zürn 1970. Vix krater: Rolley 2003. Etruscan beaked jugs: Guggisberg 2004. Figurines: Kociumaka 1991. Long-distance interactions in Late Hallstatt-Early La Tène times: Stöllner 2004.

Gold and ivory sword hilt ornaments: Gerdsen 1986, Meixner et al. 1997. Bronze situla from Straubing: Tappert and Mielke 1998. Buckle from Aul Tseia: Reeder 1999:109 (no. 7). Pectoral from Arzan: Parzinger 2007:78–79. Vani ornaments:

Kacharava and Kvirkvelia 2008:133, 135, 140. Vessels from China: von Falken-hausen 2006:251 (fig. 49 top left). Weijiaya: Michaelson 2007:96 (fig. 93). Objects from Xinjiang: Janssen-Kim 2007a, b, c, d. Pasargadae and Oxus bracelets: Curtis 2005:137, cat. nos. 152, 143, 171. Gordion horse: Farkas 2000:9 (fig. 8). Horse from northern Caucasus: Bunker et al. 1970:48 (fig. 27). Stags from Inner Mongolia and Mongolia: Bunker et al. 1970:118 (figs. 89, 90). Frieze from Georgia: Farkas 2000:10 (fig. 11). Interactions across Asia during the Bronze Age: Anthony 2007, Kohl 2007, Kristiansen 2007; exchange systems: Meicun 2008. Migrations, especially the important but often neglected phenomenon of return migration: Anthony 1990.

Europe in the Commercial and Consumption Revolution of the Second Century BC

Increasing consumption of imported commodities: Greatly expanded Roman trade during the second century BC: Morel 2007, Woolf 2009. Distribution of wine amphorae: Poux 2004:203 (fig. 118). For sites with arrangements of amphorae, see Poux 2004: Ribemont 59 (fig. 33), Braine 74 (fig. 42), Balloy 83 (fig. 47), Fontenay-le-Comte 112 (fig. 62), Corent 136 (fig. 81), Cleppé151 (fig. 87), Nordheim 161 (fig. 92). Chopping upper portions off amphorae: Poux 2004:280–291. Amphorae arranged in burials: Boiroux: Dussot et al. 1992, Poux 2004:117 (fig. 67); Clemency: Metzler et al. 1991; Welwyn: Stead 1967.

The Commercial Revolution of the Second Century BC: Rome's Expansion: Harris 2007, Morel 2007.

The Larger World of the Second and First Centuries BC: Milleker 2000. Tillya-Tepe: Sarianidi 1985. Begram: Mehendale 2011. Expansion of commercial systems throughout Asia, Africa, and Europe: Ehret 2002, Chami 2004, Sidebotham 2011, especially 206-208. Silk routes across Asia: Kuzmina 2008, Beckwith 2009, von Falkenhausen 2010, Hiebert 2011. Roman imports at Meroë in Sudan: Grzymski 2004; in India: Tomber 2008. Names on goods those of merchants: Harris 2007:533. Manching and trade: Sievers 2007: 131–132, slave chains: 123–124 (with fig. 127). *Periplus Maris Erythraei:* Casson 1989. On these sea routes generally: Casson 1991.

Visual Perception, Ceremonial Practice, and Mass Consumption

For summaries of excavation results at the *oppida,* see for Bibracte: Guillaumet 1991, Manching: Sievers 2007, Stradonice: Bren 1991, Staré Hradsko: Meduna 1991. Locks and keys on buildings at the *oppida:* Jacobi 1974b. Naturalistic representations of animals: Megaw and Megaw 1989, Wells 1989, Müller 2009.

CONCLUSION

CHAPTER 13: THE VISUALITY OF OBJECTS, PAST AND PRESENT

Roman and Post-Roman Europe

Consequences of Roman conquests for the native peoples: Woolf 1998, Wells 1999, Wamser 2000. Heimstetten group of graves: Keller 1984. Local pottery traditions continue: Flügel 1996, Struck 1996. La Tène style ornament in the second and third centuries: MacMullen 1965, Wells 1999:197, 283–284; Berger 2002; Reuter 2003, Mattingly 2008. Big changes in Roman Europe from the mid-third century on: Wells 1999, Ward-Perkins 2005, Heather 2006. Roman visual culture: Clarke 2003, Elsner 2007. Late Roman Period changes: Wells 1999, Wamser 2000, Burns 2003, Hedeager 2000, 2011. Conceptions of Rome as model for later developments: Hingley 2001. Resurgence in the late Roman and post-Roman periods of visual features on objects related to those of the Iron Age: Haseloff 1981, Leigh 1984, Roth 1986, Lindström and Kristoffersen 2001, Kristoffersen 2010.

The Spread of Literacy and the Role of Objects

Effects of writing on society: Goody and Watt 1968, Goody 1986, 2000. Expansion of literacy and texts in Rome: Woolf 1996, 2009. Late Roman and early medieval objects as media of communication: Hedeager 2000, 2011; Wells 2008.

Objects, Visuality, and Communication in Historical and Modern Times

Writing different from other media of communication: Olson 2009, Ong 1982. Difference between nonliterate and literate societies: Chaudhuri 2010. Clanchy on objects and written documents: 1993:254–260. Illuminated manuscripts: Cramsie 2010: 52. Book of Kells: Pulliam 2006. Lindisfarne Gospels: Brown 2003. Bayeux Tapestry: Wilson 1985. Luttrell Psalter: Backhouse 2000. Jan Steen and the objects in his paintings: Chapman et al. 1996. Advertisements: Messaris 1997. Reliquaries: Bagnoli et al. 2011. People's relationships with objects today: Knappett 2002; Gosden 2005; Turkle 2007; Miller 1998, 2008, 2010; Olsen 2010. Modern product design: Aimone 2004, Sudjic 2008, Sparke 2009, Cramsie 2010. "Intelligent Artefact" article: Harper et al. 2008:102–106.

REFERENCES CITED

Abels, B.-U. 1992. Eine Tonschnabelkanne von der Ehrenbürg. *Das archäologische Jahr in Bayern 1991*:94–97.

Adams, A. J. 2002. Competing Communities in the "Great Bog of Europe": Identity and Seventeenth-Century Dutch Landscape Painting. In W.J.T. Mitchell, ed., *Landscape and Power*, 35–76. Chicago: University of Chicago Press.

Adler, W. 2003. *Der Halsring von Männern und Göttern: Schriftquellen, bildliche Darstellungen und Halsringfunde aus West-, Mittel- und Nordeuropa zwischen Hallstatt- und Völkerwanderungszeit.* Bonn: Rudolf Habelt.

Aimone, S. 2004. *Design: A Lively Guide to Design Basics for Artists & Craftspeople.* New York: Lark Books.

Allen, D. F. 1972. The Fibula of CRICIRV. *Germania* 50:122–132.

Allen, D. F. and D. Nash. 1980. *The Coins of the Ancient Celts.* Edinburgh: Edinburgh University Press.

Allison, P. M. 2004. *Pompeiian Households: An Analysis of Material Culture.* Los Angeles: Cotsen Institute of Archaeology.

Almgren, O. 1923. *Studien über nordeuropäischen Fibelformen der ersten nachchristlichen Jahrhunderte mit Berücksichtigung der provinzialrömischen und südrussischen Formen.* Leipzig: C. Kabitzsch.

Alt, K. W. et al. 2007. *La Tène: Die Untersuchung, die Fragen, die Antworten.* Biel: Museum Schwab.

American Heritage Dictionary of the English Language. 1992, Third edition. Boston: Houghton Mifflin.

Andersmit, F. R. 2003. Rococo as the Dissipation of Boredom. In Farago and Zwijnenberg, 132–155.

Annaert, R. 2008. The Living and the Dead: A Bronze Age Barrow and Farmyard from Weelde. In Arnoldussen and Fokkens, 189–200.

Anthony, D. W. 1990. Migration in Archeology. *American Anthropologist* 92:895–914.

———. 2007. *The Horse, the Wheel, and Language: How Bronze-Age Riders from the Eurasian Steppes Shaped the Modern World.* Princeton: Princeton University Press.

Appadurai, A., ed. 1986. *The Social Life of Things: Commodities in Cultural Perspective.* Cambridge: Cambridge University Press.

Arnold, B. 2004. Iron Age Feasting. In P. Bogucki and P. Crabtree, eds., *Ancient Europe 8000 B.C.–A.D. 1000: Encyclopedia of the Barbarian World,* vol. 2, 179–183. New York: Thompson/Gale.

Arnoldussen, S. and H. Fokkens, eds. 2008. *Bronze Age Settlements in the Low Countries.* Oxford: Oxbow.

Auxiette, G., S. Desenne, F. Gransar, and C. Pommepuy. 2000. Structuration générale du site de Braine "La Grange des Moines" (Aisne) à La Tène finale et particularités: présentation préliminaire. *Revue archéologique de Picardie.* No. 1–2, (2000). *Les enclos celtiques—Actes de la table ronde de Ribemont-sur-Ancre (Somme),* 97–103.

Backhouse, J. 2000. *Medieval Rural Life in the Luttrell Psalter.* London: British Library.

Bagnoli, M., H. A. Klein, C. G. Mann, and J. Robinson, eds. 2011. *Treasures of Heaven: Saints, Relics, and Devotion in Medieval Europe.* London: British Museum Press.

Baitinger, H. 2002. Maskenfibel. In Baitinger and Pinsker, 290.

Baitinger, H. and B. Pinsker, eds. 2002. *Das Rätsel der Kelten vom Glauberg.* Stuttgart: Theiss.

Balcetis, E. and G. D. Lassiter, eds. 2010. *Social Psychology of Visual Perception.* New York: Psychology Press.

Baldwin, G., M. Daniel, and S. Greenough. 2004. *All the Mighty World: The Photographs of Roger Fenton, 1852–1860.* New York: Metropolitan Museum of Art.

Banck, J. 1996. Spinnen, weben, färben; feine Tuche für den Fürsten. In Biel, 40–63.

Banck-Burgess, J. 1999. *Hochdorf IV: Die Textilfunde aus dem späthallstattzeitlichen Fürstengrab von Eberdingen-Hochdorf (Kreis Ludwigsburg) und weitere Grabtextilien aus hallstatt- und latènezeitlichen Kulturgruppen.* Stuttgart: Konrad Theiss.

Bankus, M. 1995. Frühe und mittlere Bronzezeit. In: K. H. Rieder and A. Tillmann, eds., *Archäologie um Ingolstadt: Die archäologischen Untersuchungen beim Bau der B16 und der Bahnverlagung,* 53–88. Kipfenberg.

Baray, L. 2007. Le pôle aristocratique du Hallstatt D3/La Tène A ancienne de Charmoy "Le Haut des Marquettes" (Yonne). *Archäologisches Korrespondenzblatt* 37:507–525.

Barber, E.J.W. 1991. *Prehistoric Textiles: The Development of Cloth in the Neolithic and Bronze Ages with Special Reference to the Aegean.* Princeton: Princeton University Press.

Barral, P., A. Daubigny, C. Dunning, G. Kaenel, and M.-J. Roulière-Lambert, eds. 2007. *L'âge du Fer dans l'arc jurassien et ses marges: Dépôts, lieux sacrés et territorialité à l'âge du Fer.* Besancon: Presses universitaires de Franche-Comté.

Barrett, J. 2001. Agency, the Duality of Structure and the Problem of the Archaeological Record. In I. Hodder, ed., *Archaeological Theory Today,* 141–64. Oxford: Oxford University Press.

———. 2009. A Phenomenology of Landscape: A Crisis in British Landscape Archaeology? *Journal of Social Archaeology* 9:275–294.

Barsalou, L. W. 2008. Grounded Cognition. *Annual Review of Psychology* 59:617–645.

Barth, F. E. 1991. The Hallstatt Salt Mines. In Moscati et al., 163–166.

———. 2009. Ergänzende Bemerkungen zum frühlatènezeitlichen Grab 994 von
Hallstatt. *Archäologisches Korrespondenzblatt* 39:527–538.

Bataille, G. 2007. Dépôts de sanctuaires et dépôts particuliers: comparisons des
assemblages de mobiliers métalliques. In Barral et al., 699–708.

———. 2008. *Les Celtes: Des mobiliers aux cultes.* Dijon: Editions Universitaires de
Dijon.

Bauer, I. 1988. Das Verzierungsprinzip der Alb-Salem Kermik. *Jahrbuch der Schwei-
zerischen Gesellschaft für Ur- und Frühgeschichte* 71:107–121.

Baxandall, M. 1988. *Painting and Experience in Fifteenth Century Italy: A Primer in the
Social History of Pictorial Style.* New York: Oxford University Press.

Beck, H. and H. Steuer, eds. 1997. *Haus und Hof in ur- und frühgeschichtlicher Zeit.*
Göttingen: Vandenhoeck & Ruprecht.

Becker, H. 1992. Das Grabenwerk von Weichering: Ein hallstatt-/frühlatènezeitlicher
Tempelbezirk und Vorläufer spätkeltischer Viereckschanzen? *Das archäologische
Jahr in Bayern* 1991:89–93.

Beckwith, C. I. 2009. *Empires of the Silk Road: A History of Central Eurasia from the
Bronze Age to the Present.* Princeton: Princeton University Press.

Beltz, R. 1911. Die Latènefibeln. *Zeitschrift für Ethnologie* 43:664–817.

———. 1913. Die bronze- und hallstattzeitlichen Fibeln. *Zeitschrift für Ethnologie*
45:659–900.

Bender, J. and M. Marrinan. 2010. *The Culture of Diagram.* Stanford: Stanford University Press.

Berger, J. 1972. *Ways of Seeing.* London: BBC.

Berger, L. 2002. *Durchbrochene Messerfutteral-Beschläge* (Thekenbeschläge) *aus
Augusta Raurica: Ein Beitrag zur provinzial-römischen Ornamentik.* Augst: Römer-
stadt Augusta Raurica.

Berglund, B. E., M. Hjelmroos, and E. Kolstrup. 1991. Vegetation and Landscape
Through Time. In B. E. Berglund, ed., *The Cultural Landscape during 6000 Years in
Southern Sweden: The Ystad Project,* 109–112. Lund: Ecological Bulletins.

Biel, J. 1985. *Der Keltenfürst von Hochdorf.* Stuttgart: Konrad Theiss Verlag.

———. 1991. Giengen: A Middle La Tène Cemetery. In Moscati et al., 374.

———, ed. 1996. *Experiment Hochdorf: Keltische Handwerkskunst Wiederbelebt.*
Stuttgart: Schriften des Keltenmuseums Hochdorf/Enz.

Bille, M. and T. F. Sørensen. 2007. An Anthropology of Luminosity: The Agency of
Light. *Journal of Material Culture* 12:263–284.

Birngruber, E., R. Koch, and F. Leja. 1996. Ein frühlatènezeitlicher Grabfund bei Mittelburg. *Das archäologische Jahr in Bayern* 1995:80–83.

Blanchet, A. and A. Dieudonné. 1912. *Manuel de numismatique francaise.* vol. 1: *Monnaies frappées en Gaule depuis les origines jusqu'à Hugues Capet.* Paris: Librairie Alphonse Picard et Fils.

Blanton, R. E., G. M. Feinman, S. A. Kowalewski, and L. M. Nicholas. 1999. *Ancient Oaxaca: The Monte Alban State.* Cambridge: Cambridge University Press.

Blühm, A. and L. Lippincott. 2000. *Light! The Industrial Age 1750–1900, Art & Science, Technology & Society.* London: Thames & Hudson.

Böhme-Schönberger, A. 1998. Das Grab eines vornehmen Kriegers der Spätlatènezeit aus Badenheim: Neue Forschungen zu den Schwertscheiden mit *opus interrasile*-Zierblechen. *Germania* 76:217–256.

Bonnamour, L. 2000. *Archéologie de la Saône.* Paris: Editions Errance.

Bourgeois, Q. and D. Fontijn. 2008. Bronze Age Houses and Barrows in the Low Countries. In Arnoldussen and Fokkens, 41–57.

Boyd, B. 2009. *On the Origin of Stories: Evolution, Cognition, and Fiction.* Cambridge, MA: Harvard University Press.

Bradley, R. 1990. *The Passage of Arms: An Archaeological Analysis of Prehistoric Hoards and Votive Deposits.* Cambridge: Cambridge University Press.

———. 2002. *The Past in Prehistoric Societies.* London: Routledge.

Brandt, M. and T. Fischer. 1988. Ein Hortfund spätkeltischer Goldmünzen aus Hohenfels, Landkreis Neumarkt i.d. OPf., Oberpfalz. *Das archäologische Jahr in Bayern* 1987:89–90.

Bren, J. 1991. Stradonice: A Celtic *Oppidum.* In Moscati et al., 541.

Brett, D. 2005. *Rethinking Decoration: Pleasure and Ideology in the Visual Arts.* Cambridge: Cambridge University Press.

Brown, M. P. 2003. *Painted Labyrinth: The World of the Lindisfarne Gospels.* London: British Library.

Brox, J. 2010. *Brilliant: The Evolution of Artificial Light.* Boston: Houghton, Mifflin, Harcourt.

Bruce, V. and A. Young. 1998. *In the Eye of the Beholder: The Science of Face Perception.* Oxford: Oxford University Press.

Brück, J. 1999. Ritual and Rationality: Some Problems of Interpretation in European Archaeology. *Journal of European Archaeology* 2:313–344.

———. 2005. Experiencing the Past? The Development of a Phenomenological Archaeology in British Prehistory. *Archaeological Dialogues* 12:45–67.

———. 2006. Fragmentation, Personhood and the Social Construction of Technology in Middle and Late Bronze Age Britain. *Cambridge Archaeological Journal* 16:297–315.

———, ed. 2001. *Bronze Age Landscapes: Tradition and Transformation.* Oxford: Oxbow.

Brunaux, J.-L. 1988. *The Celtic Gauls: Gods, Rites and Sanctuaries.* Trans. D. Nash. London: Seaby.

————. 1996. *Les religions gauloises: rituels celtiques de la Gaule indépendante*. Paris: Editions Errance.

————. 1999. Ribemont-sur-Ancre (Somme): Bilan préliminaire et nouvelles hypothèses. *Gallia* 56:177–283.

————. 2006. Religion et sanctuaires. In Goudineau, 95–116.

Brunaux, J.-L. and C. Malagoli. 2003. La France du Nord. In P. Arcelin, P. and J.-L. Brunaux, eds., Cultes et sanctuaires en France à l'âge du Fer, 9–73. *Gallia* 60:1–268.

Buchez, N., C. Dumont, N. Ginoux, and D. Montaru. 1998. Les tombes à incinération de Villers-les-Roye "les longs champs" et de Marcelcave "le chemin d'ignaucourt" (Somme). In J.-L. Brunaux, G. Leman-Delerive, and C. Pommepuy, eds., *Les rites de la mort en Gaule du Nord à l'age du Fer, Revue archeologique de Picardie* vol. 1–2, 191–210.

Budden, S. and J. Sofaer. 2009. Non-Discursive Knowledge and the Construction of Identity: Potters, Potting and Performance at the Bronze Age Tell of Százhalom-batta, Hungary. *Cambridge Archaeological Journal* 19:203–220.

Bunker, E. C., C. B. Chatwin, and A.R. Farkas. 1970. *"Animal Style" Art from East to West*. New York: Asia Society.

Burke, P. 2001. *Eyewitnessing: The Uses of Images as Historical Evidence*. Ithaca, NY: Cornell University Press.

Burns, T. S. 2003. *Rome and the Barbarians, 100 B.C.–A.D. 400*. Baltimore: The Johns Hopkins University Press.

Buvot, P. 1998. Découverte d'un lieu de culte antique. La source de la Douix à Châtillon-sur-Seine. *Archéologia* 344:26–33.

Caesar. *The Gallic War*. Trans. H. J. Edwards. Cambridge, MA: Harvard University Press, 1986.

Capelle, T. 2002. Mobiliar. In *Reallexikon der germanischen Altertumskunde* 20:116–118.

Casadei, D., R. Cottiaux, and H. Sellès. 2005. Les structures et le mobilier du site d'habitat Hallstatt final—La Tène ancienne d'Allaines Mervilliers (Eure-et-Loir). *Revue archéologique de Centre de la France* 44:1–35.

Casson, L. 1989. *The Periplus Maris Erythraei: Text with Introduction, Translation, and Commentary*. Princeton: Princeton University Press.

————. 1991. *The Ancient Mariners: Seafarers and Sea Fighters of the Mediterranean in Ancient Times*. Princeton: Princeton University Press.

Cernuschi, P. and A. Herczynski. 2008. The Subversion of Gravity in Jackson Pollock's Abstractions. *Art Bulletin* 90:616–639.

Chadwick, J. 1990. Linear B. In J.T. Hooker, ed., *Reading the Past*, 137–196. London: British Museum.

Chami, F. 2004. The Egypto-Graeco-Romans and Panchaea/Azania: Sailing in the Erythraean Sea. In P. Lunde and A. Porter, eds., *Trade and Travel in the Red Sea Region*, 93–104. Oxford: British Archaeological Reports, International Series 1269.

Champion, T. C. 1985. Written Sources and the Study of the European Iron Age. In T. C. Champion and J.V.S. Megaw, eds., *Settlement and Society: Aspects of West European Prehistory in the First Millennium B.C.*, 9–22. Leicester: Leicester University Press.

Chapman, H. P., W. T. Kloek, and A. K. Wheelock, Jr. 1996. *Jan Steen: Painter and Storyteller*. Washington, DC: National Gallery of Art.

Charpy, J.-J. 1991. The Campagne Region under Celtic Rule during the Fourth and Third Centuries B.C. In Moscati et al., 243–250.

Chaudhuri, S. 2010. *The Metaphysics of Text*. New York: Cambridge University Press.

Chaume, B., ed. 2009. *La céramique hallstattienne: Approaches typologiques et chrono-culurelle*. Dijon: Éditions Universitaires de Dijon.

Chaume, B., L. Olivier, and W. Reinhard. 2000. L'enclos hallstattien de Vix "Les Herbues": un lieu cultuel de type aristocratique? In *Mailhac et le premier âge du fer en Europe occidentale: Hommages à Odette et Jean Taffanel. Actes du colloque international de Carcassonne*, 311–327. Lattes: Association pour la recherche archéologique en Langudoc oriental.

Chaume, B. and W. Reinhard. 2002. Das frühkeltische Heiligtum von Vix. In Baitinger and Pinsker, 221–222.

———. 2003. Les statues de Vix: Images héroïsées de l'aristocratie hallstattienne. *Madrider Mitteilungen* 44:249–268.

———. 2009. La céramique du sanctuaire hallstattien de Vix "les Herbues." In Chaume, 27–50.

Christ, K. 1995. Caesar und die Geschichte. In M. Weinmann-Walser, ed., *Historische Interpretationen*, 9–22. Stuttgart: Franz Steiner.

Clanchy, M. T. 1993. *From Memory to Written Record: England 1066–1307*. Second edition. Oxford: Blackwell.

Clark, A. 2008. *Supersizing the Mind: Embodiment, Action, and Cognitive Extension*. Oxford: Oxford University Press.

Clarke, J. R. 2003. *Art in the Lives of Ordinary Romans: Visual Representation and Non-Elite Viewers in Italy, 100 B.C.–A.D. 315*. Berkeley: University of California Press.

Collis, J. R. 1984. *The European Iron Age*. New York: Schocken.

Collis, J. 1995. The First Towns. In Green, 159–175.

———. 2007. The Polities of Gaul, Britain, and Ireland in the Late Iron Age. In Haselgrove and Moore, 523–528.

Cordie-Hackenberg, R. 1989. Eine latènezeitliche Doppelbestattung mit Holzmöbel. In A. Haffner, ed., *Gräber: Spiegel des Lebens: Zum Totenbrauchtum der Kelten und Römer am Beispiel des Treveregräberfeldes Wederath-Belginum*, 187–196. Mainz: Philipp von Zabern.

Crabtree, P. J. 2007. Biological Remains. In Johnston and Wailes, 157–169.

Cramsie, P. 2010. *The Story of Graphic Design: From the Invention of Writing to the Birth of Digital Design*. London: British Library.

Cunliffe, B. 2008. *Europe between the Oceans*. Oxford: Oxford University Press.

Curtis, J. 2005. Jewellery and Personal Ornaments. In J. Curtis and N. Tallis, eds., *Forgotten Empire: The World of Ancient Persia*, 132–149. London: The British Museum Press.

Dalton, O. M. 1925. *A Guide to Antiquities of the Early Iron Age in the Department of British and Mediaeval Antiquities*. Second edition. London: British Museum.

Darnton, R. 1984. *The Great Cat Massacre and Other Episodes in French Cultural History*. New York: Vintage.

De Bolla, P. 2003. *The Education of the Eye: Painting, Landscape, and Architecture in Eighteenth-Century Britain*. Stanford: Stanford University Press.

De Caro, S. 1996. The Northern Barbarians as Seen by Rome. In E. Björklund and L. Hejll, eds., *Roman Reflections in Scandinavia*, 25–29. Rome: "L'Erma" di Bretschneider.

Deffressigne-Tikonoff, S. and G. Auxiette. 2002. Réalité domestique ou symbolique du banquet? Les rejets d'une rosse dépotoir à Ennery "Landrevenne" (Moselle). In Méniel and Lambot, 231–246.

Dehn, R. 1992. Das "Heidentor" bei Egesheim, Kreis Tuttlingen: Ein bedeutendes archäologisches Denkmal der Hallstatt- und Frühlatènezeit durch Raubgrabungen zerstört. *Archäologische Ausgrabungen in Baden-Württemberg 1991*:102–105.

Dehn, R. and J. Klug. 1993. Fortführung der Grabungen am "Heidentor" bei Egesheim, Kreis Tuttlingen. *Archäologische Ausgrabungen in Baden-Württemberg 1992*:99–103.

Demattè, P. 2010. The Origins of Chinese Writing: The Neolithic Evidence. *Cambridge Archaeological Journal* 20:211–228.

Deregowski, J. B. 1989. Real Space and Represented Space: Cross-Cultural Perspectives. *Behavioral and Brain Sciences* 12: 51–119.

Desbat, A., V. Forest, and C. Batigne-Vallet. 2006. La cuisine et l'art de la table en Gaule après la conquête romaine. In D. Paunier, ed., *La romanisation et la question de l'héritage celtique*,167–192. Glux-en-Glenne: Collection Bibracte.

Deschmann, K. 1879. Eine heidnische Urnengrabstätte bei Zirknitz in Krain. *Mitteilungen der Anthropologischen Gesellschaft in Wien* 8:137–142.

Dietler, M. 1990. Driven by Drink: The Role of Drinking in the Political Economy and the Case of Early Iron Age France. *Journal of Anthropological Archaeology* 9: 352–406.

———. 1996. Feasts and Commensal Politics in the Political Economy: Food, Power, and Status in Prehistoric Europe. In P. Wiessner and W. Schiefenhövel, eds., *Food and the Status Quest*, 87–125. Oxford: Berghahn Books.

———. 2010. *Archaeologies of Colonialism: Consumption, Entanglement, and Violence in Ancient Mediterranean France*. Berkeley: University of California Press.

Drescher, H. 1955. Die Herstellung von Fibelspiralen. *Germania* 33:340–349.

Dubreucq, E. and J.-F. Piningre. 2007. Un dépôt d'armes du IIIe siècle av. J.-C. à Bourguignoon-les-Morey (Haute-Saône). In Barral et al., 671–680.

Duffy, S. and S. Kitayama. 2010. Cultural Modes of Seeing through Cultural Modes of Being: Cultural Influences on Visual Attention. In Balcetis and Lassiter, 51–75.

Dunning, C. 1991. La Tène. In Moscati et al., 366–368.

Dussot, D., G. Lintz, and D. Vuaillat. 1992. La sépulture gauloise de Boiroux commune de Saint Augustin (Corrèze). *Aquitania* 10:5–30.

Duval, P.-M. and V. Kruta. 1986. Le fourreau celtique de Cernon-sur-Coole (Marne). *Gallia* 44:1–27.

Echt, R. 1999. *Das Fürstinnengrab von Reinheim. Studien zur Kulturgeschichte der Früh La-Tène-Zeit.* Bonn: Rudolf Habelt.

———. 2004. Äusserer Anstoss und innerer Wandel: Drei Thesen zur Entstehung der Latènekunst. In Guggisberg, 203–215.

Edsman, C.-M. 1987. Fire. In M. Eliade, ed., *The Encyclopedia of Religion,* vol. 5, 340–346. New York: Macmillan.

Egg, M. 1996. *Das hallstattzeitliche Fürstengrab von Strettweg bei Judenburg in der Obersteiermark.* Mainz: Römisch-Germanisches Zentralmuseum.

Egg, M., M. Hauschild, and M. Schönfelder. 2006. Zum frühlatènezeitlichen Grab 994 mit figural verzierter Schwertscheide von Hallstatt (Oberösterreich). *Jahrbuch des Römisch-Germanischen Zentralmuseums* 53:175–216.

Eggert, M.K.H. 1999. Der Tote von Hochdorf: Bemerkungen zum Modus archäologischer Interpretation. *Archäologisches Korrespondenzblatt* 29:211–222.

Ehret, C. 2002. *The Civilizations of Africa: A History to 1800.* Charlottesville: University of Virginia Press.

Eicher, J. B., S. L. Evenson, and H. A. Lutz. 2008. *The Visible Self: Global Perspectives on Dress, Culture, and Society.* New York: Fairchild Publications.

Eicher, J. B., ed. 2010. *Encyclopedia of World Dress and Fashion.* vol. 10: *Global Perspectives.* Oxford: Oxford University Press.

Eliade, Mircea. 1959. *The Sacred and the Profane: The Nature of Religion.* Trans. Willard R. Trask. New York: Harper & Row.

Ellmers, D. 2010. Der Krater von Vix und der Reisebericht des Pytheas von Massalia: Reisen griechischer Kaufleute über die Rhône nach Britannien im 6.–4. Jahrhundert v. Chr. *Archäologisches Korrespondenzblatt* 40:363–382.

Elsner, J. 2007. *Roman Eyes: Visuality and Subjectivity in Art and Text.* Princeton: Princeton University Press.

Engelhardt, B. 1985. Das hallstattzeitliche Gräberfeld von Riedenburg-Haidhof, Lkr. Kelheim. In B. Engelhardt, ed., *Archäologische Denkmalpflege in Niederbayern: 10 Jahre Aussenstelle des Bayerischen Landesamtes für Denkmalpflege in Landshut,* 74–120. Munich: Bayerisches Landesamt für Denkmalpflege.

———. 2008. Ein spätbronzezeitliches Steinkistengrab von Mannsdorf. *Das archäologische Jahr in Bayern 2007*:30–32.

Ettel, P. and W. Irlinger. 2006. Die keltische Kultur. In Sommer, 172–173.

Evans, J. 1881. *The Ancient Bronze Implements, Weapons, and Ornaments, of Great Britain.* New York: D. Appleton and Company.

von Falkenhausen, L. 2006. *Chinese Society in the Age of Confucius (1000–250 BC): The Archaeological Evidence.* Los Angeles: Cotsen Institute of Archaeology.

———. 2010. Notes on the History of the "Silk Routes" from the Rise of the Xiongnu to the Mongol Conquest (250 BC–AD 1283). In V. Mair, ed., *Secrets of the Silk Road,* 58–68. Santa Ana, CA: Bowers Museum.

Farago, C. and R. Zwijnenberg, eds. 2003. *Compelling Visuality: The Work of Art In and Out of History.* Minneapolis: University of Minnesota Press.

Farkas, A. 2000. Filippovka and the Art of the Steppes. In J. Aruz, A. Farkas, A. Alekseev, and E. Korolkova, eds., *The Golden Deer of Eurasia: Scythian and Sarmatian Treasures from the Russian Steppes,* 3–17. New York: Metropolitan Museum.

Feugère, M. and C. Rolley. 1991. *La Vaisselle tardo-républicaine en bronze.* Dijon: Université de Bourgogne.

Fichtl, S. 2000. *La ville celtique: les oppida de 150 av. J.-C. à 15 ap. J.-C.* Paris: Errance.

Field, N. and M. P. Pearson. 2003. *Fiskerton: An Iron Age Timber Causeway with Iron Age and Roman Votive Offerings: The 1981 Excavations.* Oxford: Oxbow.

Fischer, F. 1959. *Der spätlatènezeitliche Depot-Fund von Kappel (Kreis Saulgau).* Stuttgart: Silberburg.

Fischer, J. 1990. Zu einer griechische Kline und weiterer Südimporten aus dem Fürstengrabhügel Grafenbühl, Asperg, Kr. Ludwigsburg. *Germania* 68: 115–127.

Fitzpatrick, A. P. 2007. Dancing with Dragons: Fantastic Animals in the Earlier Celtic Art of Iron Age Britain. In Haselgrove and Moore, 339–357.

Fleming, A. 2006. Post-Processual Landscape Archaeology: A Critique. *Cambridge Archaeological Journal* 16:267–280.

Flügel, C. 1996. Handgemachte Grobkeramik aus *Arae Flaviae*-Rottweil. *Fundberichte aus Baden-Württemberg* 21:315–400.

Fontijn, D. 2008. Everything in Its Right Place? On Selective Deposition, Landscape and the Construction of Identity in Later Prehistory. In A. Jones, 86–106.

Forge, A. 1970. Learning to See in New Guinea. In P. Mayer, ed., *Socialization: The Approach from Social Anthropology,* 269–291. London: Tavistock.

Fox, C. 1946. *A Find of the Early Iron Age from Llyn Cerrig Bach, Anglesey.* Cardiff: National Museum of Wales.

Frank, G. 2000. *The Memory of the Eyes: Pilgrims to Living Saints in Christian Late Antiquity.* Berkeley: University of California Press.

Frey, O.-H. 2002a. Frühe keltische Kunst: Dämonen und Götter. In Baisinger and Pinsker, 186–205.

———. 2002b. Menschen oder Heroen? Die Statuen vom Glauberg und die frühe keltische Grossplastik. In Baitinger and Pinsker, 208–218.

Furger-Gunti, A. and L. Berger. 1980. *Katalog und Tafeln der Funde aus der spät-keltischen Siedlung Basel-Gasfabrik.* Derendingen-Solothurn: Habegger (Basler Beiträge zur Ur- und Frühgeschichte).

Gambari, F. M. and G. Kaenel. 2001. L'iscrizione celtica sulla perla da Münsingen: una nuova lettura. *Archäologie der Schweiz* 24, 4, 34–37.

Garrow, D., C. Gosden, and J. D. Hill., eds. 2008. *Rethinking Celtic Art.* Oxford: Oxbow Books.

Gebhard, R. 1991. *Die Fibeln aus dem Oppidum von Manching.* Stuttgart: Franz Steiner.

———. 2004. Die spätkeltische Gräbergruppe von Hörgertshausen, Lkr./ Freising. In C.-M. Hüssen, W. Irlinger, and W. Zanier, eds., *Spätlatènezeit und frühe römische Kaiserzeit zwischen Alpenrand und Donau,* 113–122. Bonn: Rudolf Habelt.

Gebhard, R. and K. H. Rieder. 2002. Zwei bronzezeitliche Bernsteinobjekte mit Bild- und Schriftzeichen aus Bernstorf (Lkr. Freising). *Germania* 80:115–133.

Geertz, C. 1973. Deep Play: Notes on the Balinese Cockfight. In *The Interpretation of Cultures,* 412–453. New York: Basic Books.

Gell, A. 1992. The Techology of Enchantment and the Enchantment of Technology. In J. Coote and A. Shelton, eds., *Anthropology, Art and Aesthetics,* 40–63. Oxford: Clarendon Press.

———. 1998. *Art and Agency: An Anthropological Theory.* Oxford: Clarendon Press.

Gerdsen, H. 1986. *Studien zu den Schwertgräbern der älteren Hallstattzeit.* Mainz: Philipp von Zabern.

Gerlach, S. 2000. Grabhügel der Bronze- und Hallstattzeit bei Bastheim. *Das archäologische Jahr in Bayern 1999*:25–27.

Gerritsen, F. 2007. Familiar Landscapes with Unfamiliar Pasts? Bronze Age Barrows and Iron Age Communities in the Southern Netherlands. In Haselgrove and Pope, 338–353.

———. 2008. Domestic Times: Houses and Temporalities in Late Prehistoric Europe. In A. Jones, 143–161.

Gibson, J. J. 1966. *The Senses Considered as Perceptual Systems.* Boston: Houghton-Mifflin.

———. 1977. The Theory of Affordances. In Shaw and Bransford, 67–82.

———. 1979. *The Ecological Approach to Visual Perception.* Hillsdale, NJ: Lawrence Erlbaum Associates.

Giles, M. 2008. Seeing Red: The Aesthetics of Martial Objects in the British and Irish Iron Age. In Garrow et al., 59–77.

Gleba, M. 2008. You Are What You Wear: Scythian Costume as Identity. In Gleba *et al.*, pp. 13–28.

Gleba, M., C. Munkholt, and M.-L. Nosch, eds., 2008. *Dressing the Past.* Oxford: Oxbow Books.

Goldhill, S. 1996. Refracting Classical Vision: Changing Cultures of Viewing. In T. Brennan and M. Jay, eds., *Vision in Context*, 15–28. New York: Routledge.

Goldsworthy, A. 2006. *Caesar: Life of a Colossus*. New Haven: Yale University Press.

Gombrich, E. H. 1976. *The Heritage of Apelles: Studies in the Art of the Renaissance*. Oxford: Phaidon.

Good, I. 1995. On the Question of Silk in Pre-Han Eurasia. *Antiquity* 69:959–968.

Goodale, M. A. and A. D. Milner. 2004. *Sight Unseen: An Exploration of Conscious and Unconscious Vision*. Oxford: Oxford University Press.

Goody, J. 1986. *The Logic of Writing and the Organization of Society*. New York: Cambridge University Press.

———. 2000. *The Power of the Written Tradition*. Washington, DC: Smithsonian Institution Press.

Goody, J. and I. Watt. 1968. The Consequences of Literacy. In J. Goody, ed., *Literacy in Traditional Societies*, 27–68. Cambridge: Cambridge University Press.

Gosden, C. 2005. What Do Objects Want? *Journal of Archaeological Method and Theory* 12:193–211.

Gosden, C. and G. Lock. 2007. The Aesthetics of Landscape on the Berkshire Downs. In Haselgrove and Pope, 279–292.

Gosden, C. and Y. Marshall. 1999. The Cultural Biography of Objects. *World Archaeology* 31:169–178.

Goudineau, C., ed. 2006. *Religion et société en Gaule*. Paris: Editions Errance.

Grane, T. 2003. Roman Sources for the Geography and Ethnography of Germania. In Jørgensen et al., 126–147.

Gransar, F., G. Auxiette, S. Desenne, B. Hénon, F. Malrain, V. Matterne, and E. Pinard. 2007. Expressions symboliques, manifestations rituelles et cultuelles en contexte domestique au Ier millénaire avant notre ère dans le Nord de La France. In Barral et al., 549–564.

Green, M., ed. 1995. *The Celtic World*. London: Routledge.

Gregory, R. L. 1998. *Eye and Brain: The Psychology of Seeing*. Fifth edition. Oxford: Oxford University Press.

———. 2009. *Seeing through Illusions*. Oxford: Oxford University Press.

Grömer, K. 2006. Textilien der Bronzezeit in Mitteleuropa. *Archaeologia Austriaca* 90:31–71.

Grzymski, K. 2004. Meroë. In D. A. Welsby and J. R. Anderson, eds., *Sudan: Ancient Treasure*, 165–167. London: British Museum Press.

Guggisberg, M. A. 2000. *Der Goldschatz von Erstfeld: Ein keltischer Bilderzyklus zwischen Mitteleuropa und der Mittelmeerwelt*. Basel: Schweizerische Gesellschaft für Ur- und Frühgeschichte.

———. 2004. Keimelia: Altstücke in fürstlichen Gräbern diesseits und jenseits der Alpen. In Guggisberg, 175–192.

Guggisberg, M. A. 2006. L'art celtique: Spécificité et points de convergence. In M. Szabó, ed., *Les Civilisés et les Barbares du Ve au IIe siècle avant J.-C.*, 229–243. Glux-en-Glenne: Collection Bibracte.

———, ed. 2004. *Die Hydria von Grächwil: Zur Funktion und Rezeption mediterraner Importe in Mitteleuropa im 6. und 5. Jahrhundert v. Chr.* Bern: Bernisches Historisches Museum.

Guichard, V. 1987. La céramique peinte à décor zoomorphe des IIe et Ier s. avant J.-C. en territoire ségusiave. *Études Celtiques* 24:103–143.

———. 2009. Imaginative Designs from the Heart of France: Pottery from Clermont-Ferrand, about 120 BC. In F. Müller, 234–237.

Guillaumet, J.-P. 1991. Bibracte: An Oppidum of the Aedui People. In Moscati et al., 591.

Haffner, A. 1992. Die frühlatènezeitlichen Fürstengräber von Hochscheid im Hunsrück. *Trierer Zeitschrift* 55:25–103.

———. 2003. Le Torque: Type et fonction. In Rolley, 176–189.

———, ed. 1989. *Gräber-Spiegel des Lebens: Zum Totenbrauchtum der Kelten und Römer an Beispiel des Treverer-Gräberfeldes Wederath-Belginum.* Mainz: Philipp von Zabern.

Hahn, E. 1992. Die menschlichen Skelettreste. In F. Maier, U. Geilenbrügge, E. Hahn, H.-J. Köhler, and S. Sievers, eds., *Ergebnisse der Ausgrabungen 1984–1987 in Manching*, 214–234. Stuttgart: Franz Steiner.

Hald, M. 1980. *Ancient Danish Textiles from Bogs and Burials: A Comparative Study of Costume and Iron Age Textiles.* Trans., J. Olsen. Copenhagen: National Museum.

Hallett, M. 2006. Hogarth's Variety. In M. Hallett and C. Riding, eds., *Hogarth*, 13–21. London: Tate Publishing.

Hänsel, B. and P. Medovic. 1991. Vorbericht über die jugoslawisch-deutschen Ausgrabungen in der Siedlung von Feudvar bei Mošorin (Gem. Titel, Vojvodina) von 1986–1990. *Bericht der Römisch-Germanischen Kommission* 72:45–204.

Harding, A. 2000. *European Societies of the Bronze Age.* Cambridge: Cambridge University Press.

———. 2006. Facts and Fantasies from the Bronze Age. *Antiquity* 80:463–465.

Harper, R., A. Taylor, and M. Molloy. 2008. Intelligent Artefacts at Home in the 21st Century. In Knappett and Malafouris, 97–120.

Harris, W. V. 2007. The Late Republic. In Scheidel et al., 511–539.

Hartley, D. 1979. *Lost Country Life.* New York: Pantheon Books.

Haselgrove, C. 1997. Iron Age Brooch Deposition and Chronology. In A. Gwilt and C. Haselgrove, eds., *Reconstructing Iron Age Societies*, 51–72. Oxford: Oxbow Books.

———. 2005a. The Incidence of Iron Age Coins on Archaeological Sites in Belgic Gaul. In J. Metzler and D. Wigg-Wolf, eds., *Die Kelten und Rom: Neue numismatische Forschungen*, 247–296. Mainz: Philipp von Zabern.

————. 2005b. A Trio of Temples: A Reassessment of Iron Age Coin Deposition at Hayling Island, Harlow and Wanborough. In Haselgrove and Wigg-Wolf, 381–418.

————. 2007. The Age of Enclosure: Later Iron Age Settlement and Society in Northern France. In Haselgrove and Moore, 492–522.

Haselgrove, C. and T. Moore, eds. 2007. *The Later Iron Age in Britain and Beyond.* Oxford: Oxbow Books.

Haselgrove, C. and R. Pope, eds. 2007. *The Early Iron Age in Britain and the Near Continent.* Oxford: Oxbow Books.

Haselgrove, C. and D. Wigg-Wolf, eds. 2005. *Iron Age Coinage and Ritual Practices.* Mainz: Philipp von Zabern.

Haseloff, G. 1981. *Die germanische Tierornamentik in der Völkerwanderungszeit.* Berlin: Walter de Gruyter.

Hayden, B. 2009. Funerals as Feasts: Why Are They So Important? *Cambridge Archaeological Journal* 19:29–52.

Heather, P. 2006. *The Fall of the Roman Empire.* New York: Oxford University Press.

Hedeager, L. 2000. Migration Period Europe: The Formation of a Political Mentality. In F. Theuws and J. L. Nelson, eds., *Rituals of Power from Late Antiquity to the Early Middle Ages,* 15–57. Leiden: Brill.

————. 2011. *Iron Age Myth and Materiality: An Archaeology of Scandinavia AD 400–1000.* London: Routledge.

Heft, H. 2001. *Ecological Psychology in Context: James Gibson, Roger Barker, and the Legacy of William James's Radical Empiricism.* Mahwah, NJ: Lawrence Erlbaum Associates.

Heger, F. 1882. Grosser Fund prähistorischer Bronzen bei Dux in Böhmen. *Mitteilungen der Anthropologischen Gesellschaft in Wien* 12:80–82.

Helms, M. W. 1988. *Ulysses' Sail: An Ethnographic Odyssey of Power, Knowledge, and Geographical Distance.* Princeton: Princeton University Press.

————. 1993. *Craft and the Kingly Ideal: Art, Trade, and Power.* Austin: University of Texas Press.

Hénon, B. et al., 2002. Trois nouveaux sites d'habitat du Hallstatt final/La Tène ancienne dans la vallée de l'Aisne. In Méniel and Lambot, 49–66.

Hiebert, F. 2011. The Lost Worlds of Afghanistan. In Hiebert and Cambon, 55–64.

Hiebert, F. and P. Cambon, eds. 2011. *Afghanistan: Crossroads of the Ancient World.* London: British Museum Press.

Hill, J. D. 1995. *Ritual and Rubbish in Iron Age Wessex: A Study in the Formation of a Specific Archaeological Record.* Oxford: British Archaeological Reports.

————. 2002a. Pottery and the Expression of Society, Economy and Culture. In Woodward and Hill, pp. 75–84.

————. 2002b. Just about the Potter's Wheel? Using, Making and Depositing Middle and Later Iron Age Pots in East Anglia. In Woodward and Hill, 143–160.

Hill, J. D. 2006. Are We Any Closer to Understanding how Later Iron Age Societies Worked (or Did Not Work)? In C. Haselgrove, ed., *Les mutations de la fin de l'âge du Fer,* 169–179. Glux-en-Glenne: Collection Bibracte.

———. 2007. The Dynamics of Social Change in Later Iron Age Eastern and South-Eastern England *c.* 300 BC–AD 43. In Haselgrove and Moore, 16–40.

Hingley, R. 1997. Iron, Ironworking and Regeneration: A Study of the Symbolic Meaning of Metalworking in Iron Age Britain. In A. Gwilt and C. Haselgrove, eds., *Reconstructing Iron Age Societies,* 9–18. Oxford: Oxbow Books.

———. 2006. The Deposition of Iron Objects in Britain During the Later Prehistoric and Roman Periods: Contextual Analysis and the Significance of Iron. *Britannia* 37:213–257.

Hingley, R., ed. 2001. *Images of Rome: Perceptions of Ancient Rome in Europe and the United States in the Modern Age.* Portsmouth, RI: Journal of Roman Archaeology.

Hinz, H. 1976. Beleuchtung. In *Reallexikon der germanischen Altertumskunde* 2:207–208.

Hochstetter, A. 1980. *Die Hügelgräberbronzezeit in Niederbayern.* Kallmünz/Opf.: Michael Lassleben.

Hodson, F. R. 1968. *The La Tène Cemetery of Münsingen-Rain.* Bern: Stämpfli.

Hoernes, R. 1891. Ausgrabungen bei Oedenburg. *Mitteilungen der Anthropologischen Gesellschaft in Wien* 21, Sitzungsberichte, 71–78.

Hogarth, W. 1734/1955. *The Analysis of Beauty.* Ed., J. Burke. Oxford: Clarendon Press.

Holm, B. 1965. *Northwest Coast Indian Art: An Analysis of Form.* Seattle: University of Washington Press.

Homans, G. C. 1941. *English Villages of the Thirteenth Century.* Cambridge, MA: Harvard University Press.

Hoppe, M. 2006. Ein urnenfelderzeitliches Grab von Fechenbach. *Das archäologische Jahr in Bayern 2005:*36–38.

Hoskins, J. 1998. *Biographical Objects: How Things Tell the Stories of People's Lives.* New York: Routledge.

Hunter, F. 2001. The Carnyx in Iron Age Europe. *Antiquaries Journal* 81:77–108.

———. 2005. The Image of the Warrior in the British Iron Age: Coin Iconography in Context. In Haselgrove and Wigg-Wolf, 43–68.

———. 2008. Celtic Art in Roman Britain. In Garrow et al., 129–145.

Irlinger, W. E. and S. Winghart. 1999. Eine Statuette der Athene aus dem südbayerischen Alpenvorland sowie Siedlung- und Grabfunde der mittleren bis späten Latènezeit von Dornach, Gemeinde Aschheim, Landkreis München. *Germania* 77:71–162.

Ingold, T. 2007. *Lines: A Brief History.* London and NY: Routledge.

Iron Age Gold Hoard Saved for Ipswich Museum. *Art Fund News,* June 21, 2011.

Isherwood, C. 1939. *Goodbye to Berlin.* New York: Random House.

Jacobi, G. 1974a. Zum Schriftgebrauch in keltischen Oppida nördlich der Alpen. *Hamburger Beiträge zur Archäologie* 4:171–181.

————. 1974b. *Werkzeug und Gerät aus dem Oppidum von Manching*. Wiesbaden: Franz Steiner.

Jacobsthal, P. 1944. *Early Celtic Art*. Oxford: Clarendon.

James, S. and V. Rigby. 1997. *Britain and the Celtic Iron Age*. London: British Museum Press.

Janssen-Kim, M. 2007a. Schachtel mit Wolfsdekor. In Wieczorek and Lind, 192.

————. 2007b. Bandbesatz oder Gürtelblech mit Tigerdekor. In Wieczorek and Lind, 278.

————. 2007c. Zierblech mit Löwendekor. In Wieczorek and Lind, 278–279.

————. 2007d. Vier Zierscheiben mit Tigerdekor. In Wieczorek and Lind, 280.

Jennbert, K. 2011. *Animals and Humans: Archaeology and Old Norse Religion*. Stockholm: Nordic Academic Press.

Jenny, W. A. von. 1935. Zur Herkunft des Trompetenornamentes. *IPEK* 10:31–48.

Jerem, E. and J. Kardos. 1985. Entwicklung und Charakter der eisenzeitlichen Graphittonware. *Mitteilungen der Österreichischen Arbeitsgemeinschaft für Ur- und Frühgeschichte* 35:65–75.

Joachim, H.-E. 1995. *Waldalgesheim: Das Grab einer keltischen Fürstin*. Cologne: Rheinland-Verlag.

Joachim, W. 1999. Eine späthallstatt-frühlatènezeitliche Siedlung in Remseck-Neckargröningen. *Archäologische Ausgrabungen in Baden-Württemberg 1998*: 104–106.

Johnson, M. 1987. *The Body in the Mind: The Bodily Basis of Meaning, Imagination, and Reason*. Chicago: University of Chicago Press.

————. 2007. *The Meaning of the Body: Aesthetics of Human Understanding*. Chicago: University of Chicago Press.

Johnson, W. A. and H. N. Parker, eds. 2009. *Ancient Literacies: The Culture of Reading in Greece and Rome*. Oxford: Oxford University Press.

Johnston, S. A. and B. Wailes. 2007. *Dún Ailinne: Excavations at an Irish Royal Site, 1968–1975*. Philadelphia: University of Pennsylvania Museum of Archaeology and Anthropology.

Joly, M. and P. Barral. 2007. Le sanctuaire de Mirebeau-sur-Bèze (Côte-d'Or): Bilan des recherches récentes. In Barral et al., 55–72.

Jones, A. 2007. *Memory and Material Culture*. Cambridge: Cambridge University Press.

Jones, A., ed. 2008. *Prehistoric Europe: Theory and Practice*. Malden, MA: Wiley-Blackwell.

Jones, C. 1998. Interpreting the Perceptions of Past People. *Archaeological Review from Cambridge* 15:7–22.

Jones, M. 2009. Comment following Hayden 2009 paper, 43.

Jope, E. M. 2000. *Early Celtic Art in the British Isles*. Oxford: Clarendon Press.

Jørgensen, L., B. Storgaard, and L. G. Thomsen, eds. 2003. *The Spoils of Victory: The North in the Shadow of the Roman Empire*. Copenhagen: Nationalmuseet.

Joy, J. 2008. Reflections on Celtic Art: A Re-Examination of Mirror Decoration. In Garrow et al., 77–98.

———. 2010. *Iron Age Mirrors: A Biographical Approach.* Oxford: Archaeopress.

Jung, M. 2008. Palmettengesichter auf Attaschen etruskischer Kannen als mögliche Vorbilder latènezeitlicher Gesichtsdarstellungen? *Archäologisches Korrespondenzblatt* 38:211–222.

Kacharava, D. and G. Kvirkvelia. 2008. The Golden Graves of Ancient Vani. In D. Kacharava and G. Kvirkvelia, eds., *Wine, Worship, and Sacrifice: The Golden Graves of Ancient Vani*, 126–205. Princeton: Princeton University Press.

Kaenel, G. and F. Müller. 1991. The Swiss Plateau. In Moscati et al., 251–259.

Kalof, L. 2007. *Looking at Animals in Human History.* London: Reaktion Books.

Kappel, I. 1969. *Die Graphittonkeramik von Manching.* Wiesbaden: Franz Steiner.

Karner, P. L. 1891. Ueber einen Bronzesitula-Fund bei Kuffarn in Niederösterreich. *Mitteilungen der Anthropologischen Gesellschaft in Wien* 21:68–71.

Kastelic, J. 1965. *Situla Art.* New York: McGraw-Hill.

Kaul, F. 2003. The Hjortspring Find: The Oldest of the Large Nordic War Booty Sacrifices. In Jørgensen et al., 212–223.

Keller, E. 1984. *Die frühkaiserzeitlichen Körpergräber von Heimstetten bei München und die verwandten Funde aus Südbayern.* Munich: C.H. Beck.

Keller, F. 1866. *The Lake Dwellings of Switzerland and Other Parts of Europe.* Trans., J. E. Lee. London: Longsmans, Green.

Keller, J. 1965. *Das keltische Fürstengrab von Reinheim.* Mainz: Römisch-Germanisches Zentralmuseum.

Kellner, H.-J. 1990. *Die Münzfunde von Manching und die keltischen Fundmünzen aus Südbayern.* Stuttgart: Franz Steiner.

Kern, A., V. Guichard, R. Cordie, and W. David, eds. 2009. *Situlen: Bilderwelt zwischen Etruskern und Kelten auf antikem Weingeschirr.* Vienna: Naturhistorisches Museum.

Kilian-Dirlmeier, I. 1972. *Die hallstattzeitlichen Gürtelbleche und Blechgürtel Mitteleuropas.* Munich: C.H. Beck.

Kimmig, W., ed. 1988. *Das Kleinaspergle.* Stuttgart: Theiss.

Kimmig, W. and W. Rest. 1954. Ein Fürstengrab der späten Hallstattzeit von Kappel am Rhein. *Jahrbuch des Römisch-Germanisches Zentralmuseums* 1:179–216.

King, A. and G. Soffe. 2001. Internal Organisation and Deposition at the Iron Age Temple on Hayling Island, Hampshire. In J. Collis, ed., *Society and Settlement in Iron Age Europe,* 111–123. Sheffield: J. R. Collis Publications.

Klindt-Jensen, O. 1961. *Gundestrupkedelen.* Copenhagen: Nationalmuseet .

Knappett, C. 2002. Photographs, Skeuomorphs and Marionettes: Some Thoughts on Mind, Agency and Object. *Journal of Material Culture* 7:97–117.

Knappett, C. and L. Malafouris, eds. 2008. *Material Agency: Towards a Non-Anthropocentric Approach.* New York: Springer.

Kociumaka, C. 1991. Eine etruskische Bronzestatuette aus dem Nördlinger Ries. *Das archäologische Jahr in Bayern 1990*:62–64.

Kohl, P. L. 2007. *The Making of Bronze Age Eurasia*. Cambridge: Cambridge University Press.

Kohlberger-Schaub, T. and A. Schaub. 2007. Eine späthallstatt-frühlatènezeitliche Siedlung bei Steindorf, Landkreis Aichach-Friedberg, Schwaben. *Das archäologische Jahr in Bayern 2006*:68-70.

Kopytoff, I. 1986. The Cultural Biography of Things: Commoditization as Process. In Appadurai, 64–91.

Körber, K.T. 1905. *Neue Inschriften des Mainzer Museums*. Mainz: Verlag des Altertumsvereins.

Kos, P. and D. G. Wigg. 2002. Keltisches Münzwesen. *Reallexikon der germanischen Altertumskunde* 20:364–372.

Kossack, G. 1964. Trinkgeschirr als Kultgerät der Hallstattzeit. In P. Grimm, ed., *Varia Archaeologica*, 96–105. Berlin: Deutsche Akademie der Wissenschaften.

———. 1970. *Gräberfelder der Hallstattzeit an Main und Fränkischer Saale*. Kallmünz: Michael Lassleben.

Krahe, G. 1990. Das Grab eines bronzezeitlichen "Prominenten" von Untermeitingen. *Das archäologische Jahr in Bayern 1989*:66–71.

Krämer, W. 1964. *Das keltische Gräberfeld von Nebringen (Kreis Böblingen)*. Stuttgart: Silberburg.

———. 1966. Ein frühkaiserzeitlicher Brandopferplatz auf dem Auerberg im bayerischen Alpenvorland. *Jahrbuch des Römisch-Germanischen Zentralmuseums* 13:60–66.

———. 1982. Graffiti auf Spätlatènekeramik aus Manching. *Germania* 60:489–499.

———. 1985. *Die Grabfunde von Manching und die latènezeitlichen Flachgräber in Südbayern*. Stuttgart: Franz Steiner.

———. 1996. Prähistorische Fibelbilder. *Bayerische Vorgeschichtsblätter* 61:133–142.

Krausse, D. 1996. *Hochdorf III: Das Trink- und Speiseservice aus dem späthallstattzeitlichen Fürstengrab von Eberdingen-Hochdorf (Kreis Ludwigsburg)*. Stuttgart: Konrad Theiss.

———. 1999. Der "Keltenfürst" von Hochdorf: Dorfältester oder Sakralkönig? *Archäologisches Korrespondenzblatt* 29:339–358.

———. 2004. Komos und Kottabos am Hohenasperg? Überlegungen zur Funktion mediterraner Importgefässe des 6. und 5. Jahrhunderts aus Südwestdeutschland. In Guggisberg, 193–201.

———. 2006. The Prehistory of the Celts in South-West Germany: Centralisation Processes and Celtic Ethnogenesis in the Heart of Europe. In D. Vitali, ed., *Celtes et Gaulois: L'Archéologie face à l'Histoire: La Préhistoire des Celtes*, 131–142. Glux-en-Glenne: Collection Bibracte.

Krause, D. ed. 2008. *Frühe Zentralisierungs- und Urbanisierungsprozesse: Zur Genese und Entwicklung frühkeltischer Fürstensitze.* Stuttgart: Theiss.

Kreuz, A. 2002. Landwirtschaft und Umwelt im keltischen Hessen. In Baitinger and Pinsker, 75–81.

Kristiansen, K. 1998. *Europe Before History.* Cambridge: Cambridge University Press.

———. 2007. Eurasian Transformations: Mobility, Ecological Change, and the Transmission of Social Institutions in the Third Millennium and the Early Second Millennium B.C.E. In A. Hornborg and C. L. Crumley, eds., *The World System and the Earth System,* 149–162. Walnut Creek, CA: Left Coast Books.

Kristiansen, K. and T. B. Larsson. 2005. *The Rise of Bronze Age Society.* Cambridge: Cambridge University Press.

Kristoffersen, S. 2010. Half Beast-Man: Hybrid Figures in Animal Art. *World Archaeology* 42:261–272.

Kruta, V. 1991. The Treasure of Duchcov. In Moscati et al., 295.

Kühn, H. 1976. *Geschichte der Vorgeschichtsforschung.* Berlin: Walter de Gruyter.

Künzl, E. 2008. *Die Germanen.* Stuttgart: Theiss.

Kurz, G. 1995. *Keltische Hort- und Gewässerfunde in Mitteleuropa: Deponierungen der Latènezeit.* Stuttgart: Konrad Theiss.

Kurz, S. 2008. Neue Forschungen im Umfeld der Heuneburg: Zwischenbericht zum Stand des Projekts "Zentralort und Umland: Untersuchungen zur Struktur der Heuneburg-Aussensiedlung und zum Verhältnis der Heuneburg zu umgebenden Höhensiedlungen." In Krause, 163–183.

Küster, H. 1995. *Geschichte der Landschaft in Mitteleuropa: Von der Eiszeit bis zur Gegenwart.* Munich: C.H. Beck.

Kuzmina, E. E. 2008. *The Prehistory of the Silk Road.* Philadelphia: University of Pennsylvania Press.

Lakoff, G. and M. Johnson. 1980. *Metaphors We Live By.* Chicago: University of Chicago Press.

Lambot, B. 2002. Maison et société à Acy-Romance (Ardennes). In Méniel and Lambot, 115–124.

———. 2006. Religion et habitat: Les fouilles d'Acy-Romance. In Goudineau, 177–188.

———. 2007. Reconnaissance de manifestations rituelles et cultuelles dans les habitats du Second âge du Fer: Le cas d'Acy-Romance (Ardennes). In Barral et al., 565–578.

Lange, C. and N. Ohlsen, eds. 2010. *Realismus: Das Abenteuer der Wirklichkeit.* Munich: Hirmer Verlag.

LeCount, L. J. and J. H. Blitz. 2010. A Comment on "Funerals as Feasts: Why Are They So Important?" *Cambridge Archaeological Journal* 20:263–265.

Leigh, D. 1984. Ambiguity in Anglo-Saxon Style I Art. *Antiquaries Journal* 64:34–42.

Lejars, T. 1994. *Gournay III: Les fourreaux d'épée: Le sanctuaire de Gournay-sur-Aronde et l'armement des Celtes de La Tène moyenne.* Paris: Editions Errance.

————. 2007. La Tène: Les collections du Musée Schwab à Bienne (Canton de Berne). In Barral et al., 357–366.

Lenman, R., ed. 2005. *The Oxford Companion to the Photograph.* Oxford: Oxford University Press.

Lequoy, M.-C. 1993. Le depot funeraire de la Mailleraye-sur-Seine. In D. Cliquet, M. Remy-Watte, V. Guichard, and M. Vaginay, eds. *Les Celtes en Normandie: Les rites funéraires en Gaule (IIIème-Ier siècle),* 121–133. *Revue Archéologique de l'Ouest,* suppl. 6.

Lindenschmit, L. 1891. Das etruskische Schwert aus den Gräbern von Hallstadt und das vorgeschichtliche Eisenschwert nördlich der Alpen. *Archiv für Anthropologie* 19:309–316.

Lindstrøm, T. C. and S. Kristoffersen. 2001. "Figure it Out!" Psychological Perspectives on Perception in Migration Period Animal Art. *Norwegian Archaeological Review* 34:65–84.

Lord, A. B. 1991. *Epic Singers and Oral Tradition.* Ithaca, NY: Cornell University Press.

Lorenz, H. 1986. *Rundgang durch eine keltische 'Stadt.'* Pfaffenhofen: W. Ludwig Verlag.

Lucke, W. and O.-H. Frey. 1962. *Die Situla in Providence (Rhode Island): Ein Beitrag zur Situlenkunst des Osthallstattkreises.* Berlin: Walter de Gruyter.

Lund, A. A. 1998. *Die ersten Germanen: Ethnizität und Ethnogenese.* Heidelberg: Universitätsverlag C. Winter.

MacMullen, R. 1965. The Celtic Renaissance. *Historia* 14:93–104.

Maguire, E. A. et al., 2000. Navigation-related Structural Change in the Hippocampi of Taxi Drivers. *Proceedings of the National Academy of Sciences* 97, 8:4398–4403.

Maier, F. 1970. *Die bemalte Spätlatène-Keramik von Manching.* Wiesbaden: Franz Steiner.

————. 1976. Ein Gefässdepot mit bemalter Keramik von Manching. *Germania* 54:63–74.

Malafouris, L. 2008. At the Potter's Wheel: An Argument *for* Material Agency. In Knappett and Malafouris, 19–36.

Malafouris, L. and C. Renfrew. 2010. The Cognitive Life of Things: Archaeology, Material Engagement and the Extended Mind. In Malafouris and Renfrew, 1–12.

————, eds. 2010. *The Cognitive Life of Things: Recasting the Boundaries of the Mind.* Cambridge: McDonald Institute.

Maniquet, C. 2008. Le dépôt culturel du sanctuaire gaulois de Tintignac à Naves (Corrèze). *Gallia* 65:273–326.

————. 2009. *Les guerriers gaulois de Tintignac.* Limoges: Editions Culture & Patrimoine en Limousin.

Mannsperger, D. 1981. Münzen und Münzfunde. In K. Bittel, W. Kimmig, and S. Schiek, eds., *Die Kelten in Baden-Württemberg,* 228–247. Stuttgart: Konrad Theiss Verlag.

Mansfeld, G. 1973. *Die Fibeln der Heuneburg, 1950–1970*. Berlin: Walter de Gruyter.

Matiegka, H. 1896. Anthropophagie in der prähistorischen Ansiedlung bei Knovíze und in der prähistorischen Zeit überhaupt. *Mitteilungen der Anthropologischen Gesellschaft in Wien* 26:129–140.

Mattingly, D. 2006. *An Imperial Possession: Britain in the Roman Empire*. London: Allen Lane.

———. 2008. The Unmasking of Iron Age Identities: Art after the Roman Conquest. In Garrow et al., 214–218.

Meduna, J. 1991. The *Oppidum* of Staré-Hradisko. In Moscati et al., 546–547.

Mees, B. 2006. Runes in the First Century. In M. Stoklund, M. L. Nielsen, B. Holmberg, and G. Fellows-Jensen, eds., *Runes and Their Secrets*, 201–231. Copenhagen: Museum Tusculanum Press.

Megaw, J.V.S. 1970. *Art of the European Iron Age*. Bath: Adams & Dart.

Megaw, J.V.S. and M. R. Megaw. 1989. *Celtic Art*. London: Thames and Hudson.

———. 1990. *The Basse-Yutz Find: Masterpieces of Celtic Art*. London: The Society of Antiquaries.

Mehendale, S. 2011. Begram: At the Heart of the Silk Roads. In Hiebert and Cambon, 131–143.

Meiborg, C. and A. Müller. 1997. *Die urnenfelder- und hallstattzeitliche Siedlung "Kanal I" und das frühhallstattzeitliche Gräberfeld "Am Urnenfeld" von Kelheim*. Espelkamp: Marie Leidorf.

Meicun, L. 2008. The Art of Pottery and Cultural Exchanges Between China and the West. In T. Lawton, ed., *New Frontiers in Global Archaeology: Defining China's Ancient Traditions*, 165–189. West Palm Beach, FL: AMS Foundation for the Arts, Sciences and Humanities.

Meixner, G., K. H. Rieder, and M. Schaich. 1997. Das hallstattzeitliche Grabhügelfeld von Kinding/Ilbling. *Das archäologische Jahr in Bayern 1996*:90–93.

Méniel, P. and B. Lambot, eds. 2002. *Repas des vivants et nourriture pour les morts en Gaule*. Reims: Société Archéologique Champenoise.

Messaris, P. 1997. *Visual Persuasion: The Role of Images in Advertising*. Thousand Oaks, CA: Sage.

Metzler, J. 1995. *Das treverische Oppidum auf dem Titelberg (G.-H. Luxemburg)*. 2 vols. Luxembourg: Musée National d'Histoire et d'Art.

Metzler, J., R. Waringo, R. Bis, and N. Metzler-Zens. 1991. *Clemency et les tombes de l'aristocratie en Gaule Belgique*. Luxembourg: Musée National d'Histoire et d'Art.

Meunier, N. 2002. Analyse fonctionnelle de la céramique de la nécropole de Bucy-le-Long "Le Fond du Petit Marais" (Aisne), La Tène C1–D1. In Méniel and Lambot, 81–93.

Michaelson, C. 2007. Qin Gold and Jade. In J. Portal, ed., *The First Emperor: China's Terracotta Army*, 94–103. London: British Museum Press.

Milleker, E. J. 2000. The Year One: Empires and Trade Routes Across the Ancient World. In E. J. Milleker, ed., *The Year One: Art of the Ancient World East and West,* 3–23. New York: Metropolitan Museum of Art.

Miller, D. 2008. *The Comfort of Things.* Cambridge: Polity.

———. 2010. *Stuff.* Cambridge: Polity.

Miller, D., ed. 1998. *Material Cultures: Why Some Things Matter.* Chicago: University of Chicago Press.

Mitchell, J. P. 2007. Towards an Archaeology of Performance. In D. A. Barrowclough and C. Malone, eds., *Cult in Context: Reconsidering Ritual in Archaeology,* 336–339. Oxford: Oxbow.

Mitchell, W.J.T. 1978. *Blake's Composite Art: A Study of the Illuminated Poetry.* Princeton: Princeton University Press.

———. 1983. Metamorphoses of the Vortex: Hogarth, Turner, and Blake. In R. Wendorf, ed., *Articulate Images: The Sister Arts from Hogarth to Tennyson,* 125–168. Minneapolis: University of Minnesota Press.

Mora-Marín, D. F. 2009. Early Olmec Writing: Reading Format and Reading Order. *Latin American Antiquity* 20:395–412.

Morel, J.-P. 2007. Early Rome and Italy. In Scheidel *et al.,* 487–510.

Moreland, J. 2010. *Archaeology, Theory and the Middle Ages.* London: Duckworth.

Morphy, H. 1994. The Anthropology of Art. In T. Ingold, ed., *Companion Encyclopedia of Anthropology,* 648–685. London: Routledge.

———. 2005. Seeing Indigenous Australian Art. In M. Westermann, ed., *Anthropologies of Art,* 124–142. Williamstown, MA: Sterling and Francine Clark Art Institute.

———. 2007. *Becoming Art: Exploring Cross-Cultural Categories.* Oxford: Berg.

———. 2009. Art as a Mode of Action: Some Problems with Gell's Art and Agency. *Journal of Material Culture* 14:5–27.

Morris, E. K. 2009. Behavior Analysis and Ecological Psychology: Past, Present, and Future: A Review of Harry Heft's *Ecological Psychology in Context. Journal of the Experimental Analysis of Behavior* 92:275–304.

Morris, E. L. 2002. Staying Alive: The Function and Use of Prehistoric Ceramics. In Woodward and Hill, 54–61.

Moscati, S., O.-H. Frey, V. Kruta, B. Raftery, and M. Szabó, eds. 1991. *The Celts.* New York: Rizzoli.

Möslein, S. and J. Prammer. 2001. *Ausgrabungen und Funde in Altbayern, 1998–2000.* Straubing: Gäubodenmuseum.

Mötsch, A. 2008. Keramische Adaptionen mediterraner Bronzekannen auf dem Mont Lassois, Dép. Côte-d'Or, Burgund. *Archäologisches Korrespondenzblatt* 38:201–210.

Motyková, K., P. Drda, and A. Rybová. 1991. The Hillfort and Sanctuary of Závist. In Moscati et al., 180–181.

Moulhérat, C. and C. Rolley. 2003. L'organisation de la tombe. In Rolley, 24–28.

Mukarovsky, J. 1988. Art as Semiological Fact. In N. Bryson, ed., *Calligram: Essays in the New Art History from France*, 1-7. Cambridge: Cambridge University Press.

von Müller, A. 1964. *Die jungbronzezeitliche Siedlung von Berlin-Lichterfelde*. Berlin: Hessling.

Müller, F. 1990. *Der Massenfund von der Tiefenau bei Bern: Zur Deutung latènezeitlicher Sammelfunde mit Waffen*. Basel: Schweizerische Gesellschaft für Ur- und Frühgeschichte.

———. 2007a. Les dépôts en milieu humide dans la région des Trois-Lacs (Suisse): Un bilan de l'information disponible. In Barral et al., 347–356.

———. 2007b. Beutegut, Opfergaben und Trophäen bei den antiken Kelten. In H. Birkhan, ed., *Kelten-Einfälle an der Donau*, 361–378. Vienna: Österreichische Akademie der Wissenschaften.

———, ed. 2009. *Art of the Celts 700 BC to AD 700*. Bern: Historisches Museum.

Müller, S. 1897. *Vor oldtid: Danmarks forhistoriske archaeologi*. Copenhagen: Det Nordiske Forlag.

Müller, S. 2000. Zum Stand der Auswertung des urnenfelderzeitlichen Opferplatzes zu Füssen der "Schellnecker Wänd" bei Altessing. In M. M. Rind, ed., *Geschichte ans Licht gebracht: Archäologie im Landkreis Kelheim*, 86–94. Büchenbach: Verlag Dr. Faustus.

Müller-Depreux, A. 2005. *Die hallstatt- und frühlatènezeitliche Siedlung "Erdwerk I" von Niedererlbach, Landkreis Landshut*. Kallmünz: Michael Lassleben.

Müller-Karpe, H. 1955. Das urnenfelderzeitliche Wagengrab von Hart a.d. Alz, Oberbayern. *Bayerische Vorgeschichtsblätter* 21:46–75.

Müller-Scheessel, N. 2005. Die Toten als Zeichen: Veränderungen im Umgang mit Grab und Leichnam während der Hallstattzeit. In T.L. Kienlin, ed., *Die Dinge als Zeichen: Kulturelles Wissen und materielle Kultur*, 339–354. Bonn: Habelt.

Natsoulas, T. 2004. "To See Things is To Perceive What They Afford": James J. Gibson's Concept of Affordance. *Journal of Mind and Behavior* 25:323–347.

de Navarro, J. M. 1972. *The Finds from the Site of La Tène*, vol. 1: *Scabbards and the Swords Found in Them*. 2 vols. London: Oxford University Press.

Nedoma, R. 2002. Negauer Helm: Inschriften. In *Reallexikon der germanischen Altertumskunde* 21:56–61.

Needham, S. and S. Bowman. 2005. Flesh-Hooks, Technological Complexity and the Atlantic Bronze Age Feasting Complex. *Journal of European Archaeology* 8:93–136.

Needham, S. and A. Woodward. 2008. The Clandon Barrow Finery: A Synopsis of Success in an Early Bronze Age World. *Proceedings of the Prehistoric Society* 74:1–52.

Neidich, W. 2003. *Blow-Up: Photography, Cinema and the Brain*. New York: Distributed Art Publishers.

Nelson, R. S., ed. 2000. *Visuality Before and Beyond the Renaissance: Seeing as Others Saw*. Cambridge: Cambridge University Press.

Niblett, R. 1999. *The Excavation of a Ceremonial Site at Folly Lane, Verulamium*. London: Society for the Promotion of Roman Studies.

Nielsen, S., et al. 2005. The Gundestrup Cauldron: New Scientific and Technical Investigations. *Acta Archaeologica* 76:1–58.

Nørgaard, A. 2008. A Weaver's Voice: Making Reconstructions of Danish Iron Age Textiles. In Gleba et al., 43–58.

Nortmann, H. 2002. Modell eines Herrschaftssystems: Frühkeltische Prunkgräber der Hunsrück-Eifel-Kultur. In Baitinger and Pinsker, 33–46.

Oberman, L. M., P. Winkielman, and V. S. Ramachandran. 2010. Embodied Simulation: A Conduit for Converting Seeing into Perceiving. In Balcetis and Lassiter, 201–221.

O'Dea, W. T. 1958. *The Social History of Lighting*. London: Routledge and Paul.

Olivier, L. 1999. The Hochdorf 'Princely' Grave and the Question of the Nature of Archaeological Funerary Assemblages. In T. Murray, ed., *Time and Archaeology*, 109–138. London: Routledge.

Olsen, B. 2010. *In Defense of Things: Archaeology and the Ontology of Objects*. New York: Altamira Press.

Olson, D. R. 2009. Why Literacy Matters, Then and Now. In Johnson and Parker, 385–403.

Ong, W. J. 1982. *Orality and Literacy: The Technologizing of the World*. New York: Methuen.

van Os, H. 1995. Foreword. In P.J.J. van Thiel and C. J. de Bruyn Kops, eds., *Framing in the Golden Age: Picture and Frame in 17th-Century Holland*. Trans., A. P. McCormick, 7. Amsterdam: Rijksmuseum.

Osborne, W. 1881. Zur Beurtheilung des prähistorischen Fundes auf dem Hradischt bei Stradonic in Böhmen. *Mitteilungen der Anthropologischen Gesellschaft in Wien* 10:234–260.

Overbeck, B. 1988. Ein massiliotischer Obol aus Aubstadt. *Das archäologische Jahr in Bayern* 1987:84.

Pape, J. 2004. Importierte mediterrane Keramik in der Zone nördlich und nordwestlich der Alpen während der Hallstattzeit: Zur Frage des Weinhandels. In Guggisberg, 107–120.

Pare, C.F.E. 2004. Schwert: Hallstattzeit. In *Reallexikon der germanischen Altertumskunde* 27:537–545.

Parfitt, K. 1995. *Iron Age Burials from Mill Hill, Deal*. London: British Museum Press.

Parzinger, H., ed. 2007. *Im Zeichen des goldenen Greifen: Königsgräber der Skythen*. Munich: Prestel.

Pászthory, K. and E. F. Mayer. 1998. *Die Äxte und Beile in Bayern*. Stuttgart: Franz Steiner.

Peacock, D.P.S. and D. F. Williams. 1986. *Amphorae and the Roman Economy: An Introductory Guide*. New York: Longman.

Pernet, L. and B. Schmid-Sikimić. 2007. Le *Brandopferplatz* de Wartau-Ochsenberg (Canton de Saint-Gall) dans son contexte régional. In Barral et al., 819–834.

Pertlwieser, M. 2001. Der latènezeitliche Opferschacht und das "keltische Maennchen" von Leonding bei Linz, Oberösterreich. *Archaeologia Austriaca* 84–85:355–371.

Petronius. *The Satyricon and the Fragments.* Trans., J. P. Sullivan. Harmondsworth: Penguin, 1965.

Petrosino, N. and U. Putz. 2003. Mittel- bis spätbronzezeitliche Gefässdepots aus Minoritenhof. *Das archäologische Jahr in Bayern 2002*:38–40.

Petzl, M. 2009. Ein spätbronzezeitliches Steinkistengrab aus Burgweinting. *Das archäologische Jahr in Bayern 2008*:40–41.

Pieta, K. and J. Moravcík. 1980. Spätlatènezeitlicher Opferplatz in Prosné. *Slovenska Archeologia* 28:245–283.

Pingel, V. 1971. *Die glatte Drehscheiben-Keramik von Manching.* Wiesbaden: Franz Steiner.

Pitts, M. 2008. Globalizing the Local in Roman Britain: An Anthropological Approach to Social Change. *Journal of Anthropological Archaeology* 27:493–506.

Pleiner, R. 1993. *The Celtic Sword.* Oxford: Clarendon Press.

Pliny the Elder. *Natural History.* Trans., H. Rackham. Cambridge, MA: Harvard University Press, 1944–1947.

Poffenberger, A. T. and B. E. Barrows. 1924. The Feeling Value of Lines. *Journal of Applied Psychology* 8:187–205.

Polenz, H. 1982. Münzen in latènezeitlichen Gräbern Mitteleuropas aus der Zeit zwischen 300 und 50 vor Christi Geburt. *Bayerische Vorgeschichtsblätter* 47:27–222.

Polybius. *The Histories.* Trans., W. R. Paton. Vol. I. Cambridge, MA: Harvard University Press, 1979.

Poux, M. 2000. Festins sacrés, ivresse collective et cultes guerriers en Gaule celtique. Traces littéraires, perspectives archéologiques. In S. Verger, ed., *Rites et espaces en pays celte et méditerranéen. Étude comparée à partir du sanctuaire d'Acy-Romance (Ardennes, France).* Coll. ÉFRome 276, 305–335.

———. 2002. L'archéologie du festin en Gaule préromaine: acquis, méthodologie et perspectives. In Ménial and Lambot, 345–374.

———. 2004. *L'Âge du Vin: Rites de boisson, festins et libations en Gaule indépendante.* Montagnac: Monique Mergoil.

———. 2006. Religion et société: Le sanctuaire arverne de Corent. In Goudineau, 116–134.

Prähistorische Bronzefunde. Series publication. 1965–1990, Munich: C.H. Beck, 1990–present, Stuttgart: Franz Steiner.

Prosdocimi, A. 1991. The Language and Writing of the Early Celts. In Moscati et al., 51–59.

Pryor, F. 2010. *The Making of the British Landscape: How We Have Transformed the Land, from Prehistory to Today.* London: Allen Lane.

Pryor, F. and M. Bamforth, eds. 2010. *Flag Fen, Peterborough: Excavation and Research 1995–2007.* Oxford: Oxbow.

Pulliam, H. 2006. *Word and Image in the Book of Kells*. Dublin: Four Courts Press.

von Quillfeldt, I. 1990. Bronzezeitliche Bestattungen aus Poing. *Das archäologische Jahr in Bayern 1989*:61–63.

———. 1995. *Die Vollgriffschwerter in Süddeutschland*. Stuttgart: Franz Steiner.

Ramachandran, V. S. 2004. *A Brief Tour of Human Consciousness*. New York: Pi Press.

———. 2011. *The Tell-Tale Brain: A Neuroscientist's Quest for What Makes Us Human*. New York: W.W. Norton.

Rasmussen, T. and N. Spivey, eds. 1991. *Looking at Greek Vases*. Cambridge: Cambridge University Press.

Reallexikon der germanischen Altertumskunde. 1973–2005. Berlin: Walter de Gruyter.

Rebel, E. 2008. *Selbstporträts*. Cologne: Taschen.

Reeder, E., ed. 1999. *Scythian Gold: Treasures from Ancient Ukraine*. New York: Harry Abrams.

Reichenberger, A. 1994. "Herrenhöfe" der Urnenfelder- und Hallstattzeit. In P. Schauer, ed., *Archäologische Untersuchungen zum Übergang von der Bronze- zur Eisenzeit zwischen Nordsee und Kaukasus*, 187–215. Regensburg: Universitätsverlag Regensburg.

Reinecke, P. 1911/1965. *Mainzer Aufsätze zur Chronologie der Bronze- und Eisenzeit*. Originally published in *Altertümer unserer heidnischen Vorzeit* 5 (1911). Reprinted 1965 by Rudolf Habelt Verlag, Bonn.

Reinhard, W. 2004. *Die keltische Fürstin von Reinheim*. Gersheim-Reinheim: Stiftung Europäischer Kulturpark.

Reuter, M. 2003. Die 'keltische Renaissance' in den Nordwestprovinzen des römischen Reiches. In *Romanisation und Resistenz in Plastik, Architektur und Inschriften der Provinzen des Imperium Romanum: Neue Funde und Forschungen*, 21–26. Mainz: Philipp von Zabern.

Rice, P. 2005. *Pottery Analysis: A Sourcebook*. Chicago: University of Chicago Press.

Rieckhoff, S. 1995. *Süddeutschland im Spannungsfeld von Kelten, Germanen und Römern*. Trier: Rheinisches Landesmuseum.

Rigby, V. 2006. Weapons and Fittings with Enamelled Decoration. In Stead, 115–121.

Riggsby, A. M. 2006. *Caesar in Gaul and Rome: War in Words*. Austin: University of Texas Press.

Riis, J. A. 1890. *How the Other Half Lives: Studies Among the Tenements of New York*. New York: C. Scribner's Sons.

Riley, B. 1965. Perception is the Medium. *Art News* 64-6, Oct. 1965, 32-33.

———. 2009. At the End of My Pencil. *London Review of Books* 8, October: 20–21, 2009.

Rind, M. M. 1989. Siedlungsarchäologie im unteren Altmühltal. *Vorträge des 7. Niederbayerischen Archäologentages*, 49–84.

Robb, J. 2010. Beyond Agency. *World Archaeology* 42:493–520.

Rolley, C. 2003. Le cratère. In Rolley, 176–189.

Rolley, C., ed. 2003. *La tombe princière de Vix.* 2 vols. Paris: Picard.

Roth, H. 1986. *Kunst und Handwerk im frühen Mittelalter.* Stuttgart: Theiss.

Roymans, N. 2007. Understanding Social Change in the Late Iron Age Lower Rhine Region. In Haselgrove and Moore, 478–491.

Roymans, N. and T. Derks. 1994. *De Tempel van Empel: Een Hercules-Heiligdom in het Woongebied van de Bataven.* 's-Hertogenbosch: Brabantse Regionale Geschiedbeoefening.

Rusu, M. 1969. Das keltische Fürstengrab von Ciumeşti in Rumänien. *Bericht der Römisch-Germanischen Kommission* 50:267–300.

Rybová, A. and K. Motyková. 1983. Der Eisendepotfund der Latènezeit von Kolín. *Památky Archeologické* 74:96–174.

Sarianidi, V. I. 1985. *The Golden Hoard of Bactria: From the Tillya-tepe Excavations in Northern Afghanistan.* Trans., A. Shkarovsky-Raffé. New York: Harry N. Abrams.

Saurel, M. 2002. Boire et manger, questions de pots à Acy-Romance (Ardennes). In Méniel and Lambot, 247–264.

Schama, S. 1987. *The Embarrassment of Riches: An Interpretation of Dutch Culture in the Golden Age.* New York: Knopf.

Schauer, P. 2004. Schwert: Bronzezeit. *Reallexikon der germanischen Altertumskunde* 27:523–537.

Scheidel, W., I. Morris, and R. Saller, eds. 2007. *The Cambridge Economic History of the Greco-Roman World.* Cambridge: Cambridge University Press.

Schlott, C., D. R. Spennemann, and G. Weber. 1985. Ein Verbrennugsplatz und Bestattungen am spätlatènezeitlichen Heidetränk-Oppidum im Taunus. *Germania* 63:439–505.

Schmutz, D. 2009. Models and Independent Variations: Gold Coins. In Müller, 224–225.

Schönfelder, M. 2004. Traces organiques sur quelques armes celtiques de la Champagne. *Mémoires de la Société Eduenne des Lettres, Sciences et Arts* 57:53–64.

———. 2007. Einige Überlegungen zu Flussfunden der Latènezeit. In Barral et al., 463–472.

Schröter, P. 1998. Zwei Frauenbestattungen aus dem neuen frühbronzezeitlichen Gräberfeld von Mötzing Lkr. Regensburg, Opf. In J. Prammer and R.-M. Weiss, eds., *Ausgrabungen und Funde in Altbayern 1995–1997,* 47–51. Straubing: Gäubodenmuseum.

Searle, John R. 2010. *Making the Social World: The Structure of Human Civilization.* New York: Oxford University Press.

Sewell, W. H. 1986. Visions of Labor: Illustrations of the Mechanical Arts before, in, and after Diderot's *Encyclopédie.* In S.L. Kaplan and C.J. Koepp, eds., *Work in France: Representations, Meaning, Organization, and Practice,* 258–286. Ithaca, NY: Cornell University Press.

Shapiro, M. 1969. On Some Problems in the Semiotics of Visual Art: Field and Vehicle in Image-Signs. *Semiotica* 1:223–242.

Sharples, N. 2007. Building Communities and Creating Identities in the First Millennium BC. In Haselgrove and Pope, 174–184.

———. 2010. *Social Relations in Later Prehistory: Wessex in the First Millennium BC.* Oxford: Oxford University Press.

Shaw, R. and J. Bransford, eds. 1977. *Perceiving, Acting, and Knowing: Toward an Ecological Psychology.* Hillsdale, NJ: Lawrence Erlbaum Associates.

Shepard, A. O. 1956. *Ceramics for the Archaeologist.* Washington, DC: Carnegie Institution of Washington.

Sherratt, A. 2006. The Trans-Eurasian Exchange: The Prehistory of Chinese Relations with the West. In V. H. Mair, ed., *Contact and Exchange in the Ancient World,* 30–61. Honolulu: University of Hawai'i Press.

Shimada, I., ed. 2007. *Craft Production in Complex Societies: Multicraft and Producer Perspectives.* Salt Lake City: University of Utah Press.

Sidebotham, S. E. 2011. *Berenike and the Ancient Maritime Spice Route.* Berkeley: University of California Press.

Sievers, S. 1982. *Die mitteleuropäischen Hallstattdolche.* Munich: C.H. Beck.

———. 2004. Schwert: Latènezeit. In *Reallexikon der germanischen Altertumskunde* 27:545–549.

———. 2007. *Manching: Die Keltenstadt.* Second edition. Stuttgart: Theiss.

Smail, D. L. 2008. *On Deep History and the Brain.* Berkeley: University of California Press.

Solkin, D. 2009. *Turner and the Masters.* London: Tate.

Sommer, C. S., ed. 2006. *Archäologie in Bayern: Fenster zur Vergangenheit.* Regensburg: Verlag Friedrich Pustet.

Sparke, P. 2009. *The Genius of Design.* London: Quadrille.

Stafford, B. M. 2007. *Echo Objects: The Cognitive Work of Images.* Chicago: University of Chicago Press.

Stary, P. F. 1980. Das spätbronzezeitliche Häuptlingsgrab von Hagenau, Kr. Regensburg. In K. Spindler, ed., *Vorzeit zwischen Main und Donau,* 46–97. Erlangen: Universitätsbund Erlangen-Nürnberg.

Stead, I. M. 1967. A La Tène III Burial at Welwyn Garden City. *Archaeologia* 101:1–62.

———. 1979. *The Arras Culture.* York: Yorkshire Philosophical Society.

———. 1991. The Snettisham Treasure. *Antiquity* 65:447–464.

———. 2006. *British Iron Age Swords and Scabbards.* London: British Museum Press.

Steenstrup, J.J.S. 1895. *Det store sølvfund ved Gundestrup i Jylland 1891: Orienterende betragtninger over de tretten sølvplader talrige relief-fremstillinger.* Copenhagen: B. Lunos.

Stegmaier, G. 2009. La céramique décorée hallstattienne en Bade-Wurtemberg: Chorologie et chronologie des phases Ha C et Ha D1. In Chaume, 543–557.

———. 2010. Keramik zwischen Ost und West: Ein Beitrag zur Erforschung von Fernkontakten während der frühen Eisenzeit. *Archäologisches Korrespondenzblatt* 40:67–75.

Stöckli, W. E. 1979. *Die Grob- und Importkeramik von Manching.* Wiesbaden: Franz Steiner.

Stöllner, T. 1998. Grab 102 vom Dürrnberg bei Hallein: Bemerkungen zu den Dürrnberger Kriegergräbern der Frühlatènezeit. *Germania* 76:67–176.

———. 2004. "Verborgene Güter"—Rohstoffe und Spezereien als Fernhandelsgut in der Späthallstatt- und Frühlatènezeit. In Guggisberg, 137–158.

Struck, M. 1996. *Römische Grabfunde und Siedlungen im Isartal bei Ergolding, Landkreis Landshut.* Kallmünz: Michael Lassleben.

Sudjic, D. 2008. *The Language of Things.* London: Allen Lane.

Sutton, J. 2008. Material Agency, Skills and History: Distributed Cognition and the Archaeology of Memory. In Knappett and Malafouris, 37–56.

Szabó, M. 1991. Mercenary Activity. In Moscati et al., 333–336.

Tacitus. Vol. 1: *Agricola, Germania, Dialogus.* Trans., M. Hutton and W. Peterson. Cambridge, MA: Harvard University Press, 1980.

Tappert, C. 2006. *Die Gefässkeramik der latènezeitlichen Siedlung Straubing-Bajuwarenstrasse.* Kallmünz: Michael Lassleben.

Tappert, C. and D. P. Mielke. 1998. Eine kleine syrische Bronzesitula aus frühkeltischer Zeit. *Jahresbericht des Historischen Vereins für Straubing und Umgebung* 99, 1997, 15–31.

van Thiel, P.J.J. 1995a. Framing in the Golden Age: General Introduction. In van Thiel and de Bruyn Kops, 11–25.

———. 1995b. The Dutch Picture Frame in the Seventeenth Century: Form and Function. In van Thiel and de Bruyn Kops, 27–39.

van Thiel, P.J.J. and C. J. de Bruyn Kops. 1995. *Framing in the Golden Age: Picture and Frame in 17th-Century Holland.* Trans., A. P. McCormick. Amsterdam: Rijksmuseum.

Thrane, H. 2006. Swords and Other Weapons in the Nordic Bronze Age: Technology, Treatment, and Contexts. In T. Otto, H. Thrane, and H. Vandkilde, eds., *Warfare and Society: Archaeological and Social Anthropological Perspectives,* 491–504. Aarhus: Aarhus University Press.

Tilley, C. Y. 1994. *A Phenomenology of Landscape: Places, Paths, and Movements.* Oxford: Berg.

———. 2008. *Body and Image: Explorations in Landscape Phenomenology 2.* Walnut Creek, CA: Left Coast Press.

Tischler, O. 1882. Die Situla von Waatsch. *Correspondenz-Blatt der deutschen Gesellschaft für Anthropologie, Ethnologie und Urgeschichte* 13:231–233.

Tomalin, C. 2002. *Samuel Pepys: The Unequal Self.* New York: Alfred A. Knopf.

Tomaschitz, K. 2002. *Die Wanderungen der Kelten in der antiken literarischen Überlieferung.* Vienna: Österreichische Akademie der Wissenschaften.

Tomber, R. 2008. *Indo-Roman Trade: From Pots to Pepper.* London: Duckworth.

Torbrügge, W. 1959. *Die Bronzezeit in der Oberpfalz.* Kallmünz: Michael Lassleben.

———. 1971. Vor- und frühgeschichtliche Flussfunde. *Bericht der Römisch-Germanischen Kommission* 51–52:1–146.

Turkle, S., ed. 2007. *Evocative Objects: Things We Think With.* Cambridge, MA: MIT Press.

Uenze, H. P. 1986. Zwei ungewöhnliche Scherben der Frühlatènezeit von Schwarzach b. Nabburg. *Das archäologische Jahr in Bayern 1985*:84–86.

Urban, O.-H. 2006. Gedanken zur Interpretation der Situla von Kuffarn, Nieder-Österreich. In M. Szabó, ed., *Les Civilisés et les Barbares du Ve au IIe siècle avant J.-C.*, 221–227. Glux-en-Glenne: Collection Bibracte.

van de Vall, R. 2003. Touching the Face: The Ethics of Visuality between Levinas and a Rembrandt Self-Portrait. In Farago and Zwijnenberg, 93–111.

Veres, J. 2009. The Depiction of a Carnyx-Player from the Carpathian Basin: A Study of Two Celtic Bronze Statuettes form Eastern Hungary. *Archäologisches Korrespondenzblatt* 39:231–249.

Verger, S. 1987. La genèse celtique des rinceaux à trisceles. *Jahrbuch des Römisch-Germanischen Zentralmuseums* 34:287–339.

———. 2001. Un graffite archaïque dans l'habitat hallstattien de Montmorot (Jura, France). *Studi Etruschi* 64, 265–316.

———. 2006. La grande tombe de Hochdorf, mise en scène funéraire d'un *cursus honorum* tribal hors pair. *Siris* 7:5–44.

Villard, A. 1993. Composition et disposition du mobilier dans les tombes aristocratiques bituriges (Ier s. avant J.-C.-Ier s. après J.-C.). In D. Cliquet, M. Remy-Watte, V. Guichard, and M. Vaginay, eds. 1993. *Les Celtes en Normandie: Les rites funeraires en Gaule (IIIème-Ier siècle avant J.-C.)*, 245–265. *Revue Archéologique de l'Ouest*, supplement 6.

Virilio, P. 1994. *The Vision Machine.* Bloomington, IN: Indiana University Press.

Völling, T. 1994. Studien zu Fibelformen der jüngeren vorrömischen Eisenzeit und ältesten römischen Kaiserzeit. *Bericht der Römisch-Germanischen Kommission* 75:147–282.

Wailes, B. 1991. Dún Ailinne. In Moscati et al., 614–615.

Waldhauser, J. 1987. Keltische Gräberfelder in Böhmen. *Bericht der Römisch-Germanischen Kommission* 68:25–179.

———, ed. 1978. *Das keltische Gräberfeld bei Jenišův Újezd in Böhmen.* Teplice: Kranjské Muzeum.

Wamser, L., ed. 2000. *Die Römer zwischen Alpen und Nordmeer.* Mainz: Philipp von Zabern.

Ward, D. 1984. Feuer. In K. Ranke, ed., *Enzyklopädie des Märchens,* vol. 4, cols. 1066–1083. Berlin: Walter de Gruyter.

Ward-Perkins, B. 2005. *The Fall of Rome and the End of Civilization.* New York: Oxford University Press.

Webley, L. 2003. Iron Age Houses and Social Space: A Case Study of the Three-Aisled Longhouses of Northern Europe during the Pre-Roman and Early Roman Iron Age. In J. Humphrey, ed., *Re-searching the Iron Age: Selected Papers from the Proceedings of the Iron Age Research Student Seminars, 1999 and 2000,* 59–68. Leicester: University of Leicester.

———. 2007. Households and Social Change in Jutland, 500 BC–AD 200. In Haselgrove and Moore, 454–467.

Wehrberger, K. and G. Wieland. 1999. Ein weiteres Knollenknaufschwert und eine Aylesford-Pfanne aus der Donau bei Ulm: Überlegungen zu spätkeltischen und frührömischen Gewässerfunden von der oberen Donau. *Archäologisches Korrespondenzblatt* 29:237–256.

Weinig, J. 1991. Bestattungen der Latènezeit aus dem "Totfeld" in Oberstimm. *Das archäologische Jahr in Bayern 1990:*70–72.

Wells, P. S. 1989. Ein spätlatènezeitlicher Vogelkopf vom Kelheimer Mitterfeld. *Archäologisches Korrespondenzblatt* 19:63–67.

———. 1993. *Settlement, Economy, and Cultural Change at the End of the European Iron Age: Excavations at Kelheim in Bavaria, 1987–1991.* Ann Arbor, MI: International Monographs in Prehistory.

———. 1999. *The Barbarians Speak: How the Conquered Peoples Shaped Roman Europe.* Princeton: Princeton University Press.

———. 2001. *Beyond Celts, Germans and Scythians: Archaeology and Identity in Iron Age Europe.* London: Duckworth.

———. 2003. *The Battle that Stopped Rome: Emperor Augustus, Arminius, and the Slaughter of the Legions in the Teutoburg Forest.* New York: W.W. Norton.

———. 2006. Mobility, Art, and Identity in Early Iron Age Europe and Asia. In J. Aruz, A. Farkas, and E. V. Fino, eds., *The Golden Deer of Eurasia: Perspectives on the Steppe Nomads of the Ancient World,* 18–23. New York: Metropolitan Museum of Art.

———. 2008. *Image and Response in Early Europe.* London: Duckworth.

———. 2009. Pottery and the Visual World at Early Iron Age Hascherkeller, Germany. *Journal of Field Archaeology* 34:117–133.

———. 2010. Early Bronze Age Pottery at Hascherkeller in Bavaria: Visuality, Ecological Psychology, and the Practice of Deposition in Bronze Age A2/B1. *Archäologisches Korrespondenzblatt* 40:191–205.

————, ed. 1983. *Rural Economy in the Early Iron Age: Excavations at Hascherkeller 1978–1981.* Cambridge, MA: Peabody Museum.

Werner, J. 1954. Die Bronzekanne von Kelheim. *Bayerische Vorgeschichtsblätter* 20:43–73.

————. 1978. Zur Bronzekanne von Kelheim. *Bayerische Vorgeschichtsblätter* 43:1–18.

Werner, W. M. 1987. Klappschemel der Bronzezeit. *Germania* 65:29–65.

Wexler, B. E. 2006. *Brain and Culture: Neurobiology, Ideology, and Social Change.* Cambridge, MA: MIT Press.

Wieczorek, A. and C. Lind, eds. 2007. *Ursprünge der Seidenstrasse: Sensationelle Neufunde aus Xinjiang, China.* Mannheim: Reiss-Engelhorn-Museen.

Wilhelmi, K. 1974. Siedlungs- und Bestattungsplätze der Bronze- und Eisenzeit bei Telgte, Kr. Münster. *Archäologisches Korrespondenzblatt* 4:213–222.

Will, E. L. 1987. The Roman Amphoras from Manching. *Bayerische Vorgeschichtsblätter* 52: 21–36.

Willerding, U. 1998. Getreidespeicherung. *Reallexikon der germanischen Altertumskunde* 12:11–30.

Williams, H. 2004. Artefacts in Early Medieval Graves: A New Perspective. In R. Collins and J. Gerrard, eds., *Debating Late Antiquity in Britain, AD 300–700*, 89–120. Oxford: Archaeopress.

Wilson, D. M. 1985. *The Bayeux Tapestry.* New York: Knopf.

Wilson, T. D. 2002. *Strangers to Ourselves: Discovering the Adaptive Unconscious.* Cambridge, MA: Harvard University Press.

Winghart, S. 1992. Einige Überlegungen zu Ursprung und Herleitung des keltischen Gastmahls. *Jahrbuch der bayerischen Denkmalpflege* 45/46:9–18.

Woodward, A. 2002. Inclusions, Impressions and Interpretation. In Woodward and Hill, 106–118.

Woodward, A. and J. D. Hill, eds., 2002. *Prehistoric Britain: The Ceramic Basis.* Oxford: Oxbow Books.

Woolf, G. 1996. Monumental Writing and the Expansion of Roman Society in the Early Empire. *Journal of Roman Studies* 86:22–39.

————. 1998. *Becoming Roman: The Origins of Provincial Civilization in Gaul.* Cambridge: Cambridge University Press.

————. 2009. Literacy or Literacies in Rome? In Johnson and Parker, 46–68.

Wright, R. P. 2010. *The Ancient Indus: Urbanism, Economy, and Society.* Cambridge: Cambridge University Press.

Wyss, R. 1956. The Sword of Korisios. *Antiquity* 30:27–28.

Zanier, W. 1999. *Der spätlatènezeitliche- und römerzeitliche Brandopferplatz im Forggensee (Gde. Schwangau).* Munich: C.H. Beck.

Zeidler, J. 2003. A Celtic Script in the Eastern La Tène Culture? *Études Celtique* 35:69–132.

Zeki, S. 1999. *Inner Vision: An Exploration of Art and the Brain*. Oxford: Oxford University Press.

Zuber, J. 2006. Keltische Gräber aus Burgweinting. *Das archäologische Jahr in Bayern 2005*:56–58.

Zürn, H. 1970. *Hallstattforschungen in Nordwürttemberg*. Stuttgart: Verlag Müller & Gräf.

INDEX

◇◇◇◇◇◇◇◇◇◇◇